American Liberty & Justice

Gordon Morris Bakken
Series Editor

Editorial Board
Michal Belknap
Richard Griswold del Castillo
Rebecca Mead
Matthew Whitaker

D1521299

Also in the series

A Clamor for Equality: Emergence and Exile of an Early Californio Activist
Paul Bryan Gray

Hers, His, and Theirs: Community Property Law in Spain and Early Texas
Jean A. Stuntz

Lone Star Law: A Legal History of Texas
Michael Ariens

The Reckoning: Law Comes to Texas's Edwards Plateau
Peter R. Rose

Sex, Murder, and the Unwritten Law: Courting Judicial Mayhem, Texas Style
Bill Neal

TREASURE STATE JUSTICE

"George M. Bourquin, U.S. District Judge, Montana, 1912." Photograph by Zubick Studio, n.d., 941-199. Reprinted by permission of the Montana Historical Society Research Center—Photograph Archives, Helena, Montana.

TREASURE STATE JUSTICE

Judge George M. Bourquin,
Defender of the
Rule of Law

Arnon Gutfeld

Foreword by
Gordon Morris Bakken

Texas Tech University Press

This book is typeset in Amasis MT Std. The paper used in this book meets the minimum requirements of ANSI/NISO Z39.48-1992 (R1997). ∞

Designed by Kasey McBeath
Cover photographs by permission of the Montana Historical Society Research Center —Photograph Archives, Helena, Montana.

Library of Congress Cataloging-in-Publication Data

Gutfeld, Arnon, author.
    Treasure State Justice : Judge George M. Bourquin, defender of the rule of law / Arnon Gutfeld ; [foreword by] Gordon Morris Bakken.
        pages cm. — (American liberty and justice)
        Includes bibliographical references and index.
        ISBN 978-0-89672-844-8 (hardback) — ISBN 978-0-89672-845-5 (paperback) — ISBN 978-0-89672-846-2 (e-book) 1. Bourquin, George M., 1863-1958. 2. Judges—Montana—Biography. 3. United States. District Court (Montana)—Officials and employees—Biography. 4. Civil rights—United States—History. I. Bourquin, George M., 1863-1958. II. Title.
        KF368.B68G68 2013
        347.73'2234092—dc23
        [B]   2013036281

13 14 15 16 17 18 19 20 21 / 9 8 7 6 5 4 3 2 1

Texas Tech University Press
Box 41037 | Lubbock, Texas 79409-1037 USA
800.832.4042 | ttup@ttu.edu | www.ttupress.org

In fond memory of K. Ross Toole and John W. Caughey—mentors

For Sara, Hila, Andy, Mikey, Kate, and Eli

Forever grateful

Arnie

CONTENTS

ILLUSTRATIONS

FOREWORD

ederal District Judge George M. Bourquin of Montana consistently and forcefully defended the individual rights of minorities in the face of governmental and popular pressures. Some of his decisions had important national ramifications. Judge Bourquin understood that liberty of thought and action as well as the right of dissent must be guaranteed to all and protected. He believed that the real test of a democracy was in protecting unpopular dissent and minorities exercising their constitutional rights. He denounced some dissenters' ideas but just as forcefully defended their right to be heard. Bourquin also sat on bench trials of a wide variety of case. He did the job of judging and he did it well.

This volume is one of the few to fully explore the work of a federal judge in the American West. In these pages readers will find Bourquin's judicial career resonating with that of other federal judges, yet this is one of only a few full examinations of a federal judge's work.

A few federal district judges have drawn scholarly attention. Roger Tuller's *Let No Guilty Man Escape* (2001) focused on Isaac Parker's cases in Indian Territory and his notoriety as the "hanging judge." Presiding from 1875 to 1896 over the US Court for the Western Judicial District of Arkansas, Isaac Charles Parker was responsible for law and order in Indian Territory. Driven by a sense of responsibility to the law rather than a Biblical sense of justice, Parker administered justice in a territory dominated by outlaws. Tuller set straight the record of decades of popular accounts of law west of Fort Smith. He demonstrated that Parker rose from a frontier Missouri lawyer to the House of Representatives. He actively sought appointment to the federal bench and with that appointment administered law in Indian Territory. He sent seventy-nine felons to the gallows, earning the sobriquet "the hanging judge." But at the end of his life, Parker advocated the abolition of the death penalty.[1]

Christian G. Fritz's *Federal Justice in California* (1991) focused on the judicial career of Ogden Hoffman.[2] Hoffman presided over the federal district court for the Northern District of California, handling more than nineteen thousand cases in forty years. During his four decades on the bench, Hoffman heard admiralty cases involving sea captains, seaman and their claims for wages, and injured passengers. He also heard the claims of Chinese immigrants, a critical political issue amid the racist "the Chinese must go" movement of the late nineteenth century. Hoffman also handled land grant conflicts and bankruptcy cases, as well as criminal, common law, and equity dockets. Fritz's analysis of the institution never loses sight of Ogden Hoffman, bachelor, New Yorker, and distinguished member of a distinguished family. Gutfeld's account of George M. Bourquin resonates powerfully with Fritz's work, putting a twentieth-century judge in a very different western setting.

Louise Fisch's study of Reynaldo Garza is set in Texas and chronicles the rise of the first Mexican American appointed to the federal bench.[3] Garza was an upwardly mobile middle-class Mexican American growing up amid anti-Mexican prejudice. He retained a bicultural ethnic identity while successfully integrating into Anglo culture. He was helped by Lyndon Johnson to achieve his dream of ascending to the bench.

Jace Weaver's *Then to the Rock Let Me Fly* focused on Luther Bohanon's judicial career.[4] President Kennedy appointed Luther Bohanon to the Oklahoma District Court bench in 1961. On the bench, Bohanon mandated the integration of Oklahoma City's public schools. He ended segregation in public housing within his jurisdiction. He also decided cases establishing the right of Native Americans to sue for compensation under federal statute. His rulings were unpopular in Oklahoma, yet most stood the test of appellate courts.

Harry H. Stein's biography of Gus J. Solomon focused on his liberal politics, Jews, and the federal courts in Oregon.[5] A legal and political activist in the 1930s and 1940s, he was appointed to the US District Court for Oregon in 1958. He sat as the longest serving federal judge in the state. Solomon was an activist for Jewish issues throughout his career and promoted liberal causes. He worked hard to streamline pleadings and developed a reputation for being fairly hard on lawyers. Stein argues that he developed an idiosyncratic judicial autocracy. He combined judicial restraint with the search for justice. Solomon was a strong proponent of civil rights, emphasizing equal opportunities rather than equal results. Solomon defended the First Amendment, but he disagreed with the ACLU's support of Nazi demonstrators in Skokie, Illinois. Solomon consistently construed treaties to protect Native American rights.

Other judges of the federal bench have biographies, but few in the American West.[6] This analysis of Federal District Judge George M. Bourquin of Montana adds to the growing literature on federal judges, puts a face on federal justice in Montana, and enriches our understanding of the breadth of impact federal justice had in the American West. Further, Bourquin's fidelity to the rule of law resonates powerfully with the judicial struggles to establish the rule of law in Rhode Island and New Hampshire. D. Kurt Graham's *To Bring Law Home: The Federal Judiciary in Early National Rhode Island* (2010) demonstrates how the federal bench promoted national values and the rule of law. Rhode Island's federal bench was instrumental in enforcing federal statutory and constitutional law. In particular, the federal bench took the enforcement of debt seriously. "But more important is the fact that these cases fit into a larger pattern. In dealing with questions involving wages, prize, the slave trade, federal revenue, contract disputes, diversity of citizenship, or equity, the federal courts were the voice of national authority."[7] So too, Bourquin made clear the federal voice in Montana.

The New Hampshire struggle to enshrine the rule of law involved legislators wanting to eliminate written judicial decisions, special debtor interests seeking a free ride, and judges struggling to legitimate the rule of law. John Phillip Reid's *Legitimating the Law: The Struggle for Judicial Competency in Early National New Hampshire* (2012) analyzes the issues, political machinations, personal antagonisms, and establishment of a rule of law. Reid opined, "Significant as lawyers are in the common-law tradition, judges are even more important. The methodology is the same except that judges often leave a written record explaining their rulings, and they have the reasonings of other judges from over the centuries with which to measure their own judgments and to which to conform their own rulings. This methodology helps to explain the persistent strength of rule-of-law over the centuries in common-law jurisdictions."[8] Judge Bourquin's struggle for the rule of law in Montana is part of a larger process to bring legal and constitutional principles to public approbation.

Gordon Morris Bakken
California State University, Fullerton

PREFACE

ore than forty years ago, when I was gathering materials in preparation for writing my MA thesis at the University of Montana, I first encountered the legal writings of Federal District Judge George M. Bourquin of Montana. After completing the MA, I was referred by my mentor, K. Ross Toole, to his mentor, John Walton Caughey at the University of California, Los Angeles, where I received my PhD. Both my thesis and dissertation focused on civil liberties violations in Montana during World War I and the "Red Scare" that followed.

I decided then to produce a biography of Judge Bourquin because I was fascinated by his courage, by his unusual and beautiful prose, and by the impact he had on national legislation. In the four decades that followed, I authored numerous books and more than eighty articles, but wherever I researched, whether in Montana, New York, Seattle, San Francisco, Los Angeles, Washington DC, or Cambridge, Massachusetts, I looked for materials relating to the life and career of Judge Bourquin. I finally concluded that the dearth of source materials rendered a birth-to-death biography of Bourquin impossible and abandoned my efforts.

My decision not to produce a biography of Bourquin changed after I arrived in New York City on a sabbatical in late September 2001. Observing the reactions of the American administration and public to the events of September 11, 2001, I became convinced of the importance of telling and analyzing Judge Bourquin's fearless stance and the power of his convictions in defense of individual liberties and freedom of expression in the face of mass hysteria. I concluded that his numerous legal decisions rendered between 1912 and 1934 constituted a sufficient and ample base for an extremely topical and important legal biography of this outstanding jurist. Numerous studies have been published of defense of civil liberties by legal ideologues from the left, liberal side of the political and legal spectrum. This study is unique as it presents an analysis of an unrelenting, spirited defense of civil liberties, during crisis times, in the finest Edmund Burke tradition coming from a traditional, Jeffersonian-libertarian side of the political spectrum.

Very few studies and certainly no book length studies have been written about federal judges in the early-twentieth-century American West. Therefore I felt that it was very important to analyze the dilemmas they faced. A number of studies have been written of frontier judges and the issues they confronted, but hardly any studies of federal judges who acted in the post-territorial period of transition when the far western states moved from frontier law to full adaptation and application of twentieth-century American legal realities.

Some prominent western political figures have been studied in depth. Students of American history are well acquainted with political figures such as William E. Borah, George W. Norris, Barry Goldwater, and Mike Mansfield. The study of Judge Bourquin and other figures who did not become household names in America is imperative for an understanding of the deeper nuances of the western political and legal experience.

Judge Bourquin served as a federal judge during a time when the federal government assumed an ever-increasing role over the well-being and destiny of the West. At that time local and state governments in the West were notoriously weak, and many of the most essential decisions regarding the welfare and development of the region were made by federal authorities and by the private sector. The judicial career of judge Bourquin provides us with a unique opportunity to examine the manner in which the judicial system has produced sagacious heroes in every generation dedicated to the rule of law.

Numerous persons assisted me in getting this manuscript to print. Some stand out for their special contributions. I am grateful to fine editors such as John Walton Caughey and Norris Hundley of the *Pacific Historical Review*, Brad Williams of *Western Legal History*, and numerous other editors, too numerous to be listed, who recognized the historical and legal significance of Judge Bourquin's judicial career and who published my many articles on him in their fine journals.

I wish to thank Professor Aviam Soifer, dean, School of Law, University of Hawaii, for his immense assistance and for his constant encouragement and fine advice; Professor David Mesher, of California State University, San Jose, for his friendship and help; Professor Oren Gross of the University of Minnesota Law School for sharing with me some of his vast knowledge; Professor Stanley Kutler of the University of Wisconsin for his help and sound advice; Professor Gordon Bakken for his thorough reading of the manuscript and his numerous helpful comments. Special thanks to Professor Enrique Ucelay-Da Cal of the Autonomous University of Barcelona, whose comments, corrections, and advice were extremely helpful. I am deeply indebted to Judith Keeling, editor-in-chief, the Editorial Committee, the staff, and the readers of the Texas Tech University Press for the efforts they invested to improve the manuscript.

I recognize, and greatly appreciate, the courtesy and assistance extended to me by the many librarians at Tel-Aviv University; the National Archives in Washington DC; the Widener Library at Harvard University and the Harvard Law School; the New York Public Library; and the Montana Historical Society in Helena, especially the late Dave Walter, who was extremely helpful.

My love and thanks to my family for their continuous support of my efforts. The computer mastery of my daughter Hila, my daughter-in-law Andrea, and my son Mikey constantly solved problems. My wife Sara's encouragement and help in ways too numerous to count accompanied me along the entire process. They are all responsible for the completion of this project.

Arnon Gutfeld
Ramat-Aviv, Israel, 2013

TREASURE STATE JUSTICE

INTRODUCTION

I n late March 1917, just before the United States declared war on Germany, Justice Oliver Wendell Holmes wrote to Felix Frankfurter, then on the faculty of Harvard Law School: "Patriotism is the demand of the territorial club for priority, and as much priority as it needs for vital purposes, and other such tribal groups as the church and trade unions. I go whole hog for the territorial club—and don't care a damn if it interferes with some of the spontaneities of the other groups."[1]

Holmes, whose opinions on free speech had not yet crystallized, was guided by this rationale in his support of the governmental persecution and prosecution of the opponents of the war.[2] His legal brethren agreed with him. But in the fall of 1919 he changed his mind and expressed a strong dissent in *Abrams et al. v. United States* in staunch support of free speech: "Only the emergency that makes it immediately dangerous to leave the correction of evil counsels to time warrants making any exception to the sweeping command, 'Congress shall make no law abridging the freedom of speech.'"[3] Holmes's dramatic switch largely resulted from his alarm about the threat of political authoritarianism overwhelming the United States, a fear well illustrated by the Red Scare of 1919–20.

Federal District Judge George M. Bourquin of Montana, on the other hand, did not need time to change his mind. Consistently, clearly, and forcefully he defended the individual rights of various minorities in the face of huge governmental and popular pressures. Some of his decisions had important national ramifications. Judge Bourquin understood, long before Holmes realized it, that liberty of thought and action as well as the right of dissent must be guaranteed to all and had to be protected from the encroachments and intents of the ruling majority to severely limit these rights. Judge Bourquin believed that the real test of a democracy was the manner in which it protected unpopular opinions, minorities, and dissent. He denounced some dissenters' ideas but just as forcefully defended their right to be heard.

Judge Bourquin was among those rare defenders of liberty who seemed divorced from self-interest. To him, the law was part of the on-going battle between civilization and barbarism: the main line of protection dividing the populace from the ongoing threat of a descent into savagery. He believed that laws protecting individual rights must have much broader general applications than other legislations and had to protect the individual from what he called "government despotism." Judge Bourquin was committed to the idea that freedom mattered as much to those within the system as to those outside it. Roger Baldwin, one of the founders of the American Civil Liberties Union, once commented that the leading activists of the ACLU always had been "well bred and well fed."[4] Bourquin was well aware of the responsibilities that his comfortable position entailed.

After September 11, 2001, the relationship between First Amendment protections and national security once again became a major issue in the United States. The furor over Attorney General John Ashcroft and the USA PATRIOT Act makes Judge Bourquin's forceful defense of individual rights, his opposition to the government's disregard of these rights, and his rulings regarding civil liberties, property rights, Native American rights, ethics in the legal profession, and the public good particularly topical and significant. His words offer guidance as to what must be done now and in the future in the never-ending struggle against intolerance and the disregard of constitutional rights, especially during crisis times.

George M. Bourquin served as a federal district judge in Montana between 1912 and 1934. He studied law in the 1890s and practiced law in various capacities during the first decades of the twentieth century. Throughout his entire career he put much emphasis on the study of judicial philosophy and legal history. But Greek mythology, the Bible, and the ideas and writings of the founders of the American Republic were also ever-present in his judicial decisions.

During his career, the reigning judicial vision that guided American legal thinking was known as "classical legal thought," "legal formalism," "legal orthodoxy," or "laissez-faire constitutionalism," and by sundry other labels. Those were the various ideas, beliefs, and values that heavily influenced many in the legal profession from the post-Reconstruction amendments era until the "Constitutional Revolution" of 1937.[5]

Those adhering to legal formalism believed that law was based on general principles that were the basis of a doctrine that set the norms that could be employed to settle any issue contested. Its followers viewed it as a science similar to mathematics. The principle that overshadowed all others was human liberty, which was defined as the means to secure life and person and the ability to exercise individual will. Above all, the US Constitution was seen as protecting the sanctity of property and contracts. Inherent in legal formalism is a belief in an inevitable clash between the rights of the individual and the power and authority of government.[6]

Judge Bourquin enthusiastically adopted this basic tenet of legal formalism, and it guided him in his long legal and short political career. Bourquin was forever on guard against what he regarded as governmental despotism, including government usurpation of power. A close examination of Bourquin's decisions between 1912 and 1937 reveal that legal formalism heavily influenced his approach to and interpretation of the law. Yet being a highly independent judicial persona, he at times rejected important elements of that legal doctrine along with some of its assumptions. The basic assumptions of this judicial vision were closely related to how its adherents regarded rights, liberty, authority, power, and the values of the foundation of Americans as a people. This also influenced adherents' thoughts as to how the basic components of the American governmental system—the American Republic—should be viewed. It was a philosophy that had very practical jurisprudential applications.[7]

Legal formalism began during the era that preceded the birth of the American Republic and grew with the Declaration of Independence, the state constitutions, and the Articles of Confederation. It is especially apparent in the major compromises agreed upon in the US Constitution. In all of these documents the influence of the Enlightenment, the English judicial system, common law, and the belief in the superiority of the Anglo-Saxon people are evident. Legal formalism added substance and authority to the major decisions of Chief Justice John Marshall and Justice Joseph Story.[8]

Although Bourquin admired Thomas Jefferson and enthusiastically endorsed his ideology of government with limited authority, this did not prevent him from referring to Marshall often and with deep reverence as "the Great Marshall." Bourquin, a stern person very much aware of humans' bestial propensities, did not share Jefferson's faith in the people, but like many who subscribed to legal formalism, he believed that law and its strict enforcement was the single shield that protected civilization from barbarism.

Similar to the legal formalists, Judge Bourquin regarded the Constitution as one of the most brilliant documents—if not the greatest document— ever produced. It was a document whose strict interpretation should serve to introduce order and stability to daily human endeavors. In a sense, it served as a supplement to the Bible as a living guide to life in America. It was the writings of the Founding Fathers and the subsequent rulings of the great justices that defined the rule of law and the limits and boundaries of the legitimate judicial, legislative, and executive powers.

In some crucial areas Bourquin adopted very different positions and did not fit the mold of the typical legal formalist. Unlike some of the followers of legal formalism, he had little faith in the people. Along with many of his fellow formalists, he distrusted majoritarian legislatures that catered to voters and demagogues who, forgetting sacred and constitutional maxims, thrived on the base instincts of the populace. Bourquin often referred to the people as the "mob" or the "herd" and left no doubt as to how dangerous he considered them.

Furthermore, many of his fellow judges and others in the legal profession identified with the interests and values of the successful "captains of industry" during the age of laissez-faire and the triumph of private enterprise that lasted until the mid-1930s. Bourquin, however, remained true to his higher principles. Most judges and other members of the legal profession demonstrated xenophobia and despised immigrants, whom they considered a serious threat to America's traditional values. Bourquin delighted in protecting the rights of Native Americans, immigrants, and radicals and was dedicated to the proposition that if the rights and opinions of the unpopular were not protected, no one's rights were safe.

Bourquin abhorred socialism, communism, anarchism, and dictatorships, but this did not prevent him from steadfastly defending the right of unpopular minorities to freedom of speech and thought. His most important and historically significant rulings occurred during the tumultuous days of World War I and the Red Scare that followed. Whereas most judges and attorneys did their utmost to support the war effort and to demonstrate their "patriotism," Bourquin was one of the very few judges who protected freedom of expression during times of crisis.

Bourquin was a conservative and a formalist who during times of national emergency never compromised on First Amendment guarantees and protections and fought governmental excesses. In the post-frontier West of the early twentieth century he steadfastly protected the rights of Native Americans. In Montana, which exemplified corporate rule and a colonial economy, Bourquin often supported the rights of laborers and unions and opposed the wholesale use of injunctions during strikes. He also defended the "public good" against the powerful railroads. In the face of great hostility and hysteria he often stood alone in defending legitimate dissent with which he disagreed, and he did all of it within the context of his legal formalist beliefs.

Property and contracts had an exalted place in legal formalist thought, as they were explicitly singled out and protected in the Constitution.[9] Contracts and property, in the minds of the formalists, were the foundations of American civilization. Thus, judges considered one of their major responsibilities to be the protection of the Constitution from the majoritarian threats of legislators and elected representatives. Like other formalists, Judge Bourquin viewed this as one of the most important duties of the courts. To the formalists, Andrew Carnegie and the poorest of his employees were equal before the law. This they considered evidence of their belief in the ideal of equality, but in fact formalist judges were followers of the Protestant ethic and often chose to protect and enhance the fortunes and interests of the "elect."

The United States underwent major changes after the Civil War that involved political, economic, and social dislocations. Antebellum America was a backward agricultural-frontier society that contained the seeds of industrialization. According to Morton Horowitz, the legal system was already being reshaped to the advantage of elite industrial and commercial interests and to the disadvantage of the traditional agricultural concerns and rights of the Jacksonian-exalted "common men."[10]

Postbellum America was drastically different from what historian Daniel Boorstin called the "lost world of Thomas Jefferson." Industrialization, urbanization, and massive immigration were the major processes in a nation that was soon to become a leading world power. Yet with all the upheavals and transformations one element remained constant: the Constitution as the basis of the American system. The ideas and values of the formalists remained the same, but it was clear that adjustments were imperative in order to fit the Constitution to the new realities. The first major changes came with the passage of the Reconstruction amendments. With the abolition of slavery the government clearly interfered with traditional property rights. Slowly and increasingly during the age of laissez-faire that ensued, many realized that unchecked American capitalism carried within it the seeds of its own destruction. Opportunities for competition and success were essential for the preservation of the system. Vast powers accumulated by some individuals and monopolies made the American economic and social scene similar to Europe's.

In America, as in Europe, labor became the cheapest commodity. American tradition protected business enterprise and property because the American economic battle was perceived as mostly between the "haves" and the "will haves," not between the "haves" and the "have-nots" as in Europe. This was the guarantee and the safeguard of the economic and political status quo in America. As the American scene and America's problems began to resemble Europe's, some in America began to advocate "European" solutions such as socialism and syndicalism to solve the country's economic and social ills.

A growing number of jurists, economists, and social reformers gradually came to the realization that within the democratic context only one force existed that could check the evils inherent in unregulated and unlimited economic and political power, and that was the federal government. From the 1880s until 1937, the legal-political debate centered on what powers should be delegated to the government in order to oversee and regulate economic activities. Most in the legal profession believed that it was their duty, especially the judges, to preserve the sanctity of contracts and property against the onslaught of reform-minded legislators.

Thus the Supreme Court of the United States became a major arena in which the future civil and social course was debated and decided. Against the background of rapid and drastic dislocations, the Supreme Court, the lower courts, and the bar set the guidelines for action for American society. Their main goal was to preserve the supremacy, rule, and values of old-stock Americans. They aimed to enhance productivity and economic activity while maintaining a measure of opportunity for individual success that in their mindset paralleled individual liberty. At the foundation of American society was a contract, mostly economic, that had to be protected.

From the Reconstruction amendments era until 1937, the Supreme Court, in a long series of highly controversial and contradictory decisions, attempted to establish a modus vivendi between governmental power and individual liberty. These important decisions[11] generated numerous legal debates at that time and still are generating fierce debates among legal and constitutional experts and historians.[12] In these cases, the Supreme Court defended the rights of business, although at times the court did an about-face and protected labor unions. Melvin I. Urofsky, a professor of public policy and law at Virginia Commonwealth University, has demonstrated that the court was not hostile to the Progressive movement and its political goals, as many believed, and that it upheld more Progressive legislation than it struck down.[13] These decisions that attempted to stay within the bounds set by the principles of legal formalism while adjusting to the new industrial, social, and urban realities were laden with inconsistencies, ambivalences, and contradictions.

For the most part, Bourquin adhered to legal formalism, but on civil rights and labor issues he at times took different positions. Nonetheless, he was always careful to explain and defend them in the context of his Jeffersonian outlook and interpretation of the Constitution. Bourquin admired Oliver Wendell Holmes, Jr., and often cited him, even though Holmes was a central figure in the onslaught on formalism.[14] Not once did Bourquin mention or cite Supreme Court Justice Louis D. Brandeis, who repeatedly challenged traditional legal formalism.

In similar fashion, Bourquin repeatedly invoked Jefferson and other founders, but not once did he mention Alexander Hamilton or any of the Federalist papers, though original intent was one of his favorite subjects. It was in Federalist 78 that Hamilton brilliantly resolved the basic dilemma of legal formalism in which nonelected judges denied popular sovereignty and the will of the people through their representatives: "the Courts were designed to be an intermediate body between the people and the legislatures. . . . To keep the latter within the limits assigned to their authority."[15]

The reign of legal formalism ended after the "packing of the Court" crisis of 1937. It was the Charles Evans Hughes Supreme Court that during President Franklin D. Roosevelt's first term struck down most of the New Deal welfare state legislation and began the process that dismantled legal formalism. The court abandoned substantive due process and liberty of contract and adopted a new vision of congressional regulatory power. It recognized the need for governmental power as a legitimate and necessary overseer and regulator of the economy; the welfare of the citizenry became the basis for the establishment of the modern American welfare state. In the 1930s, when many European democracies turned to totalitarianism because of the severe economic crisis, the United States rejected both socialism and totalitarianism and maintained and preserved its constitutional democracy.[16]

Bourquin was a federal district judge who held office in the early-twentieth-century West. Unlike nineteenth-century frontier judges, he did not deal with cowboys, trappers, or mining camp laws and issues. When he ruled on issues of mining law, it was not on laws that originated from voluntary agreements among miners but mostly on federal and state statutes. These and others were among the subjects that defined the uniqueness of western law and differentiated it from issues in eastern courts.[17]

Other difficult problems faced by frontier and western judges were present in Bourquin's court. He encountered and ruled on issues that dealt with Native Americans and that resulted from the history of the clash between the Native American and white civilizations in the West. The dilemmas faced by the courts were unique in that "jurisdiction might be determined not only by the citizenship of the victim or the accused, but by the status of fathers and grandfathers of the victims or the accused."[18] To highlight the difference, John Phillip Reid gave the following example: "Telephone companies were located in Indian Territory, and railroads had rolling stocks, employees, and stations there, yet they could not enforce a contract nor could they be sued for torts in local courts."[19]

Treaties such as the Louisiana Purchase, the Treaty of Guadalupe Hidalgo, and those signed with Native American tribes and nations were at the foundation of some of the issues raised in Bourquin's court. Though many layers of western legal history as defined by Reid were not part of nor were present in Bourquin's court, he definitely belonged in the category of a western judge. Some of his issues, worldviews, and legal philosophies were influenced or shaped by his experience and western environment.

A native of Pennsylvania, he moved to Colorado as a youth, where he worked as a cowboy and miner. Subsequently, he moved to Montana in the early 1890s, at the time that it became a state. He read law in the frontier tradition and worked as a lawyer in emerging post-frontier towns such as Butte and Helena. He held federal appointments, a local judgeship, and finally became a federal judge. Though his parents never mastered the English language, he had an outstanding and unusual command of the language. His western experience and success made him a fierce nationalist but never blindly "super-patriotic." As a true westerner, he was forever suspicious of concentrations of power, be it the federal government or East Coast–based giant corporations. He, in the frontier tradition, worshiped the individual, his rights, and his responsibilities. He was an unusual western judge in his approach to Native Americans. Unlike many of his neighbors, he understood, sympathized with, and at times even idealized the nature and history of Native American civilizations. Yet this did not prevent him from adopting a paternalistic approach toward them.

It is difficult to compare Bourquin with other western judges, since most studies of western judges focus on those who performed their duties during the nineteenth century. One theme was common to all of them—they faced extremely difficult tasks in new and harsh environments. Fine studies of nineteenth-century western judges are relatively numerous when compared to research on twentieth-century judges. Among them are Roger Tuller's *Let No Guilty Man Escape*, on Judge Isaac Parker;[20] Paul Kens, *Justice Steven Field*;[21] Christian Fritz's biography of Ogden Hoffman in California;[22] and Michael Brodhead's study of the career of Judge David J. Brewer.[23] All of these deal with nineteenth-century judges whose problems and tasks were quite different from those of a twentieth-century western judge. This highlights the need to study the careers of more twentieth-century judges in the American West, and the list of important and worthy candidates is not short.

The biographical material on Bourquin is scant. I have relied heavily on information in Montana newspapers and on interviews conducted with members of his family and with some contemporaries, as well as on Burton K. Wheeler's autobiography.

The aim of this work is not to relate the life story of the judge but rather to study and analyze his legal decisions. These offer a historically important addition to the history of civil liberties in particular and to law in general in the United States and western legal history. In addition, it analyzes the topical and crucial issues of civil liberties during crisis times and Bourquin's impact on the development of national legislation on the subject. The study focuses on topics as diverse as the extraordinary impeachment trial of a judge for "patriotic" reasons and on property rights, legal ethics, and the rights of labor, all in the context of the legal and political realities of the "colonial" economy of the early-twentieth-century American West. One chapter is devoted to the highly unusual, original, and precedent-setting rulings by Bourquin on the rights and history of Native Americans. The final chapter relates what occurred when the judge attempted to translate his judicial philosophy into political reality—namely, his failed campaign for the US Senate. It was an unusual campaign in which two philosophies clashed—a microcosm of the clash between the past and modernity. It was a forerunner of many similar political clashes, but because of Bourquin's role in it, the issues were beautifully and clearly defined. In this sense, what follows is a "legal biography" of a highly significant and important judicial and political persona.

In 2005, Clemens P. Work published *Darkest Before Dawn: Sedition and Free Speech in the American West*. This study relied extensively on my book *Montana's Agony: Years of War and Hysteria, 1917–1921* and on over a dozen of my articles that focused on events in Montana during World War I and the Red Scare. *Darkest Before Dawn* contributed to our knowledge of the fate of those accused and convicted of sedition.[24] The contribution of the present study is that it analyzes Bourquin's opposition to hysteria and to the suppression of free speech and expression in terms of jurisprudence. Specifically, I demonstrate how he used the First, Fourth, and Fifth Amendments in molding a jurisprudence of liberty. This legal biography also addresses his decisions in a large array of topics all within his opposition to what he described as governmental despotism. It is the story of a unique, highly original, and important western judge.

Chapter I
THE PERSON ON THE BENCH

George Bourquin's life story belongs to an era long gone, to the world that came immediately after the end of America's far northwestern frontier era. It was a world in which the law and judges such as Bourquin assisted in defining and creating the basis for life in the post-frontier West. His legal reasoning included a rare, generally neglected side of the American civil liberties story. An ideological Jeffersonian, in the Edmund Burke tradition, who was often contemptuous of the "people," the masses, and the "herd," Bourquin also believed that unless courts protected each individual's rights, no one's rights were safe. Unlike many "legal technicians," he was a well-read individual whose decisions were usually written in idiosyncratic, even poignant prose.

Bourquin's great love and mastery of the classics also influenced both the style and the content of his written decisions. Those close to Bourquin insisted that "his manner of addressing himself was straight out of the classics."[1] His use of history, law, philosophy, psychology, and political science made him a cultural critic as well as a legal interpreter. He also clearly was an iconoclast, insisting on interpreting the Constitution in the spirit in which he believed it had been written. Yet Bourquin's most significant characteristic, which I have distilled from a study of almost 250 opinions published between 1912 and 1937, was his ability to combine civil libertarianism and political conservatism.

Bourquin's contemporaries described him as vain, arrogant, and irascible. He was an imposing figure in stature and in personality. His oratorical prowess impressed people who heard him speak. "He was what some of us used to call 'a slave driver,'" wrote Burton K. Wheeler, then a district attorney and later a US senator from Montana, but Wheeler also described Bourquin as "a model of judiciary integrity."[2] This is high praise coming from a person who had a long, complicated relationship with Bourquin, first because of their relative positions within the federal judiciary system and later as severe political and ideological adversaries.

Bourquin hated wasting precious courtroom time and had nothing but contempt for ill-prepared attorneys. He once held twenty-three lawyers in contempt in one day, but this was under extenuating circumstances. The case involved the arraignment of a number of people on Prohibition violations. Several attorneys were late for court, unprepared, and seemed not to know why they were there. Bourquin asked the same question of each one, and the invariable answer was: "I don't know, Your Honor." He then held them in contempt, imposed a slight fine, excoriated them, and said: "For God's sake, if you come into my court, come in prepared and know what you're doing." This sounds Draconian, but actually the judge was simply asserting his authority on a new court.[3]

Bourquin drove himself as he drove others. He was an extremely hardworking, conscientious judge who regularly tried four or five cases in a single day. In spite of his heavy schedule, Bourquin's decisions and his instructions to juries were, as a local Montana newspaper later recalled, "given careful consideration. Litigants knew that his judgments were humane, righteous and according to the law."[4] He was an austere individual with no intimate friends. When Bourquin dined at a restaurant he asked the waitress to turn up the other chairs around his table so that no one would join him.[5] On the other hand, he could demonstrate a sense of humor. On one occasion, a defendant charged with a minor liquor violation was tried before him without a jury. When the time came for the court to render judgment, Bourquin said: "The court finds you not guilty, but don't do it again." According to many, one of his favorite statements was: "This court may be wrong, but it is never in doubt."[6] His prose was colorful and almost Victorian, displaying individuality, independence, and a strong emphasis on the rights of the individual vis-à-vis the authorities.[7]

Another of his traits was his stubborn independence that his granddaughter claimed shortened his life to a "mere ninety-five years."[8] Bourquin's suspicion of the federal government caused him to question any encroachment upon individual rights; this was particularly clear in his attitude toward Prohibition. He thought that Prohibition was a "silly" law and "beneath the dignity of the federal court."[9] His conservative libertarianism also led him to characterize Prohibition as "an absolutely disgraced act of the government trying to regulate personal conduct." As a frontier individualist, his attitude was, "If a man wants to visit whores, or drink whiskey, or smoke cigars, just don't do it in my face."[10]

Bourquin was born in 1863 on a farm near Tidioute, in Warren County, Pennsylvania. His father, Justin, arrived in the United States from Switzerland in 1842 at the age of twenty. Justine was a graduate of a teachers' academy with an excellent command of French. Yet despite his broad education he spoke no English and thus could not pursue an academic career in the United States. Instead, he became a farmer and a blacksmith. Research into the history of the family in Switzerland and in France (*Bourquin* refers to a native or inhabitant of Bourg-Fidèle), going back to 1340, reveals that numerous ancestors were well educated and held important political and religious positions. Many of them were dissenters, iconoclasts, and opponents of authorities and consensus.[11]

Justin and Celestine had ten children, of whom George was the ninth. At eight, George was a big, tall boy, taking his first steps in the English language through his friends at play and at school. Yet his education was limited. His elder brother Julius went to work at fourteen to assist the family. School seemed a temporary interlude. It was intended to last until one could master the reading, writing, and basic mathematical skills that would enable him to function in the very practical world of the rural United States at the end of the nineteenth century.[12] The Bourquin children attended a one-room school where children of all ages studied together. Despite difficult conditions George seemed to achieve impressive results, and he stayed in school until he was seventeen. Then he was asked to stay on as a teacher. After a year, however, he felt the need to see the world.

He decided to move to Aspen, Colorado, where four of his brothers were making their living as engineers, operating equipment in the mines. There, during the next three years, George worked as a cowboy, a miner, and a smelter man in Aspen and in Leadville. In June 1884, he moved to the Montana Territory and settled in Butte. That city was in the midst of an economic boom resulting from the discovery of vast lodes of copper, gold, silver, and other rare metals in its vicinity. He continued to work in the silver mines of Walkerville, near Butte, and advanced from processing the ore to operating sophisticated equipment. Yet this was not enough to satisfy his drive. He enrolled in the Montana School of Mines in Butte and searched for other ways to advance.[13]

At that time and place, upward mobility seemed possible through two routes: commerce or public office. Bourquin chose the second. In 1888 he ran for the office that monitored silver production in Silver Bow (Butte) County. He failed but did not give up. In 1889, he apprenticed with a local lawyer and at the same time tried to gain access to Butte's political circle. In 1890, he established connections with state Republican politicians.[14]

President Benjamin Harrison appointed him to the position of Receiver of the Public Money in the federal land office in Helena, the state capital. He was responsible for accounting to the federal treasury all the expenditures and income of the government in Montana. He also monitored silver production. Bourquin held this position for four years.[15]

While in Helena, he did not neglect his law studies, which were then undertaken in a completely different manner from today. A lawyer's office was usually located in the back of a store, most often the town's barbershop. The apprentice studied the theoretical legal material on his own. He was required to work for his mentor, producing documents, serving court orders, running the office, and even cleaning it.

The two jobs that Bourquin held gave him the confidence he needed in his personal life, and in 1891 he married Mary Mitchell Ratigan, a young woman from a family rooted in western Ireland. They settled in Helena, where their three sons were born.[16] The young Mrs. Bourquin was Catholic, just like George's mother. His father's religion is unknown, but it can be safely assumed that he was Catholic as well. Bourquin lived as a Catholic but did not frequent church services and never declared his religious persuasion.[17] His wife was in charge of the household, which was run as a Catholic home. Although Butte had large Catholic and Protestant populations with a legendary rivalry between them, Bourquin apparently never got caught in the crossfire. He resigned from the federal land office in 1894 and applied for bar membership. The bar, too, was quite different then. It included those who practiced law, but members did not have to pass a bar examination. They were accepted on the basis of an interview conducted by a several lawyers. If the interviewers agreed that the applicant was worthy, he was admitted to the practice of law. The examining board simply declared that the candidate was of good moral character and had the knowledge and mental capacity to join the law profession.[18]

Bourquin established his practice in Helena. In 1899, however, for reasons that are unclear, he returned to Butte. His granddaughter Marilyn believed that Butte simply offered greater opportunities, although the people there were tough and even brutal.[19] Butte held out the promise of riches because of its extensive mining activities. A young and determined man could not find similar opportunities in the relatively more civilized Helena. Precisely because it was a developing town, characterized by conflicts, Butte may have presented a broader potential client base.

Bourquin did not remain a practicing lawyer for very long, however. Five years after arriving in Butte he was elected as a judge of the district court in Silver Bow County. Four years later, after finishing his term as judge in 1908, he opened a law office with two associates: Kirk, Bourquin and Kirk.[20] He remained there for only four years. In 1912, President William H. Taft appointed him the federal judge for the District of Montana. As to the circumstances of this nomination, his grandson stated: "I don't know how he got the federal appointment. He must have politicked. He was a young lawyer and he was apparently a tough guy."[21] It also can be presumed from his initial appointment to a federal position in Helena that he was active and respected in Republican Party circles in Montana.

On June 9, 1912, Bourquin began his tenure as federal district judge.[22] That is remembered as a tumultuous year, with the sinking of the *Titanic* and the aftermath of the second Morocco crisis. In Europe, conflicts that ultimately contributed to the outbreak of World War I gathered steam. There were also vast changes beginning in the United States. The main domestic issue was the relationship of the government to the big trusts. In the 1912 presidential election, President Taft faced three major candidates: Theodore Roosevelt, the head of a new Progressive Party; Eugene V. Debs, the leader of the Socialist Party; and Woodrow Wilson, a political science professor standing at the helm of the Democratic Party. All four candidates embraced progressive ideologies, preaching virtuous governing and greater morality in society.[23]

Though born in Pennsylvania, Bourquin viewed himself as a westerner. According to his family, Bourquin "thought that Washington was a remote and disgusting place, overrun by Easterners. It was Easterners who controlled the giant Anaconda Copper Mining Company that controlled Butte and Montana. There was little doubt that his frontier pride was manifest in his judicial rulings."[24]

Despite harsh criticism of Bourquin during World War I and the era that followed, many remembered him as Montana's finest judge. In a memorial tribute printed in Butte's *Montana Standard*, Bourquin was credited with having "left his mark on the history of Montana during his twenty-two-year career and having done more than any other federal judge of the Montana districts, the members of the bar and especially for the public." Furthermore, his "legacy to the Montana judiciary and Bar," the paper added, "was exemplary behavior which others at least claimed to desire in some small way to emulate."[25]

Posthumously, Bourquin's peers also praised him. Judge J. J. Lynch, a retired Silver Bow County (Butte) judge who had worked with Bourquin, noted: "Judge Bourquin was a keen student of law and history, was a philosopher who delved deeply into the humanities and was a fine author who was never at a loss for words."[26] The memorial tribute claimed that in comparison to Bourquin "no judge ever had a clearer conception of the basic principle of right and wrong." Bourquin earned a national reputation as a judge who concluded cases quickly and accurately. He was called to New Jersey, California, Arizona, and other states to help clean up clogged federal court calendars. His memorial tribute characterized him as "one of America's most colorful, sound, and able judges."[27]

Behind Bourquin's extraordinary judicial work ethic lay his belief that "justice delayed is justice denied." Bourquin was also a keen student of the human condition and as such once directed a jury as follows: "Remember that self-interest is the mightiest thing that moves a man; ask yourselves whether self-interest caused any witness to depart from the truth."[28] The "truth," as Bourquin understood it, was always of paramount concern in his court. Perhaps the final sentence of Bourquin's memorial tribute, though a standard remark in the rhetoric of eulogy, was not an exaggeration: "There was only one judge Bourquin in the world. . . . There will never be another like him."[29]

During Bourquin's entire career Montana was ruled by the Anaconda Copper Mining Company and was the outstanding example of a "company state" in the American West.[30] Montana certainly needed political reforms. The state's giant corporation possessed extraordinary powers that it did not hesitate to employ in order to crush labor's dissent. The Pinkerton Agency and goon squads intimidated and prevented legitimate labor protest. Numerous politicians served as agents of big business. The inhabitants of the mining towns lived in buildings provided by the mining companies that had inadequate sanitation. The employees were totally dependent on the goodwill of their employers. In Bourquin's view, the supremacy of the law was the most important value and a vehicle to protect individual rights. He was not a favorite of Anaconda. Bourquin firmly believed that only one thing stood between a civil society and barbarism, and that was enforcement of the law.

Bourquin was meticulous about his judicial ethics.[31] He would not permit anyone to sit next to him during a trial, lest they influence him or even seem to do so. Undoubtedly, he paid a personal price for such behavior. He did not have any close friends, but this did not seem to bother him. He preferred an isolated life. Wheeler described Bourquin as a very nervous and irritable person. He had a reputation for dealing harshly with anyone who sought to influence him in the slightest way. In his courtroom, he put great emphasis on proper conduct.[32]

Bourquin's decisions were written in flowery prose. His views were basically conservative and often directly reflected the influence of the western environment on his thinking. He was forever suspicious of the federal government, viewing it with the arrogant pride of a westerner, a sentiment mixed with the traditional local hostility toward entrepreneurs from the East who came west to exploit its natural resources for a quick profit. This was well represented by Anaconda Copper, which basically owned the town of Butte.

As a judge, Bourquin was not detached from the violence of the booming post-frontier town. A bootlegger by the name of John O'Leary was brought to trial in his court. Originally O'Leary was to stand trial in Butte, but no one had any illusions that he could be convicted there. The town in those days was small and tightly knit, almost tribal. O'Leary knew everyone, including the jurors. He probably supplied some of them with illegal booze. Therefore his trial was moved to Helena, where Bourquin happened to be sitting. When the bailiff called out "John O'Leary, come forward," a blast of gunfire sounded in the courtroom. O'Leary had a gun in each hand and was shooting in all directions. Luckily, no one was injured. The recoil of the guns sent the shots upward. O'Leary fled but was caught and brought before Bourquin, who sentenced him to a lengthy jail term.[33]

In contrast to his judicial decisions, Bourquin's political speeches could not be considered masterpieces. One might even say they were banal. As a stump speaker, he was not held in high regard. For example, a cartoon entitled "Pastime for Autumn Leisure" published in the *Daily Missoulian* on October 16, 1934, showed a politician addressing a crowd. It presented the judge, and above him the Founding Fathers, looking at a scoreboard with the caption: "Quoted in Campaign Speeches." It was a close race between Jefferson and Lincoln. The meaning was clear: Bourquin was preaching about history but was barely addressing the pressing contemporary issues.

After Bourquin lost the election he continued to show a great deal of interest in politics, but he did not make any effort to return to that arena. Instead, he started a new hobby, traveling throughout the country.[34] His declared goal for these trips was to check out business opportunities, as well as to visit his brothers and sisters and their children. It seemed that he enjoyed travel. In November 1958, during one of these trips, he passed away at the age of ninety-five. He was staying with his family at his birthplace in Pennsylvania. During the visit, he had decided to purchase a farm, perhaps out of nostalgia for the kind of life he had growing up. He asked one of his sisters to go with him on what he called "farm hunting." The weather was bad, and she tried to discourage him.

Bourquin, however, insisted, and they traveled throughout Pennsylvania checking out farms for sale.[35] During the trip he caught a cold, which became pneumonia, and he died soon after.

Bourquin's coffin was brought to Butte and lay in state at the federal courthouse. A dignified old man with long white hair entered the courthouse and looked at the judge in the open coffin. He turned to one of Bourquin's sons and said, "You do not know me." "True," the son answered. "I am John O'Leary," the man said as he left.[36] He came to pay a final tribute to a person who brought life into law and law into life.

Chapter II

THE GENESIS OF THE NATIONAL SEDITION ACT OF 1918

A s the guns of August 1914 began to roar and the world war commenced in Europe, President Woodrow Wilson advocated neutrality. The United States was ostensibly heeding George Washington's admonition to stay clear of foreign entanglements. Acting in this manner, it seemed that the United States could maintain its freedom and independence from Europe's problems. Soon, however, American strategic and economic interests dictated participation in the European conflict. Those interests were coated with idealistic, lofty slogans. America's elites concluded that avoidance of participation in the affairs of Europe did not further their needs and their vision of America's role in the world. Their aims could not be achieved through a policy of neutrality. To the American leadership the strategic imperatives were clear. They presented their interests as grand ideals and as the fulfillment of America's special destiny. They believed that America's divine goals could be attained only if Americans took command of civilization's fortunes in the global war.

Most Americans were convinced that World War I was the "war of the sons of light" against the evil "children of darkness." They embraced a vision of a holy crusade against the godless Huns. In order to fulfill America's Manifest Destiny they had to bring the blessings of democracy, independence, and freedom to the world. On April 2, 1917, in asking the US Congress to declare war, Wilson made it clear that the United States was fighting "for the intimate peace of the world and for the liberation of its peoples" and "to make the world safe for democracy." Wilson was the biblical trumpeter and messenger of a supposedly unselfish America that wished "no conquest, no dominion" but instead fought as the champion of the rights of humankind.

Some in America, such as Senator George Norris of Nebraska, opposed American participation in the war and insisted that it was "sold" to Americans by the "merchants of death." Yet Wilson, and many in leadership, saw a great opportunity in the war to create consensus in a nation that was torn by vast and radical changes. Fundamental transformations catalyzed by the Civil War changed America from a backward, homogenous, basically agricultural society to an advanced urban, industrial, and incredibly diverse society. The modernization process changed Jeffersonian America into an industrial world power. America became a colossus.

By 1914 America had experienced great social, economic, and political strife and sought new mechanisms to fit American society to the new realities. War and patriotism could provide much-needed unity and cohesion. Wilson hoped that the war might minimize the great chasms within American society. He labored to provide a focus for the nation that would submerge differences of origin, class, and race. Rapidly, the war became a holy crusade. It is highly significant and instructive that after World War II Winston Churchill authored *The History of World War II*, whereas Dwight D. Eisenhower's book was titled *Crusade in Europe*. Other nations fight wars; the United States engages in holy crusades.

In 1917, an intense campaign began against those who did not show enthusiastic and wholehearted support of the war. Vicious attacks on labor unions, German Americans, Irish Americans, and other hyphenated Americans soon followed, as did a crusade against "foreign ideas" and immigration in general. Free immigration was curtailed in 1924. New definitions of nationality, patriotism, and loyalty dominated the era. Loyalty was now defined as uncritical support of governmental policies and national leaders. Everything else was easily transformed into sedition, treachery, and subversion. Supporters of "alien ideas," such as socialism and communism, were labeled anarchists and radicals and were suppressed harshly. The Russian Revolution in November 1917 intensified fears, as the leaders of that movement called for a worldwide revolution of workers. The logic of absolute loyalty continued long after the war ended, in the era known as the Red Scare.

During the war, the president and government assumed vast powers. The government took over the railroads. It also took control of food supplies and ran numerous agencies. It began to plan and oversee industrial production and allocation of raw materials. The armed forces commanded enormous budgets, and the government oversaw American shipping. Government agencies directed propaganda and supervised all communications. The president and government agencies assumed complete power in all matters even remotely connected with the war effort.[1]

During World War I and the Red Scare that followed, patriotic fervor swept the United States. The hysteria that engulfed the state of Montana was extraordinary. The significance and importance of the extreme occurrences in Montana, however, far transcended its borders. Burton K. Wheeler aptly described the madness that characterized Montana during World War I and the years immediately following. As district attorney, he was close to the events and was under enormous pressure to prosecute alleged traitors, slackers, and spies.[2] According to Wheeler, "Montana was going crazy with reports of slackers and rumors of spies."

In early June 1917 a disaster occurred at a copper mine in Butte. An assistant foreman accidentally ignited a fire that caused an explosion in the Speculator mine. Despite heroic rescue efforts, 164 miners perished on the night of June 8, 1917. "Because the foreman had a German name it was widely believed that this was an act of sabotage directed by the Kaiser."[3] This was part of a newspaper campaign to promote hysteria under the guise of patriotism, in order to delegitimize organized labor's demands for higher wages and safer working conditions in the copper mines. The Anaconda Company, the state's largest employer, described every miner's strike as an "enemy plot."[4] Anaconda also owned many of the state's newspapers.[5] Labor in Montana had a long and distinguished history, and Butte was known as the "Gibraltar of Unionism." By 1914, however, the Anaconda Copper Mining Company had crushed labor's powers.

In the beginning of the war, there was much unrest and numerous strikes. Yet patriotism gave employers a fine opportunity to silence labor's demands.[6] "All labor leaders, miners, and discontented farmers were regarded by the super-patriots as pacifists and ipso facto agents of the Kaiser."[7] Members and supporters of the syndicalist, radical Industrial Workers of the World (IWW) were considered the greatest threat to the capitalist order and were mercilessly persecuted. The IWW organized unskilled laborers in the mining camps and in the lumber industry. It promised to create the "One Big Union" that would organize the "one Big Strike" that would "bring capitalism to its knees." The IWW opposed World War I since it believed in class wars only and not in national wars, and it promised to undertake violent action to prevent American soldiers from participating in the war. The reaction to the IWW was a national campaign, as members were considered traitors and agents of Germany and of godless anarchism.[8] In this atmosphere, in Butte, persons unknown lynched Frank Little of the General Executive Board of the radical, syndicalist Industrial Workers of the World. It was widely believed that the murderers were members of the Anaconda Company's "goon squad."[9] A central feature of the hysteria and irrationality in Montana was the numerous reports of German airplanes in the forests of western Montana. Wheeler explained: "There were increasing reports of enemy airplanes operating out of mountain hideaways south of Missoula in the Bitterroot valley. Just how and why the German high command expected to launch an invasion of the United States through western Montana, six thousand miles from Berlin, never made the slightest bit of sense to me."[10]

Reports were so numerous and fears so rampant that Wheeler was forced to assign an agent to investigate the rumors. He recalled that "there were persistent stories in the Flathead Reserve that airships were seen crossing the country and were always going south." A newspaperman wrote a story for the wire that a German base existed "in the wilds west of Missoula and a woman reported a burning airship near Hamilton." The *Daily Missoulian* insisted that Germans had a "wireless plant in the mountains." Wheeler received a directive from the Department of Justice in Washington DC to investigate "possible infiltration by the Huns."[11] In Helena, the state capital, things were not much different. The *Helena Independent* offered a hundred dollar reward to anyone who "could find the airplane flying over the city."[12] An editorial in the paper asked: "Are the Germans about to bomb the capital of Montana?" and "Do our enemies fly around over the high mountains where formerly only the shadow of the eagle swept?" Wheeler added that "this state of mind got utterly out of control two weeks later as the *Independent* proudly reported that an 'Helena citizen, unnamed, had fired the first shots discharged in America at an airplane.'" Governor Sam V. Stewart got into the act and promised to follow the plane next time with an expert rifleman.[13] Hundreds of stories circulated about individuals who allegedly were German spies and about mysterious cars with an even more "mysterious wireless."[14]

Liberty Committees were organized in most towns to deal directly with those who did not demonstrate sufficient zeal in purchasing Liberty Bonds. In Red Lodge, for example, two Finnish IWW leaders were beaten; in Billings, a city councilman was forced to march with the flag, and a meat market owner who dared to tear up a Liberty Bond subscription form was forced to kiss the flag.[15]

Rumor had it that a train full of Belgian children, whose arms had been cut off by the Germans, would come through Billings. Someone who said he did not believe the story was severely beaten and expelled from town. Prominent citizens, businessmen, and lawyers participated in this vigilante activity. A judge refused to issue warrants for their arrests. Instead, the person who had been beaten was arrested, accused of sedition, and convicted under a state sedition law. The Montana Supreme Court later overturned the conviction. A great deal of mob violence, deportations, and beatings of Nonpartisan League (NPL) organizers followed.[16]

George Bourquin was presiding over the federal district court in Montana during those troubled times, which he referred to as the "tumultuous years."[17] His rulings and interpretations, especially his interpretations of the federal Espionage Act of 1917, had important ramifications far beyond Montana. Real and perceived internal threats, coupled with fears that an external menace would subvert the nation, spurred the federal government to embark on a moral crusade that resulted in massive repression. Patriotic uniformity of thought became the yardstick of good citizenship. The courts served as a vehicle for the suppression of dissent, collaborating in the effort to "remove" the "other" from the nation's boundaries and to preserve the purity of the American way of life. Dissenters served as scapegoats in an atmosphere Bourquin likened to times when patriotism descended into fanaticism. To the judge, the era's excesses were reprehensible.[18] The newly organized Montana Council of Defense soon brought the hysteria in Montana to a fever pitch. Book burnings, public floggings, widespread harassment, witch hunts, and even inquisitions occurred with the official stamp of an agency of the state.[19]

A special session of the Montana legislature convened to combat the treacherous and seditious. Governor Stewart addressed the session and asked for legislation to provide "the mighty means of throttling the traitor and choking the traducer." He reported that "every disloyal utterance and every treasonable act is duly reported to the German people. . . . The tender mother is startled by the mere suggestion that [her] boy may not come back, the father clenches his fists at the very suspicion that any of his own acquaintances might conspire to encompass the destruction of his son and heir."[20] Analyzing the speech, historian K. Ross Toole summarized: "Stewart's address is remarkable for the high pitch of its frenzy and the mixture of tear jerking sentimentality and violent references to 'traitors in our midst,' 'poisoned tentacles, and vipers, circulating the propaganda of the Junkers.'"[21] Stewart was confident that the special session would act to protect that "mother" so that she would not awaken to find that disloyalty had destroyed her boy and "that the timber of her manhood has decayed, that the luster of her womanhood [has been] tarnished."[22]

The session unanimously passed a sedition act and a criminal syndicalism act. Joint resolutions calling for the resignation of Bourquin and

Wheeler were introduced. The resolution to remove Wheeler lost by a vote of thirty to twenty-nine. The resolution on Bourquin was tabled. According to Wheeler, the Bourquin resolution did not even reach the floor because of "his reputation for dealing with any interference with process of his court through stiff contempt penalty . . . [and] . . . also the mining companies had no desire to antagonize him because they had important claims cases pending before him."[23]

The special session turned instead to the impeachment of Judge Charles L. Crum.[24] It was in this session that the Montana Council of Defense became legal. The council was endowed with extraordinary powers, leaving to it responsibility for the security and welfare of the state of Montana.[25] It used these powers to spread war propaganda, promote the sale of Liberty Bonds, and search for traitors, "slackers," draft dodgers, and other nonconformists.[26]

The "patriots" of Montana sought to crush opposition to the war and to the status quo through strict enforcement of the Espionage Act of 1917. However, District Attorney Wheeler refused to be stampeded into mass indictments against those considered seditious. In January 1918, the first men indicted under the Espionage Act appeared in court. George M. Bourquin presided.

Bourquin exasperated the Justice Department and many residents of Montana through his rulings in "slacker" cases. His conduct in court included unusual procedures. In one case, at the conclusion of the testimony and arguments, Bourquin told the jury that he would allow the case to go to them but that his personal opinion was that the evidence was not adequate to justify finding against the defendant. In another case, upon the return of a verdict of guilty, Bourquin directed the defense counsel to demand a new trial because he was of the opinion that the evidence presented had not been sufficient to support the verdict. After losing a series of cases, Assistant District Attorney James Baldwin asked for more time to prepare; Judge Bourquin granted his request but allowed him only an hour and a half.[27]

Bourquin came under heavy attack. James H. Rowe, chairman of the local draft board of the city of Butte, described Bourquin as "the one United States District Judge who apparently regards delinquency under the Selective Service law with the amiable unconcern with which a normal citizen might view the eccentricities of a harmless and benignant mental defective. By some fatal coincidence," Rowe continued, such a man "is presiding . . . over this very federal district where relentless and certain punishment of evasion of the duties of citizenship is a paramount

"The Richest Hill on Earth, Butte, Montana." Photograph by N. A. Forsyth, ca. 1909. Stereograph Collection, ST 001.100. Reprinted by permission of the Montana Historical Society Research Center—Photograph Archives, Helena, Montana.

necessity." Rowe complained about the judge's rulings and saw them as nullifying "every attempt of the city and state to enforce the Selective Service Law."[28]

District attorneys throughout the country used the Espionage Act to suppress dissent. This act defined as actionable the making of "false statements" intended to interfere with the operations or the success of the armed forces or to promote insubordination within their ranks. It also made it a federal crime to obstruct the recruitment and enlistment of men for the military.[29]

In late January 1918, the first Montana case of alleged violation of the Espionage Act came to court. Ves Hall, a rancher from Rosebud County, had been arrested for uttering seditious remarks. He claimed that he would flee the United States to avoid the draft and that he hoped Germany would defeat the United States. He described President Wilson as a "British tool, a servant of Wall Street millionaires, and the richest and crookedest ——— ever President." Hall also said that the Germans had a right to sink ships and kill Americans without warning.[30]

Assistant District Attorney Homer G. Murphy, who prosecuted the case in Wheeler's absence from the state, charged that Hall had violated section three of the act in that he did

> "make and convey false reports and false statements with intent to inter-
> fere with the operation and success of the military and naval forces of
> the United States and to promote the success of its enemies" and that he
> did "cause and attempt to cause insubordination, disloyalty, mutiny, and
> refusal to duty in the military and naval forces of the United States, and
> obstruct the recruiting and enlistment service of the United States to the
> injury of the service of the United States."[31]

The *Helena Independent* of January 27, 1918, reported that Murphy "made a hard fight to convict the man." Evidence was produced, as cited by the court in handing down the opinion, that was conclusive—"that . . . [Hall] . . . had been guilty of doing about all the . . . lying, falsifying and vilifying with which . . . [he] . . . was charged."

Wheeler had considered it to be a weak case. On January 14, 1918, he asked the Department of Justice for authorization to obtain a steno-graphic record of the testimony. "It is desirable to preserve the records in this case by reason of the rulings of the court herefore in slacker cases."[32] This view proved to be prophetic. On January 27, Bourquin granted de-fense attorney Matt Canning's motion for a directed verdict and acquitted Ves Hall.[33]

Bourquin explained that his ruling was based on his belief that it was necessary to interpret the Espionage Act "to the end that a precedent be established." He found Hall's traitorous statements "unspeakable" but still could not justify a verdict of guilty. Hall had made his statements in a small Montana town of sixty people, sixty miles from the nearest railroad, with "none of the armies or navies within hundreds of miles." Furthermore, Hall made them in a hotel kitchen, at a picnic, in the street, and in a "hot and furious saloon argument." Bourquin found no proof of intent to interfere with the military. He illustrated his decision with the

President Taft visits Montana. Photograph by N. A. Forsyth, 1909. Stereograph Collection, ST 001.98. Reprinted by permission of the Montana Historical Society Research Center—Photograph Archives, Helena, Montana.

statement that if A shot B with a .22 pistol from a distance of three miles, A could not be convicted of attempted murder.

Actually, if A believed he could kill B by using the .22 at that distance, and the prosecution was able to prove intent, A could in fact be convicted of attempted murder. Bourquin's zealousness in protecting a US citizen's rights in the face of draconian efforts by the government to curtail basic civil liberties rested on shaky legal grounds. His causal argument was almost as shaky as some of the super-patriots' claims that the Espionage

WALKERVILLE

Walkerville, a suburb of Butte, Montana. Copy by Smithers, ca. 1880. PAc 98-57.103.
Reprinted by permission of the Montana Historical Society Research Center—
Photograph Archives, Helena, Montana.

Act authorized jailing dissenters to prevent them from making illegal statements. Bourquin's paramount interest was to maintain civil liberties in a time of mass hysteria. He ruled that Hall's threats were not unlawful because they were ineffectual. Bourquin thus anticipated future doctrinal developments in which First Amendment protections often receive special judicial consideration.

Bourquin emphasized that the government could prosecute only matters that had been clearly defined as crimes by Congress. Referring to the "madness" (Bourquin's term) of the times, he commented that the public, in its clamor for the trial and conviction of the "disloyal," operated under the mistaken impression that any slanderous or disloyal remark was just cause for prosecution. As Bourquin put it: "The patriotism that inspires such criticism is less a passion than passionate."[34]

Bourquin believed that Hall had intended to obstruct the recruiting and enlistment services of the United States, but he found that this was not a crime under the Espionage Act. The act was not intended "to suppress criticism or denunciation, truth or slander, oratory or gossip, argument or loose talk." Loose talk and slander of the president were not federal crimes, and Hall could not be punished for them. Bourquin added that such slander might be punishable by law:

> But since the sedition law had its share in the overthrow of the Federalists and in the elevation of Jefferson to the Presidency and his party to power, Congress has not ventured to denounce as crimes slander and libels of government and its officers. The genius of democracy and the spirit of our people and times seem yet unable to avoid greater than benefits from laws to that end.

Bourquin's strict interpretation of the act and his zealous protection of individual rights and free speech infuriated supporters of the war. Bourquin lent his staunch support to the position held by District Attorney Wheeler, whose reappointment was pending. The judge condemned those who unjustly criticized district attorneys for failure to prosecute when the merits of a case did not warrant it. He reasserted that the Espionage Act was not intended to suppress criticism, and he continued with a defense of Wheeler: "United States attorneys throughout the country have been unjustly criticized because they do not prosecute where they cannot. In instances their proper failure to prosecute has been made the subject of complaint to the Department of Justice to oust them or defeat reappointment."[35] The decision in the Hall case created a furor that led to immediate action on the local level and provoked significant action on the national level as well. Less than a week after the decision, Governor Sam V. Stewart announced that a special session of the Montana legislature would convene on February 14. The governor felt strongly that a law should be enacted to stop the activities of the disloyal element in Montana. He wrote: "Feeling is running high and I really expected some killing as a result of the construction of the law in the Hall case."[36]

William J. Campbell, a fanatic member of the Montana Council of Defense and the editor of the *Helena Independent*, observed that the decision in the Hall case was only the latest in a series of similar decisions by Judge Bourquin that pushed the people of Montana to the brink of violence. He predicted bloodshed, hangings, and unheard-of violence, for he believed that Montanans had reached the end of their patience. Campbell concluded a letter to Senator Henry L. Myers with the statement: "There

"The Great Steel Hoist, Original Mine, Butte, Montana." Photograph by N. A. Forsyth, n.d. Stereograph Collection, ST 001.152. Reprinted by permission of the Montana Historical Society Research Center—Photograph Archives, Helena, Montana.

is going to be trouble, deep, wide, and serious and don't you forget it." He asked the senator to look into the prospect of having Bourquin removed from the state for the duration of the war: "Men . . . are determined to rid the state of Wobblies, slackers, disloyalists and traitors. . . . I am ever expecting . . . trouble . . . in the state where sedition runs wild.[37]

Guy E. LaFollette, managing editor of the *Helena Independent*, wrote the attorney general in Washington accusing Bourquin of bias in favor of Germany's cause. He denounced him for never having punished any Wobbly or traitor and added, "relief, it is hoped, may be obtained by a special session of the legislature." LaFollette explained that Bourquin's home was in Butte, which he described as a haven of German spies and propagandists who had influenced the judge. He declared that the judge had become ever more belligerent since the drafting of his son. LaFollette speculated as to what could be done: Impeachment involved too long a process, and death was not likely, as he felt Bourquin to be "an exceedingly healthy specimen of whatever he is." He asked that the Department of Justice transfer the judge to another district because "Montana is 'fed up' with Bourquin." LaFollette also predicted the lynching of those whom Bourquin had set free.[38]

Bourquin's decision in the Hall case provoked an editorial barrage in Montana. Newspapers clamored for the passage of acts to halt sedition. On January 29, 1918, the *Great Falls Tribune* complained that "the ruling makes it practically impossible to punish any man for sedition" and recommended that Congress change the law. The *Anaconda Standard* of January 31 of that year lamented that, as a result of the decision, it was impossible to punish sedition or treason in Montana. William J. Campbell wrote in the *Helena Independent* on February 3: "The Independent can interpret public opinion very well indeed, and to say the decision of Judge Bourquin was a disappointment to the people of Montana is putting it mildly." The newspapers welcomed the call for a special session of the legislature. On February 3, the *Great Falls Tribune*, one of the few independent newspapers in Montana, stated: "There will be satisfaction to the patriotic people of Montana that . . . in . . . the coming session of the legislature there is promise of effective means for the punishment of loudmouthed traitors. Legislation for that is . . . made necessary by a recent court decision of Judge Bourquin." At the opening session of the legislature, Governor Stewart declared that some of the laws of the state were "inadequate, insufficient and lacking." He emphasized the necessity of protecting soldiers against financial losses that resulted from their service in the army. He asked for the legalization of the state Council of Defense and the Home Guard Organization in Montana. He also asked the legislature to act upon the national Prohibition amendment. However, the major portion of his opening speech dealt with the need to curb sedition in Montana. The governor insisted that Montana's statutes did not contain adequate provision for the punishment of those guilty of sedition, treasonable and disloyal acts and utterances. He called for some suitable statutes to be enacted to rectify the situation. He felt that otherwise various people in numerous communities would be provoked into becoming a law onto themselves and as a result "unwarranted and illegal violence may occur. . . . There is no law to curb the pernicious activities of individuals and organizations guilty of sabotage, criminal syndicalism, and industrial and political anarchy. At this critical time it is important that the people have protection from such dangerous activities."[39]

All the legislation requested by Governor Stewart passed with the exception of a Home Guard measure. On February 23, 1918, the governor signed into law the Montana Criminal Syndicalism Act.[40] Criminal syndicalism was defined as any philosophy that advocated "crime, violence, force, arson, destruction of property, sabotage and other unlawful acts or methods" as a means to achieve industrial or political revolution.[41] Another bill intended to suppress free speech became law on February 23, 1918. Introduced by Representative William J. Crismas of Carbon County, it was identical to the bill Senator Myers of Montana had submitted in the US Senate on August 13, 1917. Myers emphasized that he had introduced the bill

> on account of a lynching that had occurred in Montana just a short time before. . . . A man named Little was lynched at Butte, Montana. It was reported that he referred to the United States soldiers as "Uncle Sam's scabs in uniform." There was no effort by officers of the law to punish him; and, as a result, one morning he was hung by a mob. Having that in mind and fearing a repetition of such occurrences unless we had more and better law to suppress, prevent and punish such utterances, I introduced a bill on the subject. . . . There is going to be more of mob law and lawlessness unless we speedily enact a measure of this kind.[42]

The Myers bill had been referred to the Judiciary Committee, and there it had died.[43] It was not ignored by the extraordinary session of the House and Senate of Montana, however. The act, as passed by the Montana legislature and later by the US Congress, made it a crime to "utter, print, write or publish any disloyal, profane or scurrilous or abusing language" about the government, the Constitution, or the armies of the United States. Furthermore, anyone who showed "contempt, scorn, contumely, or disrepute" toward the army, navy, flag, or government could be fined a sum not to exceed $10,000 and sentenced to a prison term of not more than twenty years. The same punishment was to be meted out to any person who "shall willfully utter, print, write or publish any language intended to incite, provoke or encourage resistance" to the US government. Any instigation to curtail production in any industry essential to the war effort was to be punished in the same manner.[44]

Joint resolutions by the state legislature calling for the resignations of

Bourquin and Wheeler had been introduced in the special 1918 legislative session. The first resolution was tabled and the second defeated by only one vote.[45] The judge and the district attorney thus fared better than did Judge Charles L. Crum of the Fifteenth Judicial District of Montana, who had acted as a character witness for Ves Hall.[46]

While the legislature of Montana debated the Sedition and Anti-Syndicalism Acts,[47] the Department of Justice in Washington DC began to react to Bourquin's decision in the Hall case. The Justice Department had received a large volume of mail from Montana citizens and the Montana congressional delegation criticizing Bourquin and inquiring as to whether his decision could be appealed. John Lord O'Brian, special assistant to the attorney general, wrote to Attorney General Thomas W. Gregory:

> In the annexed memoranda you suggested that Mr. Warren [special assistant to the attorney general] and I consider amending the Espionage Act in some way adequate to get around Judge Bourquin's ruling in Montana. . . . We are both of the opinion that the only type of amendment which could dispose of Judge Bourquin's interpretation would be an amendment declaratory of the purpose of the Section and in substance providing that questions of individual intent should be questions of fact for the jury. . . . I am of the further opinion that even if such an amendment could be prepared and passed it would not dispose of the attitude of Judge Bourquin. In enforcing the draft law, for example, he has been far more unreasonable and stubborn than in the case of the Espionage law. The record of his rulings in our files show unmistakably that the real trouble with him is that he is distinctly against the proper enforcement of any of the war statutes and is out of sympathy with their purpose.

The Justice Department realized that Bourquin's precedent endangered its objectives and sought some corrective action. After a thorough investigation of events in Montana, the Justice Department concluded that Bourquin's attitude and his decisions handicapped enforcement of the Selective Service law. In some instances, he had sentenced offenders to only one day in jail. The Justice Department also concluded that complaints against the judge were "well founded, and his occupancy of the bench at this time is a most unfortunate thing for the people of Montana."[48]

Military intelligence was also interested in the situation in Montana. On May 22, 1918, Colonel F. G. Knabenshue, an intelligence officer in the Western Division of the War Department, recommended to his superiors

"A Great Day in Butte, Miners' Union Day." Photograph by N. A. Forsyth, n.d. Stereograph Collection, ST 001.077. Reprinted by permission of the Montana Historical Society Research Center—Photograph Archives, Helena, Montana.

that Wheeler's reappointment be delayed. The War Department forwarded the letter to the Justice Department, which replied that there was a factional fight in Montana and asked the War Department to disregard the report. The officer had recommended that "Judge Bourquim [sic] should be transferred and [a] man 500% American be sent to Butte . . . also [that the] reappointment [of] Mr. Wheeler [be] killed." This report was sent to A. Bruce Bielaski, chief of the Bureau of Investigation in the Justice Department. The Justice Department conducted a special investigation of Wheeler and concluded that he did his job well: "it is the view of this department that responsibility for the unfortunate conditions in Montana rests not upon him [Wheeler] but upon the United States District Judge [Bourquin]."[49]

Senator Thomas J. Walsh of Montana repeatedly inquired as to whether the decision in the Hall case could be appealed. Assistant Attorney General O'Brian explained to Walsh that because of the directed verdict it would be double jeopardy to try Hall again on the same charge. Instead the Department of Justice decided to amend the Espionage Act of 1917. With the aid of Governor Stewart, Senators Walsh and Myers of Montana persuaded national legislators of the need to suppress all forms of dissent in order to curtail mob violence.[50]

On January 16, 1918, Representative Edwin W. Webb of North Carolina, chairman of the House Judiciary Committee, presented a bill, HR 8753, to amend the federal Espionage Act of June 15, 1917. His intention was to prevent any obstruction to the sale of Liberty Bonds. Between March 14 and April 2 of that year, the Senate Judiciary Committee considered the House bill. Senator Walsh fought successfully to incorporate the Montana Sedition Act into HR 8753. The amended bill, he argued, would be an effective instrument for the suppression of dissent and for limiting the freedom of speech. A heated debate ensued on the Senate floor. Senator Walsh referred his colleagues to the decision by Judge Bourquin in the Ves Hall case to illustrate the need for the bill; in his opinion, it was essential for allied victory.[51]

Opponents of the bill maintained that the Walsh amendment was dangerous to constitutional guarantees of the freedom of expression. The amendment provided punishment for anyone who supported or favored the cause of any enemy of the United States. Senator Thomas W. Hardwick of Georgia, for example, warned that the proposed legislation was twice as drastic as the "abominated and execrated Alien and Sedition Act of 1798 that destroyed the Federalist Party and changed the course of American history." He was afraid that the Sedition Act could do the same to the Republican and Democratic parties. Senators Joseph K. Vardaman of Mississippi and Joseph I. France of Maryland claimed that the act was unnecessary. Senator Hardwick summed up the arguments of the opposition with a direct challenge to the motivations behind the Walsh amendment:

> I understand that the real—in fact, the only—object of this section is to get some men called I.W.W.'s who are operating [in] a few of the Northwestern states, and you Senators from those states have been exceedingly solicitous to have legislation of this kind enacted. . . . I dislike to be confronted by a situation in which in the name of patriotism we are asked to jeopardize the fundamental rights and liberties of 100,000,000 American people in order to meet a situation in a few Northwestern States.[52]

During the debate, the senators discussed the murder of Robert Prager by a mob of coal miners in Collinsville, Illinois, on April 4, 1918. Prager had allegedly voiced his opposition to war with seditious remarks about the administration's policies. Senator Myers argued that the bill was essential to stop mob rule and reminded the senators of the murder of Frank Little in Butte.[53]

Prompted by patriotic zeal to enhance the successful prosecution of the war, the senators adopted HR 8753. The bill was returned to the House, and a conference committee was established. On May 7, 1918, after a short debate, the House approved the bill 293 to 1. Two days later, both houses agreed to a federal sedition and anti-sabotage bill, and President Wilson signed it into law on May 16, 1918.[54]

The Sedition Act was designed to stop dissent. On May 28, 1918, the *Anaconda Standard* correctly interpreted its significance: "There is no freedom of speech any longer for the disloyal or pro-German. A man can talk all he pleases if he talks right." Thus, an alleged violation of a federal law in a small town in Montana, a courageous decision by a judge who could not be intimidated by a patriotic mob, and the extraordinary hysteria that engulfed a state and a nation contributed in large measure to the passage of one of the most stringent anti–free speech acts in American history.

The events of 1917–18 left an indelible impression on many of the primary actors involved. Burton K. Wheeler, for example, wrote: "One reason why I was oppose [sic] to F.D.R. packing the Supreme Court in 1937 was because of my experience during that time [World War I]—the local courts were crazy; only . . . Judge Bourquin and a few other local Federal Courts stood up."[55] Wheeler was correct; very few in the legal profession opposed the national hysterical "patriotic" orgy.[56]

Brutal stifling of the rights guaranteed by the Constitution followed the passage of the Sedition Act of 1918.[57] The act stemmed from local and national fears of radicals compounded by astute manipulation of patriotic feelings by business interests within a nation at war. President Wilson's Mediation Commission concluded that the unrest in the mining and lumber industries had not been the result of treasonable plots by the IWW but rather was triggered primarily by employers dealing with "unremedied and remediable industrial disorders."[58] The Justice Department, recognizing the wide scope of the act and the danger to individual liberties inherent within it, urged district attorneys to enforce the act with discretion. The department did not want wholesale suppression of legitimate criticism of the government.[59] On March 3, 1921, Congress repealed the Sedition Act. The nation, in the process of returning to "normalcy," could afford to do without it.

On May 3, 2006, Governor Brian Schweitzer of Montana signed pardons for seventy-eight people who had been convicted of sedition during the anti-German hysteria that engulfed Montana during World War I. Schweitzer declared that these posthumous pardons, the first in Montana's history, "should have been done a long time ago."[60]

Chapter III

CIVIL RIGHTS CASES IN TIMES OF CRISIS

J udge George Bourquin continued to preside over the federal district court in the District of Montana during the anxious years following World War I known as the period of the Red Scare. During World War I, real and perceived threats from within the country coupled with fears that an external menace might be about to subvert the nation spurred the federal government into embarking on a moral crusade that produced massive repression. During this time, the courts became a vehicle for suppression of dissent and eagerly collaborated in efforts to remove the "others" from the nation's boundaries in an attempt to preserve the purity of the American way of life. The logic of absolute loyalty continued long after the war ended.

Dissenters served as scapegoats in an atmosphere Bourquin likened to periods when patriotism descended into fanaticism. To this judge, the era's excesses were reprehensible.[1] Yet most courts in the United States ignored or rejected the individual rights guaranteed by the Constitution.[2] Few judges or elected officials proved willing or able to risk their positions and face ostracism by defending individual liberties. Following his rulings in cases during World War I, Bourquin remained one of those few during the Red Scare period as well.

An additional example of the judge's activism in ensuring that constitutional guidelines and the separation of powers in the American system of government were preserved is the case of *Ex parte Beck*[3] that came to court as World War I was winding down in 1917. Under the Selective Service Act, the draft tribunal had charged John Beck, a nondeclarant, with desertion and ordered him court-martialed in a military court. Bourquin ruled that the tribunal had no right to do that and had exceeded its authority by deciding that Beck had not offered sufficient proof of his alien status. An alien, the judge pointed out, was not entitled to an exemption by the draft tribunal, and, more importantly, did not qualify for the draft under US law. Draft tribunals did not have the power to grant exemptions to people not within their jurisdiction or to determine their nonalien status.[4] Thus the issue was not that the tribunal had refused to exempt Beck as an alien; it had usurped the power of the courts when it arbitrarily decided that Beck's alien status was even in question.[5]

Bourquin relied on a decision by Chief Justice John Marshall that established the invalidity of such a tribunal when it overstepped its jurisdiction.[6] In *Wise v. Withers*, Marshall had ruled that Wise, a justice of the peace in the District of Columbia, was exempt from military duty. Wise had previously been court-martialed and fined but had refused to pay the fine; Marshall found that the court-martial tribunal had no jurisdiction over Wise because federal law exempted all US officers from military duty. Bourquin considered Beck's case to be stronger.[7] The judge was at his constitutional best when he reviewed the argument of the army respondent, Major Roote. Roote contended that if he honored the court's decision he would be disobeying his commanding officer, the president, who ordered him, through the Selective Service Act, to imprison all deserters. Bourquin answered that the president "is required by law and duty to uphold and execute as the law of the land any such decree until reversed. All law requires him to do so, and no law, military or civil, permits him not to do so."[8]

Indirectly, Bourquin identified and limited the concept of executive privilege, an idea still ambiguous today. The president, as commander in chief, was not above the law and had to obey it like anyone else. Once again, the judge denied the potential tyranny of the federal government in favor of the constitutional guarantees of habeas corpus.

Bourquin's defense of civil liberties continued in the case of E.V. Starr regarding free speech in 1920. A bill intended to suppress free speech in Montana had become law on February 23, 1918. The act, as passed by the Montana legislature and later by the US Congress, made it a crime to "utter, print, write or publish any disloyal, profane or scurrilous or abusing language" about the government, the Constitution, or the armies of the United States. Furthermore, anyone who showed "contempt, scorn, contumely, or disrepute" toward the army, navy, flag, or government could be fined a sum not to exceed $10,000 and sentenced to a prison term of not more than twenty years. The same punishment was to be meted out to any person who "shall willfully utter, print, write or publish any language intended to incite, provoke or encourage resistance" to the US government. Any instigation to curtail production in any industry essential to the war effort was to be punished in the same manner.[9]

Under these state laws, E. V. Starr was convicted and sentenced in a Montana state court to not less than ten years nor more than twenty years of hard labor for stating: "What is this thing [the flag] anyway? Nothing but a piece of cotton with a little paint on it and some other marks in the corner there. I will not kiss that thing. It might be covered with microbes."[10]

In late 1919, Starr applied to the Montana Supreme Court for a writ of habeas corpus, which was denied. He then turned to the federal district court. On January 31, 1920, during the height of the Red Scare, Judge Bourquin handed down his decision. Starr claimed that the Montana laws under which he had been convicted were repugnant to the federal Constitution and that his sentence violated the Thirteenth and Fourteenth Amendments. Bourquin disagreed, ruling that federal law neither pardoned the offense nor drew it within federal jurisdiction.[11] Yet Bourquin did not stop there. He announced that Starr "was more sinned against than sinning." Starr had been victimized by what Nietzsche had called the "herd." According to Bourquin, Starr "was in the hands of one of those too common mobs, bent upon vindicating its peculiar standards of patriotism and its odd concept of respect for the flag." Forcing a person to kiss the flag, the judge stated, was "a spectacle for the pity and laughter of gods and men." Those who had forced this act upon Starr had degraded the "sacred banner" and brought it into contempt. They, and not Starr, should be punished.[12] Bourquin left no doubt as to his views on the uses and abuses of patriotism. In his decision in *Ex parte Starr*, Bourquin wrote:

> Patriotism is the cement that binds the foundation and the superstructure of the state. The safety of the latter depends upon the integrity of the former. Like religion, patriotism is a virtue so indispensable and exalted, its excesses pass with little censure. But when, as here, it descends to fanaticism, it is of the reprehensible quality of the religion that incited the massacre of St. Bartholomew, the tortures of the Inquisition, the fires of Smithfield, the scaffolds of Salem, and is equally cruel and murderous. In its name, as in that of Liberty, what crimes have been committed![13]

Bourquin "turned the screw," as it were, on Dr. Samuel Johnson's well-known dictum that "patriotism is the last refuge of scoundrels." He be-

lieved that patriotism was an exalted value but one too easily manipulated by the "herd" to suit its baser needs. He would not allow such a
distortion of patriotism in his courtroom. He called the sentence "horrifying" and cited it as an example of what Oliver Wendell Holmes, Jr., had
criticized in his famous dissent in the Abrams case.[14] Bourquin concluded
that in a "frivolous" charge, such as that against Starr, "a nominal fine
would serve every end of justice."[15] In spite of Bourquin's private beliefs,
he could not accept Starr's claims. For Bourquin, obedience to the law
was the supreme consideration. He could not entirely relieve Starr and
advised him to appeal to the pardoning authorities.[16]

As patriotic fervor continued after World War I, Bourquin continued
to rule in accordance with his worldview that was forever watchful of
governmental excesses. As such, Bourquin granted a petition of citizenship previously denied a Norwegian immigrant who, during World War
I, had claimed alien status.[17] Lasse A. Siem claimed exemption from the
draft because of physical unfitness, the burden of dependents, and his
alien status. Siem was examined and rejected by the armed forces as
physically unfit. Throughout the war he worked as a copper miner, toiling
in an industry vital to the war effort. This, according to the judge, was
praiseworthy. Unlike others, Siem "did not hide nor take to the woods."
Writing in 1922, Bourquin further noted that "as the war and its emotions
recede, it should be recognized that a great number of natives secured
statutory or strategic exemptions to escape active service and secured
positions in a department with a 'military tinge' and no or little 'military
hazard.'" After the war, he continued, these same men assumed positions
of leadership in civilian life based on the "strength of their military record." Bourquin found Siem's service neither less valuable nor less haz-
ardous. "No one condemns them. Why condemn him[?] Why demand
more of an alien, who yet owes this country little, than of them, who now
owe this country much, everything."[18] He called on the US Naturalization
Service to recognize that Siem fulfilled the requirements of "good, moral
character" and had an "attachment to the Constitution." The judge concluded that it was "peculiar logic to hold otherwise."[19]

In the Siem case, Bourquin believed that "it was the government that
violated both law and morals." The government's contention that Siem's
insistence on the right of exemption demonstrated his unfitness for citizenship "savors much of the tyrant's bitter complaint that his victims refused to die quietly and disturbed his sleep by their indecent wails of agony."[20] The judge praised Siem's claim for exemption from military service.
He was a citizen of Norway, a neutral country, and his first obligation was

to his native land. Siem claimed that he was attached to, and had affection for, the US Constitution. Bourquin ruled that "between affection and duty, everywhere, in all circumstances, law and good morals dictate choice of duty." Thus Siem's conduct before declaring his intention to become a citizen demonstrated that he was a principled person worthy of becoming a US citizen. For Siem to have acted differently would have been contrary to the law of nations. It was not reasonable to infer that Congress intended to compel or persuade aliens to violate their allegiances or to offend their native lands. Bourquin observed that "the inference does violence to the relations between nations, and it must be rejected especially since the law of nations is part of our law."[21] Bourquin also objected to the criteria that the naturalization examiner employed to determine whether an applicant was worthy of citizenship. An alien, for example, could be refused citizenship because he could not pass an examination in constitutional law that "90 per cent of the native-born would flunk" and that "might well drive the presiding judge to the books."[22]

Bourquin claimed that the "distinguishing and supreme obligation of citizenry and its permanent allegiance is military service." He traced the origins of this obligation to the feudal system, "wherein the vassal makes oath of fealty to his lord and serves him in war, as a consideration and payment for the land and protection that he receives from his lord." This applied fully to the alien once he was admitted to citizenship but not before.[23] Bourquin concluded with a question that did not require a reply: "If the government confiscates the services of mules admitted not to be its own, in a court of law, the owner may recover the reasonable value thereof, not being limited to compensation the government may assume to pay; and if government confiscates the services of men admitted not its citizens, can they likewise recover?"[24] There is little doubt as to how Bourquin would have ruled in the hypothetical situation he put forth. He clearly expressed his stance by insisting there were other nations in the world in addition to the United States that had values and sensitivities and that encouraged the loyalty of their citizens. By being loyal to Norway, Siem had done nothing to forfeit his right to become an American citizen.

After a long series of decisions in which Bourquin repeatedly chastised the government for violating the rights of radicals and aliens, the Department of Labor should not have been surprised by Bourquin's refusal to deport Nicholas Radivoeff. In a ruling he made in *Ex parte Radivoeff* in 1922, Radivoeff was a "radical" alien and the secretary of the Butte branch of the IWW.[25] Bourquin believed that Radivoeff's rights had been violated, even though the judge conceded that pamphlets bought from the defendant contained "I.W.W. and communist philosophy" and had passages that seemingly approved of sabotage in opposition to capitalism. Few judges at the time were concerned with the rights of communists, "Wobblies," and aliens.[26]

Bourquin, however, would not allow the government to disregard due process of law when its deportation procedures did not protect the basic rights of a person who happened to be an alien. He found that Radivoeff had been denied a fair hearing, that the warrant for his arrest was not based on any probable cause, that the alien was made to be a witness against himself, and that the hearings were quasi-secret rather than open. In addition, the evidence presented was not within the scope of the warrant issued and Radivoeff had not been given time to secure counsel. The government refused to produce a former Department of Labor inspector whose statements were admitted into evidence. The government demanded to know what the defense hoped to prove by cross-examining the inspector and required a commitment from the accused to cover the costs of producing the inspector at the trial. In effect, the Department of Labor demanded that the alien prove he was innocent in advance.[27] Nothing could have been more antithetical to Bourquin's approach in interpreting the Constitution when individual rights were at issue.

Bourquin had no doubt that the IWW member in question advocated the destruction of property, but he regarded the proceedings against Radivoeff as unfair and prejudiced and as a basic denial of due process of law. Not only were general principles of law violated, he maintained, but so were the Labor Department's rules—rules that became law as far as the government and the alien were concerned.[28] Referring to one of his earlier rulings, he noted that "the vast power of the Secretary of Labor, judicial in its nature, [is] capable of infinite abuse and tyranny, little restrained by the Constitution, procedure, publicity, responsibilities and traditions that hedge about the court, and little controlled, save by his honor and conscience."[29] Bourquin admonished the Department of Labor to administer the law "not arbitrarily and secretly, but fairly and openly, under the restraints of the tradition and principles of free government applicable where the fundamental rights of men are involved."[30] To that end, he added "that trials resulted in justice, with what is of only lesser importance, an appearance of justice."[31]

Bourquin would not stand for a situation in which "the frequent great injustice in deportation proceedings in part has been incited by a theory that obsessed the department . . . enough to accuse the alien to justify deportation."[32] The government did not need to prove the alien guilty. It acted as if it were the alien's responsibility to prove he was innocent.[33] Bourquin concluded that deportation proceedings had to be fair and had to be supported by substantial evidence. Otherwise, he noted, the proceedings became evil and dangerous. It was the role of the courts to guarantee "public, humane, and just administration of the law."[34]

Not all deportation cases involved alleged radicals. Any group of outsiders was fair game. In *In re Tam Chung*, an earlier decision about the deportation of a Chinese student in 1915, Bourquin had recorded his fears about the extraordinary powers vested in the secretary of labor in such matters. Tam Chung, who lived with his family in Butte and occasionally helped at the family restaurant in return for food and lodging, had been found working without a permit. He thus was ordered deported. There was evidence that the seventeen-year-old had been instructed daily by a tutor, who described him as a "diligent student of good behavior."[35] To begin his ruling, Bourquin offered a few skeptical comments:

> Perhaps Congress could have broken our plighted faith and treaty law stipulating the Chinese students should loaf in their leisure and not labor for their living—could have placed Chinese students who here turn to honest labor for a livelihood on the plane of panders and prostitutes so far as deportation is concerned; but, happily, not having done so, it needs no argument to demonstrate that the Secretary of Labor cannot—that it is not given to him to violate the national promise, repudiate the treaty, and convert it into a mere scrap of paper.[36]

Under the rules of the Chinese Exclusion Act of 1888, the United States had agreed that Chinese students had rights, privileges, immunities, and exemptions accorded to the citizens and subjects of a most favored nation. However, Tam Chung was to be deported under the rules adopted by the secretary of labor, pursuant to the act.[37] Bourquin felt that a US government official could not and should not "violate the national promise." The only limits to the secretary's vast powers in deportation matters were his honor and his conscience. In this particular case, however, Bourquin held that the secretary had exceeded those limits.[38] The judge provided a long list of precedents supporting his ruling, concluding forthrightly that the deportation of Chinese, without the ability to go to court, "is at least food for disquieting thought."[39]

Bourquin often came under heavy attack because of his controversial decisions. The common theme of his legal thinking was to protect the individual from the excesses of governmental power. Indeed, in cases that came before him involving "loyalty", the "Red Scare," and "Indians," the common legal ground was his desire to limit the scope of governmental authority pertaining to individuals, minorities, and any group that could be construed as the "other." For Bourquin, the way society dealt with those outside the popular consensus was a true test of democracy.

Bourquin's concern for the ordinary individual was paramount precisely because of his strict constitutional interpretations. He believed that individuals needed to be protected both from themselves and from governmental excess. Furthermore, he extended this paternalism to Native Americans and other endangered minorities. When George Norman, an immigrant, alien "other," was denied citizenship by the government, Bourquin defended his civil rights in *In re Norman* in 1919. As a farmer, Norman had been exempted from active service during World War I, yet because he had not served he was later denied citizenship. Bourquin delivered a scathing critique of the hypocrisy of judges who would question the patriotism of those who received draft deferments, writing, "that the judge of the state court that partial exemption stamped Norman as unfit for admission to the same citizenship that the judge enjoys, is incomprehensible."[40]

Bourquin found that Norman had been abused through the exercise of "mere arbitrary power," yet he did not overturn the earlier judge's ruling because he had to honor a technical legal barrier. Bourquin explained that the state court's denial of leave to file a naturalization petition was res judicata and therefore could not be litigated again.[41] Bourquin's solution was to suggest that Norman continue to cultivate a "good moral character" and refile for citizenship in five years.

Bourquin's ongoing theme of protecting the rights of the individual in clashes with the state was most forcefully demonstrated in *Ex parte Jackson*.[42] This was, perhaps, the most important case involving individual rights that Bourquin ruled on. He handed down this decision in February 1920 in the midst of the Red Scare, when most judges were effective tools for the suppression of radicals.[43] Bourquin used a deportation procedure against John Jackson, a member of the anarcho-syndicalist Industrial Workers of the World, as an opportunity to air his views on civil liberties, emphasizing that no emergency, even war, warranted the violation of the rights of personal security, safety, and the orderly due process of law.[44]

John Jackson petitioned Bourquin for a writ of habeas corpus to protest the decision of the federal government to deport him from the United States. He was held for deportation after immigration inspectors, according to Bourquin, had been guilty of an illegal raid of his premises and after they ignored due process by proceeding against the petitioner —without warrant—through an unlawful search and seizure. Jackson's alleged offense was "advocating or teaching the unlawful destruction of private property and who at the time of entry [to the US] was categorized as someone likely to become a public charge."[45]

Jackson was a Wobbly who persistently protested working conditions and wages in the mining industry in Montana. In one of these IWW protest meetings, the possibility of a strike was discussed. Federal agents raided the meeting. In an ironic reversal of the charges against Jackson, Bourquin found that only the raiders created disorder, by breaking and entering, destroying property, searching and arresting people, seizing papers and documents, and cursing, insulting, and beating members of the union by order of the commanding officer. In general, Bourquin wrote, the inspectors "perpetrated a reign of terror, violence, and crime against citizen and alien alike," whose "only offence seems to have been peaceable insistence upon and exercise of a clear legal right."[46]

Bourquin stated that it was the immigration inspectors who had acted illegally in their treatment of Jackson, illustrating Michel Foucault's premise that discourse could be "disarmed" of its power by institutions. The irony was in the fact that the institution of the judiciary, represented by Bourquin, "disarmed" institutional discourse, which was governmental in origin.[47] The judiciary disarmed the prosecutorial arm of the federal government. The judge could find no evidence to support the government's case. Pamphlets of the IWW advocating armed insurrection and resistance to government were not found in the petitioner's home but rather in a general meeting place. Bourquin declared the "deportation proceedings [to be] . . . unfair and invalid in that they are based upon evidence and procedure that violate the search and seizure and due process clauses of the Constitution."[48] Bourquin also was unable to sanction a deportation after the government, in its arrogance, "at bar freely discloses its own wrong by which it seized the evidence. The law and courts no more sanction such evidence than such methods, and no more approve either than the thumbscrew and the rack."[49] Bourquin delivered an impassioned opinion in defense of civil liberties. He was especially agitated by methods that called to his mind a particularly dark era in human history. He considered the actions and rhetoric of the founders of the Republic living safeguards against the excesses of government: "The Declaration of Independence, the writings of the fathers, the Revolution, the Constitution, and the Union, all were inspired to overthrow and prevent . . .

governmental despotism. They are yet living, vital, and potential forces to those ends, to safeguard all domiciled in the country, alien as well as citizen."[50]

In this decision Bourquin also displayed the wealth of knowledge he employed in his judicial persona. Not content to deliver decisions as a technician analyzing precedent divorced from human society, he particularly liked to refer to historical memory to safeguard the civil rights of his contemporaries: "For in emergency, real or assumed, tyrants in all ages have found excuse for their destruction [of civil liberties]. Without them [safeguards], democracy perishes, autocracy reigns, and the innocent suffer with the guilty."[51] He also explained excesses of mob behavior through historical simile, seeing the hysteria and hatred disseminated by the "super patriots" in times of war as an endless historical repetition.[52]

Bourquin defended democracy and its privileges, viewing the courts as the last bastion of liberty in America in times of frenzy and xenophobia, yet his attitude toward the masses of humanity was as dark as that of some of the Puritan founders of the Massachusetts theocracy in the early seventeenth century. Much like Walt Whitman in *Democratic Vistas*, Bourquin feared the cowardice, viciousness, and antidemocratic tendencies of the "mob" or "herd." Bourquin insisted that the "Reds" were of less danger to America than those who would deny them their liberties and seek to deport them. "These latter," he wrote, "are the mob and the spirit of violence and intolerance incarnate, the most alarming manifestation in America today."[53]

For Bourquin, "lynch law" was not law at all. He viewed the judiciary as an institution that had to protect the common man from his own frailties. It could not do so by refusing the accused the right to interrogate inspectors who presented evidence against him or by demanding from him the costs of producing a government official that testified against him. The government also presented no evidence that Jackson was a "public charge." What happened in this case, according to Bourquin, was that the government chose to ignore the fact that "the inalienable rights of personal security and safety and due process of law are the fundamentals of the social compact, the basis of organized society, the essence and justification of government, the foundation, key, and capstones of the Constitution."[54]

Based on the inspectors' conduct, Bourquin halted the deportation proceedings. Bourquin had little doubt that some of those who advocated "stone wall, shooting at sunrise, and other lynch law" sincerely cared for America's welfare. But those "super-patriots," in the name of love of country, disregarded basic constitutional values. He also recognized that many of them seemed to gain power, prestige, and money by harping on the powerless threats of anarchy and revolution of those he called the "miserable, bated, bedeviled 'Reds.'" As to the idea of Jackson being a public charge, Bourquin pressured the immigration inspector into admitting that Jackson made a good salary. What had disturbed the inspector —and revealed that the true issue of the trial was Jackson's suspect patriotism—was that he had "never purchased any War Savings Stamps or Liberty Bonds."

Such admissions disclosed the xenophobic atmosphere surrounding the proceedings.[55] Responding to this atmosphere of suspicion and intolerance, Bourquin issued the writ of habeas corpus sought by Jackson, and the Justice Department appealed. The appeal was dismissed, and Jackson was never deported.

Like World War I, the ensuing Red Scare was a dark period for basic American freedoms. The dream that a saner, better world would emerge from the Great War had been shattered. Consensus in America was replaced by emotional and extreme reactions, ostensibly to preserve basic American values. The results, however, triggered mass hysteria and governmental repression. Disregard for liberty and due process was rampant; the gagging of dissent became the order of the day. Individual rights were either ignored or repressed, often in the name of the law.

At a time when state and national government officials sought to consolidate their powers on the premise that national security demanded increased deference to central authority, Bourquin was outspoken in his opposition. To him, it was an outrage that judges refused to second-guess the wishes of an inflamed citizenry, made manifest through the repressive acts of government officials. Bourquin thought it the duty of the courts to protect the citizenry from government excesses, or what he called "government despotism," and at the same time protect the "herd" from their base instincts by safeguarding the laws, which were the only barrier between civilization and barbarism. His distrust in his fellow beings in all their social manifestations mixed with his enduring faith in the Constitution motivated him to be a kind of civil libertarian in the most trying of times.

George Bourquin did not permit governmental power or public opinion to alter his commitment to the rule of law. Serving at a time of great intolerance, Bourquin demonstrated the importance of an individual who would not abandon his convictions. He would not permit his beloved legal system to become politicized, nor would he allow a subversion of the Bill of Rights. His fealty to American liberties had nothing to do with an antiwar posture or with sympathy for Germany. Prior to America's entrance into World War I, Bourquin had said: "I hope to see the day when Berlin will be a cow-path and the Allied flag will be flying over the Krupp factory."[56] Yet Bourquin's conduct on the bench provided an outstanding example of integrity. He rarely allowed his private opinions to interfere with his judicial persona or with his interpretation of constitutional liberties. Thus, despite his inherent conservatism, Bourquin insisted on defending the civil rights of "unpatriotic" citizens, immigrants, and many "others." In Bourquin's case, justice truly was unusually blind.

Chapter IV
THE IMPEACHMENT OF JUDGE CRUM

O n January 26, 1991, the Montana Senate, by a vote of forty-six to zero, passed Resolution No. 2. The resolution exonerated Charles L. Crum, judge of the Fifteenth Judicial District in eastern Montana, from his wrongful impeachment on March 22, 1918.[1] The senate resolution was a direct result of an article by Dave Walter in *Montana Magazine*. Walter's article told the story of Crum's impeachment and focused on Crum's personality, background, and family life, as well as on his tragedy.[2] State senator Harry Fritz of Missoula, a University of Montana historian, cosponsored the senate's unique resolution, which attempted to undo and rectify a historical injustice.[3]

Crum's impeachment is an outstanding example of the fear, hatred, and paranoia that swept Montana and the nation during the World War I period. The transcript of the Crum impeachment trial provides a special opportunity to examine and analyze the words used by common people who testified during the trial and attempted to damn the judge, thereby demonstrating their own patriotism. Through the trial record, it is possible to study the background of the hysteria and to consider what was regarded as appropriate for patriotic language and behavior during World War I.

Our interest in the Crum case, then, is not based on the interesting history of an individual judge. Rather, close attention to the transcript illuminates aspects of the cultural and political fabric of a trying time in American history. It was a time when immigrant "outsiders"—perceived as "others"—did everything they could to present themselves as purely American. That Judge Crum was of German descent was an integral, though unstated, part of the impeachment proceedings against him. The trial provided "good" German immigrants in a western state a showcase in which to display their undivided loyalty to the United States. In spite of the hysterical atmosphere, Bourquin decided to appear as a character witness for Crum.

Judge Crum's crimes were that he was of German parentage and did not seem to demonstrate sufficient zeal for the war. Moreover, he served as a character witness for Ves Hall during his trial. Unlike Bourquin, who was a federal judge, Charles Crum was a state judge who could be brought to account directly by the representatives of the people of Montana.

On March 20, 1918, the senate of the state of Montana, sitting as a High Court of Impeachment, convened in the matter of the impeachment of Charles L. Crum. This followed the Montana House of Representatives' decision on February 25, 1918, to present articles of impeachment against Judge Crum.[4]

During the house debate, it became clear that many Montana representatives had had "enough" of "pro-German traitors," and they were willing to spend large amounts of money to guarantee that the disloyal would not "go scot free without trial or attention from the court."[5] After a unanimous House vote to present impeachment articles, the leading newspaper in the state capital, which was one of the most influential in Montana and the paper that represented the views of the state's ruling elite, printed the following melodramatic account:

> Solemn, earnest, grim and determined—standing up to their stern obligation and duty with courage and high spirit—the men and women of the house of representatives, in movements that will be historic in Montana, yesterday morning voted that Charles L. Crum, incumbent of high office, wearer of the ermine of the judiciary, arbiter of the fortunes of his district, . . . should be brought to the bar of the senate of Montana, there to be tried upon charges of disloyalty to his state and to his country, of high crimes and misdemeanors, of malfeasance in office, of seditious utterances and acts approaching in gravity that most heinous of all crimes in the penal category—treason to the United States.[6]

The clamor for action against the "disloyal" in Montana increased until it reached panic proportions. Fully a decade before Lindbergh crossed the Atlantic—and so well before transatlantic flights were feasible—there were repeated reports of German planes landing in Montana.[7] Many in Montana considered the courts to be the best instrument to combat dissent. Burton K. Wheeler, at that time US district attorney, described how hundreds of cases were brought to his office for prosecution, many by local police authorities. Wheeler recalled that "most of them were inspired by old grudges, malicious gossip, barroom conversations."[8] He refused to prosecute. In fact, it was Bourquin who actually triggered the Hall case by suggesting that Wheeler send him some sedition cases in order to defuse the attacks on the federal district attorney's office. Felkner (Fritz) Haynes, a Rosebud County attorney who acted as special prosecutor during one of Wheeler's absences from the district, presented the charges against Ves Hall. After Bourquin acquitted Hall, Wheeler commented that few other judges in the country would have written such a decision in the face of the great demand to punish the "disloyal."[9]

After Hall's acquittal, a local patriotic group in Rosebud County, incensed by Crum's testimony on behalf of Hall, demanded his resignation. He categorically refused. Only after charges against him were presented to the Montana House of Representatives did Crum decide to do so. Yet the political atmosphere in the state was so aroused that Crum's resignation did not stop the impeachment proceedings. Wheeler summed up Crum's story as a tragedy for a "fine and honorable man."[10] Many representatives in the house sought to find some way to attack Bourquin and Wheeler for dereliction of duty, but the Montana legislature simply did not have jurisdiction over federal officials. The legislature, however, had the capacity to act vindictively against a state official such as Crum.

An analysis of the impeachment trial shows that Crum was actually tried for what amounted to crimes of heresy. His perceived radical "otherness" derived from his German heritage but also from his implied socialism and anti-imperialism. The characterization of various statements he made as heresies resulted from his unwillingness to assign to secular objects—such as the flag—sacramental status. Thus, paradoxically, the charges against him were specific but also undefined and even unsaid.

The main offenses said to have been committed by the judge were stated briefly. Crum allegedly had said that the United States was duped by England to enter the world war on her behalf unnecessarily. The judge was thus considered a traitor to his country.[11] Even those who supported Crum, such as the citizens of Roundup, Montana, were confused as to the nature of the impeachment trial against him. An attorney, G. J. Jeffries, for example, defended Crum as if he were on trial for treason: "I believe that [it] is necessary to secure a fair and impartial trial, especially where the public mind is in the condition it now is and where a man is on trial for treason."[12]

In fact, Crum was not on trial for anything like treason. The only sanction available to a senate trial was to remove the judge from office and to prevent him from seeking a position of public trust in Montana again.

"The Federal Building, Butte, Montana." Photograph by N. A. Forsyth, n.d. Stereograph Collection, ST 001.075. Reprinted by permission of the Montana Historical Society Research Center—Photograph Archives, Helena, Montana.

In the minds of both friends and enemies, it was Crum's loyalty as a "hyphenated American" of German ancestry that was actually on trial. The whole legal point of the impeachment trial was moot. Why bother to impeach someone who had already resigned? Clearly, public punishment for "otherness" was more important to the senate than the removal of a judge who already had removed himself. He had become a useful political target because of his background. Crum was also charged with siding with Germany in the *Lusitania* affair and with having no sympathy for American civilian casualties. He allegedly accused President Wilson of being a "tool, hireling and puppet of the British Empire and of Wall Street and of the bankers and financial interests of the United States who had made loans to prosecute the war."[13] In the subtext of the impeachment trial, the judge also was accused of being a socialist, a revolutionary, and someone who opposed "imperialist" and anti-labor legislation and policies. Crum was supposed to have claimed that the very act of declaring war and sending the armed forces abroad, to fight beyond the borders of America, was unconstitutional. Therefore, it was claimed that he did his utmost to convince people to disobey the draft laws.[14]

Judge Crum may have committed a crime, but not one for which anyone could be impeached. He threatened the prosecuting attorney of Rosebud, Felkner Haynes, with a loaded revolver: "You have circulated in Montana reports that I am a traitor and I will kill you like a dog," Crum declared.[15] Certainly, this was a mistake. Subsequently, Haynes admitted that he was the one who "got the ball rolling" in the investigation of Judge Crum.

Some witnesses said that Crum attempted to disqualify two members of the Over-Seas Club from serving on the jury in his court because of that organization's support of England against Germany.[16] Crum surely despised that organization's motto:

We sailed wherever ship could sail
We founded many a mighty state,
Pray God our greatness may not fail
Through craven fears of being great.[17]

One might juxtapose this verse by Alfred Tennyson with Crum's vision of dead American bodies in the trenches of Europe, young men who perished in a war that he believed was none of America's affair. On matters of ideology, clearly the Over-Seas Club and Judge Crum vehemently disagreed.

An additional charge against the judge was his act of feeding and clothing three jailed members of the Industrial Workers of the World (IWW) against the explicit orders of the sheriff of Rosebud County.[18] The last two charges were so obviously trumped up that one courageous state senator, Fred Whiteside, actually voted for acquittal on these charges. He noted that for a German defendant, Joe Holtz, to challenge a member of a jury, at the suggestion of Judge Crum, because the potential juror belonged to the Over-Seas Club, might be Crum's method of ensuring an impartial jury.[19] According to Whiteside, however, even more important was the issue of feeding the prisoners. Crum was charged with interfering in feeding prisoners bread and water. "Now there is no law that authorizes officers of the county to confine prisoners in that way," Whiteside said, "and if the matter was called to the attention of the Judge, it certainly was his duty to see that the law was observed." Of his "not guilty" vote, Whiteside declared: "It is a strange circumstance indeed, if a man is to be impeached because he has enforced the law."[20]

Perhaps the whole point of this trial was that in America, a public official could, in a time of great stress, be impeached in Alice-in-Wonderland fashion precisely because he had "enforced the law." In Crum's case, concern for the constitutional rights of the individual in an atmosphere of war mongering was too much for many in Montana to bear. This was especially so because the judge had advised Ves Hall to leave Forsyth to avoid prosecution for sedition.[21]

The judge had also dared to criticize the United States in a public speech that was deemed criminal because "said speech" was delivered with a tone and inflection of the voice that, it was charged, showed clearly the malignity on the part of Crum against the United States and its participation in the war. He was accused of saying that "WWI was a rich man's war."[22] Criticism of the war in terms of capitalism was anathema to the Montana patriots. No one was interested in hearing that a son might die in a war for "Wall Street" or J. P. Morgan. Therefore, it seemed legitimate to cite Crum's tone of voice as a reasonable ground for impeachment. It also seemed fair to accuse Crum of being "disloyal and unpatriotic" because he refused to adopt the properly militant "tone" of his neighbors. [23]

Crum was not the only one to worry seriously about his credibility in Montana. Governor Stewart, for example, seemed nervous in explaining why he initially agreed to Crum's resignation in return for discontinuing the impeachment proceedings. In the middle of the impeachment proceedings, a letter of explanation by the governor that revealed his deep fear of appearing unpatriotic enough to "spoil" the senate's proceedings was read: "My only reason for withholding the acceptance of the resignation [Crum's] was that I did not desire to hinder or embarrass the members of the pending proceedings," Stewart explained.[24] It's clear from the governor's letter that he was preoccupied with his own political survival, even if it meant that he had to ignore the agreement he had with Crum not to proceed with the trial if Crum resigned. Since he had already resigned, Crum saw no reason to defend himself in the senate, which pleased most of the senators. As one noted, "it is trifling with this august body now sitting as the highest court in this state to, at this time, appoint anyone to go out and defend Judge Crum, either in this body or beyond it."[25] Only Senator Whiteside noticed the perversity of "trying dead issues,"[26] but he objected to no avail. The impeachment of someone who had already resigned continued.

One of the witnesses, D. J. Muri, clerk of the district court, testified to what seemed to be an even more serious crime. Muri accused the judge of claiming that many Americans would fight on the side of Germany and that "the United States' flag would be a rag."[27] Like the senate High Court of Impeachment, Muri here sacralized a secular object. Criticizing President Wilson also became an implied impeachable offence.[28] Muri just "happened to be" the chairman of the executive committee of the One Hundred Club, a patriotic organization of "one hundred percent Americans."

Another revealing charge was that Crum denied the superiority of Western civilization. Elizabeth Snook, deputy clerk of the court, accused Crum of being a kind of Huck Finn in reverse, claiming that the judge said he planned to "sell out what he had and take his family to the Fiji Islands, where they were civilized."[29] Snook's origins were carefully established. The revelation that she, too, was of German descent was meant to show that there were "good" Germans. Judge Crum was simply not one of them. Otherwise, he would never have been seen in conference with a number of people later accused of violating the Espionage Act, as Snook testified he had been.[30]

The examination of another "good" German, a Presbyterian minister by the name of A. T. Klemme, supposedly showed that Judge Crum also suffered from inflexibility. Klemme had supported Germany until he saw the light.[31] He thus stood in contrast to the judge, who would not abandon his heretical beliefs, even under great pressure. Thus, the impeachment trial presented the struggle between these two men of German origin in terms of heresy. A question posed to Klemme by house member Ronald Higgins was: "Did Judge Crum ever attempt to reconvert you to your former views concerning the war?"[32] Conversion generally takes place, after all, in the realm of religious activity. Nationalism, with full public observance, had become a full-fledged civic religion.

G. Flege, a bookkeeper for the Bank of Commerce, was another example of a "good immigrant" and a "loyal" naturalized citizen, though he was from Norway. Flege merely repeated the charges by others regarding Crum's disloyalty. The judge again stood accused of supporting Germany, justifying the *Lusitania* incident, and hating England. The war was being fought, Flege reported the judge saying, to support the "Robber

Barons" and thus was as unjust as America's imperialistic policies had been in the Spanish-American War. The most significant part of Flege's testimony was its aftermath. When Flege had completed his testimony and was about to step down, Senator Gwen F. Burla began to interrogate the witness as to his process of obtaining citizenship, specifically how many years were still to pass before he received his final citizenship papers.[33] These questions suggested that those who did not comply with the majority might well have a completely different experience in procuring American citizenship. The threat of sanctions against otherness was left hanging in the air.

R. A. Martin also was called to testify against Crum. His profession was the "sheep business," he explained, an activity that fit the atmosphere of the impeachment hearing. As the father of a boy serving in France, Martin said he had little patience with the judge's alleged hatred of battle and his claim that American children were sent abroad to be slaughtered in Europe for a cause that had nothing to do with the average American. Judge Crum, it seemed to him, was a foreigner, a Marxist sympathizer, and a peace activist, all completely unacceptable either in a judge or in anyone else.

From the point of view of many, the legitimacy of being a judge, part of the American legal system, had to be denied Crum. Otherwise, American jurisprudence in its entirety could be tainted by even tacit acceptance of the judge's views and values. To further discredit Crum, George Farr, an attorney from Miles City, testified. His examination by state representative Ronald Higgins, who acted as a manager on behalf of the Montana House of Representatives in the impeachment proceedings, was meant to suggest that Crum was a spy for Germany who possessed privileged information. Higgins's questions to Farr implied that Crum was able to discuss with authority the amount of German submarine tonnage "as facts within his own knowledge," rather than "prophecy."[34] Higgins's strategy was clever. He realized that it was not necessary to accuse the judge of being a spy directly. Innuendo would suffice to ensure impeachment. All that Higgins had to do was prove Crum's "otherness." When Elizabeth Snook was recalled to add that she had heard the judge conversing in German, it bolstered the impression of Crum as dangerously different. It didn't matter that Snook was unable to understand German. Lack of expertise actually enhanced her testimony.

Crum also stood accused of admiring the American Progressive movement, especially its most noted representatives, Senators Robert La Follette and William J. Stone, who were accused by some in the Wilson administration of pro-German sympathies. By standing up for their

American patriotism, Crum was implicitly accused of the opposite. Even Progressives now played the role of outsiders.[35]

Prior to the impeachment proceedings, One Hundred Club members took it upon themselves to conduct their own investigation of Judge Crum. While there had been severe criticism in the newspapers regarding his stance on the war, District Judge A. C. Spencer accused Crum of judicial malpractice, by paying back an attorney in a civil suit who had done him an "awful good turn."[36] Members of the Club apparently had to be coerced into voting against the judge. The large majority initially refused to vote, but as Bussert, the chairman of the club, testified: "When the question was put for vote three or four would vote on one side and four or five on another side, and I finally had to threaten that if they did not vote, I would count them as one side or another, and worked with them to get a full, free expression from everybody on the different questions that had been answered by Judge Crum."[37] Even within a patriotic association, there apparently was some initial reluctance to condemn the judge, though such hesitations were quickly overcome by coercion. The vote to ask Crum to resign eventually became unanimous. The club's oath of membership once again blurred the sacred and the profane. The oath of the One Hundred Club ended as follows: "In token of my sincerity in these declarations I do now kiss the flag of the Republic spread upon the open pages of the Holy Bible."[38] One of Judge Crum's crimes was to distinguish the flag from the Bible.

One community was a voice of sanity during these impeachment proceedings. The town of Roundup published a number of resolutions in defense of Judge Crum. Apparently what the townspeople objected to most was that the charges against Crum were published in the newspapers before the impeachment proceedings began.[39] Therefore, the case seemed to be decided beforehand.[40] By forcing a witness named Jarrett, who was an attorney from Roundup, to read the resolutions out loud, Higgins manipulated matters so that Jarrett, Roundup, and the resolutions could in effect be put on trial. The senate's obsession with the resolutions suggests that the senators hardly cared whether they were giving Judge Crum a fair and balanced hearing. Their focus was on the basic "otherness" of this public official. The most revealing question put to Jarrett in connection with the Roundup resolutions was asked by Senator C. L. Mershon: "Mr. President I would just like to ask what proportion of Roundup citizens are foreign born citizens or naturalized citizens?"[41] The fact that there were only two hundred such citizens, and that the majority of them were Austrian rather than German, did little to mitigate the impact of the question. Only the town of Roundup could pass such resolutions, it was strongly implied, through manipulation by its "foreign" citizens, who were unaccustomed to true American ideals. In fact, Roundup was actually struggling for the American ideal.

The clearest perversion of American justice within this entire impeachment involved the testimony of Mrs. Tillman. She was called in connection with her having signed the Roundup resolutions. Because Mrs. Tillman had no intention of incriminating Judge Crum for disloyal or unpatriotic behavior, anything positive she had to say about the judge was quickly dismissed as hearsay. Higgins cleverly insisted that Mrs. Tillman prove that Crum did not make various incriminating statements: "But further than your belief that he did not say or do these things, Mrs. Tillman, you cannot enlighten this senate, can you, upon these matters?"[42] Where was the burden of proof? The unsaid often has an important place in textual analysis, as in the very transcript of this trial. However, it should have had no such place in supplying proof in the American legal system.

Higgins continued his unorthodox prosecution of the case by requesting that "the ladies retire from the senate chamber" because the testimony to follow would surely "shock" their sensibilities.[43] Higgins was doing more than exhibiting his sexism, disguised as chivalry. This gesture was an a priori condemnation of the judge because Higgins clearly suspected that crimes even more heinous were about to be discussed. What followed, however, was the usual body of charges: the *Lusitania* episode, draft laws, Crum's warning of a new revolution, the slander of Wilson, and sympathy for Russia.[44] Despite his earlier resignation, Judge Crum was "convicted." This brief review of the charges and testimony against Judge Crum show that the official charges brought against him had little to do with his actual "crimes."

The Crum impeachment in Montana provides an important lesson about the excesses that can be committed in a democracy that feels itself to be in jeopardy. The testimony in the Crum trial affords a unique opportunity to examine attitudes and views of people who clearly were swayed by the ideology of America's dominant institutions.

The courageous Montana federal judge George M. Bourquin aptly summed up the position of the courts during World War I. Paraphrasing the playwright George Bernard Shaw, Bourquin noted: "During the war, the courts in France, bleeding under German guns, were very severe; the courts in England, hearing but the echoes of those guns, were grossly unjust; but the courts in the United States, knowing naught save censured news of those guns, were stark, staring, raving mad."[45]

Chapter V

GEORGE BOURQUIN ON "PUBLIC GOOD" AND "PROPERTY RIGHTS"

The principle of the "public good" may have been short-lived in American jurisprudence outside the realm of theory, but reference to the public interest appears in many of Bourquin's important decisions—this despite his firm defense of individual civil liberties in other kinds of cases and his general unease with upholding rights of sovereignty. In the conflict between individual economic liberties and conditions of reasonable government—what in effect Bourquin struggled with in cases involving the public good—perhaps what influenced Bourquin most was his belief that the public interest took precedence over individual rights of property. Bourquin seemed somewhat uneasy in the positions he took and may have felt that common law often had little to do with the needs of the common people. Nonetheless, be believed common law ought to be obeyed. Bourquin believed that, unless specifically inconsistent with constitutional or statutory enactments, the public good—the "good" that was shared or was beneficial for most members of a given community—needed to be accorded legal consideration. For Bourquin, the ultimate issue in law was constitutionality. He believed that the legislative practice of regulating the prices of mundane business transactions arbitrarily "is repugnant to the due process clause of the Fourteenth Amendment."[1] As important to Bourquin as law for the public interest was his fear of the potential tyranny of legislatures in usurping the power of the people to conduct capitalistic business practices. Bourquin regarded this as guaranteed by the Constitution as an inalienable right. Although he accepted the validity of emergency legislative powers in certain situations, Bourquin still viewed those powers with suspicion, noting that "it is inconceivable that [government's] all-embracing provisions, now when the war is over, save as a fiction perpetuating rather dictatorial powers, are necessary to public health, peace and safety."[2]

Bourquin was unwilling to allow the state "dictatorial powers" or public opinion to dictate changes in constitutional practice without a constitutional amendment. The "people reserved to themselves the power to regulate prices in ordinary business and employment in the state constitutions, but with the Fourteenth Amendment, they suspended that power so long as the 'due process' clause endures."[3] The American governmental system perpetuated checks and balances to prevent legislatures from enacting regulatory laws that would impinge on the Constitution's guarantee of the inalienable right of people to conduct free enterprise. Bourquin thought he would protect the collective rights of the public by affirming the rights of the individual.

Bourquin also ruled to prevent government excess and the abuse of power. His pessimistic, suspicious view of human nature permeated his legal thought. He mistrusted the tendency of power to invest excessive authority in any branch of government, including the judiciary. He quoted John Marshall's dictum that "all power wherever reposed is abused." This generally guided Bourquin's interpretation of the law. In addition, he expressed special responsibility to uphold the public good in light of the potential for judicial abuse of power. Yet just as he was sensitive to an excess of power, he also was unwilling to dilute the ability of the judiciary to expedite justice. His deep distrust of the motivations and actions of humans guided him in his legal interpretations to protect the public interest. Eventually, power used would become power abused—by the executive, legislative, or even the judiciary—unless there were proper legal restraints. The public always suffered from these abuses.

In explaining the connection between the common law and the public good, Bourquin noted: "It is, in fact, a reservation or exception to the general course of law in favor of the public or for its good. From its nature its origin may be said to be higher than, superior to, and to antedate the common law—of the fundamentals of all government."[4] He traced the public good concept back to the Magna Carta, seemingly in an effort to make the idea more palatable. For an example of Bourquin's thinking, we can examine *American Bonding Co. v. Reynolds* (1913). The American Bonding Company owed money to the state and to individuals; the issue was what debts had to be paid first. Bourquin upheld the right of a state to payment priority over private creditors. Indeed, in the last analysis, Bourquin recognized the privileged status of Montana law. By recognizing the privileged status of the state law he ignored the English legal tradition practices that preferred the individual. In this case the interest of the state was the public interest, and he concluded that the "statutes of the latter [Montana] provided that, where they declare the law, there is no common law."[5]

Bourquin almost belabored the point that the tradition of state priority in matters of debt was in the public interest. It was as if he needed to reassure himself that supporting the state's claim over individual creditors was within the realm of "justice." Why else did he underscore his argument that the right of the state came from common law while noting that Montana law took precedence over earlier tradition? Bourquin supported this notion of the public good and even invoked the authority of the kings of England to do so. However, Bourquin's own reasoning clearly left him dissatisfied.

In *A. M. Holter Hardware Co. v. Boyle* (1920), Bourquin embarked upon a stringent defense of the due process clause of the Fourteenth Amendment. The suit was brought by Holter Hardware to prevent the enforcement of state legislation that established a trade commission to regulate ordinary business, including, "curiously enough, burial plots in cemeteries for gain." Superficially, the judgment may seem to strike out against the public good because Bourquin ruled against state regulation. In Bourquin's view, however, to fetter free enterprise through arbitrary machinations of government was the antithesis of the public good;[6] thus curtailing state regulation in specific instances could be considered, at times, the promotion of the "common good." Bourquin strongly believed that the legislature should not exercise arbitrary powers, including regulation, arguing that if that were allowed the inalienable rights guaranteed by the Constitution would be left to the whims of the legislatures. However, he stated, "Emergency, opinion, morality, changes wrought by time and circumstances, often justify the exercise of powers that Legislatures have; but they create no new powers."[7] It was clear that Bourquin realized that his rulings in these cases were problematic.

In *United States v. Smith*, in 1922, Bourquin again reaffirmed public rights by upholding individual privilege vis-à-vis the government. Bourquin upheld the right of one Charles Smith to enjoy grazing privileges on government land, despite the fact that the secretary of agriculture had refused Smith a permit. The government sought to prosecute Smith for grazing livestock without a permit. Smith claimed that the government violated the spirit of its own decree by refusing to grant him the grazing license. Only after his application was turned down did Smith decide to "trespass" on government land.

In finding for the defendant, Bourquin elaborated the difference between individual and governmental rights. In Bourquin's view, "those who ask equity must do equity, governments as well as persons. Indeed, for the sake of good example, governments, more than persons, are bound to respect a court's decree."[8] According to the law, the secretary of agriculture could deny grazing privileges to an applicant, "provided, however, that it was not intended by the terms of the decree to enjoin or restrain the defendant from enjoying and using the privileges granted bona fide settlers as to the grazing of live stock upon said lands under the rules and regulations provided by the Secretary of Agriculture."[9] Bourquin demanded that governmental grants of privilege not be arbitrarily denied to any individual. He viewed the secretary's decree essentially as a matter of contract: "The rule is that a party who fails to comply with the terms of a decree or contract favorable to the other party is disabled to complain of the latter's like failure in respect to the terms favorable to him."[10] Indeed, Bourquin believed that the government had been the first party to violate an implied "contract" with Charles Smith.

Bourquin went beyond the confines of the usual legal constructs, however, when he insisted that governments, "more than persons, are bound to respect a court's decree." Bourquin believed that governments were to be guided by the notion of the public good. No government should impose more rigid interpretation of the law on its citizens than it was prepared to assume for itself. Ever suspicious of governmental intentions, Bourquin demanded that governments govern by example. No institution could be above the law: "If plaintiff's department conceives it has the power of a tyrant, and exercises it like a tyrant, therein will be no aid from a court of equity."[11] Bourquin insisted he would not allow the "little" man to be overwhelmed by the immense powers of government.

The ideological underpinnings of Bourquin's language went beyond jurisprudence to the American myth of the frontier. The tone of Bourquin's decision in *United States v. Smith* suggested his outrage at the government's attempt to act against its own decree and to limit the efforts of "bona fide settlers." Not only did Bourquin support the rights of the individual in this instance, but he also tapped directly into the image of unfair government practice aligned against the inherent right of Americans to expand into the "wilderness," perhaps the ultimate expression of the public good.[12] The inherent right to settle was not to be taken lightly by governmental authority.

In *Yellowstone Park Transportation Co. v. Gallatin County* (1928), Bourquin struck a compromise in a dispute over jurisdiction between Gallatin County and the federal government concerning an area of land "set apart" by the United States for Yellowstone National Park. Bourquin had to decide between the public good of the nation as a whole and the public welfare of one county.

Though the act that created Yellowstone Park had provided that the specified land was to be reserved and withdrawn from settlement, occupancy, or sale, the county had not lost its territorial integrity or its right to assess taxes within that area. Bourquin rejected the plaintiff's complaint that the act implied changing the original borders of Montana and somehow changed its territorial boundaries. Bourquin noted: "If Congress had intended these anomalous results, it could have plainly said so."[13] Bourquin instead was adamant that the Yellowstone legislation had in no way created a "no man's land" in terms of Montana's territorial sovereignty. The people's sovereignty could never be destroyed to create a recreation area, which could not be compared to the appropriation of land for an army base. In this case, Bourquin believed that the "'exclusive control' [granted the United States over this area] imported only administrative authority to care for the proprietary interests of the United States in the lands, and not the legislative and judicial jurisdiction or political dominion, which is beyond the power of Congress to vest in the Secretary [of the Interior]."[14]

Bourquin attacked the problem linguistically. He claimed that "set apart" is a more or less synonym for "dedicated," and that both terms signified not segregation from Montana but from other public lands, their last antecedent in the text of the legislation. Thus they definitely served to appropriate the lands to the particular object of the reservation.[15] By claiming that "set apart" meant "dedicated," Bourquin tried to maneuver between the claims of Gallatin County and the United States.

In *Northern Pac. Ry. Co. et al. v. Board of Railroad Commissioners of Montana* (1929), Bourquin, in the process of denying the Northern Pacific's motion to convene a three-judge court to reinstate an injunction against Montana's board of railroad commissioners, lashed out against the Supreme Court interference in district court matters. In this case, four railroads attempted to enjoin the Board of Railroad Commissioners of Montana from enforcing an intrastate rate order until the Interstate Commerce Commission could hear the railroads. The railroads were granted a temporary restraining order, but before the three-judge court could be convened, as stipulated under the law, the Board of Commissioners moved to dismiss the suit and to dissolve the restraining order on the grounds that the complaint was insufficient. The railroads' complaint was dismissed because the regulation of rates was not found to be "forbidden, unreasonable, or unjust."[16] The railroads, however, applied to the Supreme Court, and Justice Willis Van Devanter advised the district court that its dismissal of the railroads' complaint without convening a three-judge panel "probably" was in violation of the law. The initial restraining order against the commission should be reinstated, he said. Few things could enrage Bourquin more than an attempt by the Supreme Court to challenge the district court's authority. But here also Bourquin treaded on extremely shaky legal grounds.

Bourquin upheld the rights of the "little man" vis-à-vis the railroads and sought to mitigate the power of the "three-judge" statute to infringe on the judicial integrity of a single district court judge. Once again, the public good manifested itself in the protection of individual consumer rights—this time in relation to the powerful railroad companies. In this instance, Bourquin was a westerner lashing out against entrenched economic power and the excessive power of the federal government that he forever suspected, feared, and abhorred.

Bourquin, in no uncertain terms, denied the Supreme Court's right to interfere in the legitimate business of the district court. Because the Supreme Court could not order the district court to reinstate the injunction, Bourquin "assumed" the Supreme Court had granted the order itself. He then insulted Supreme Court Justice Van Devanter directly. If Justice Van Devanter had issued the order himself, Bourquin's reply was that, "Although precedent may be found for anything . . . none has been found for authority in a Supreme Court Justice to issue an order to a District Court to reinstate a restraining order in present, if in any, circumstances."[17]

Having disposed of the matter of appropriate division of responsibility between the Supreme Court and the district courts, Bourquin asserted that the proper reason to convene a three-judge panel in such cases was to "to remedy a well-known evil, viz. the activities of sovereign states too frequently enjoined by a single judge too prone to sign on the dotted line upon the request of public utilities."[18] Bourquin was unwilling to allow the railroad companies to distort the statute's intention. For him, this section of the law was not created to impede the work of regulatory commissions but rather to prevent big business from obstructing the public good. A single judge, in Bourquin's view, had the right to determine if a case had sufficient merit to be heard in the "three-judge" forum. To do otherwise would be "sheer futility and absurdity." If the intention of the law was to protect the people from the public utilities' excesses, Bourquin would not allow the utilities or the railroads to exploit the rule for their own purposes. When the utilities or the railroads attempted to stall judicial due process, by manipulating this section of the law in order to delay or to prevent rate regulation, the "consumer . . . as usual, 'pays the [inflated] freight.'" The railroads, by this perversion of justice, "are safe." [19]

This state of affairs was anathema to Bourquin. He therefore denied the railroads' motion to convene a three-judge court. The suit was not pending, therefore, but rather "as dead as Julius Caesar" or as futile as Glendower's attempt to call "spirits from the vastly deep."[20] Bourquin's literary references suggest how much he enjoyed demonstrating that "the mighty have fallen" in his court. Bourquin tried to stand up to both the railroads and the Supreme Court.

Great Falls Gas Co. v. Public Service Commission of Montana (1930) also involved a motion to deny the legality of an injunction issued as a restraining order, this time against the Public Service Commission of Montana. Judge Bourquin now found himself simultaneously defending and protesting the power of the judiciary. In principle, he supported prohibiting a single judge from hearing injunction motions without an "application to a judge of the Supreme Court of the United States, or to a Circuit or District Judge, and hearing and determination by three judges."[21] For practical reasons, however, as well as the need to avoid the implied "repeal [of] prior general statutes," Bourquin found that "it is hardly necessary to point out the downright absurdities involved in construction of this special statute to include process, pleading, jurisdiction, [and] incidents to progress of the suit."[22]

Bourquin applauded the spirit of the injunction law, enacted "when the evils of government by injunction were notorious, viz. the activities of sovereign states paralyzed, their statutes overturned, organized labor oppressed, jury trials superseded by contempt proceedings, and all by a too complaisant judiciary in behalf of great corporations."[23] The potential for abuse of the process of injunction by a single member of the judiciary was clear, he explained, because "those who come and go upon the bench are average and not supermen, to whom respect is due solely to the extent their decisions merit it, and not at all because of that anachronism, the gowns of antiquity to which they tenaciously cling."[24]

Bourquin would not yield to a legislature if it enacted a law that overturned the delicate balance of power between the branches of government. By issuing an injunction against a state commission, Bourquin paradoxically tried to check governmental abuse of authority by the very weapon that government previously used to indulge in its own "tyranny."

If the government had used injunctions to eradicate the power of labor unions and others, that same power, through the agency of a pliable solitary judge, could now be turned against the state to limit its authority to regulate prices. So Bourquin had no qualms about the use of injunctions per se. Rather, he feared "the suspicion and abuse attaching when granted by a single member of the judiciary." This was the legal tightrope Bourquin walked as he attempted to mitigate the potential for constitutional abuse by the various branches of government.

Despite Bourquin's belief that the state government had the right to regulate commerce through regulatory commissions, and in some cases even to set minimum rates, he denied that privilege in the *Great Northern Utilities Co. v. Public Service Commission* case of 1931. Bourquin recognized that the commission intended to interfere with "cut-throat competition" by forcing the company to sell its gas at a higher rate than it wished, and he refused it that right. Just as the federal government had the right to regulate commerce under the Constitution's Fifth Amendment, the states had a similar right. Because the very economic existence of the Great Northern Utilities Company was at stake, Bourquin found in its favor.

Bourquin's decision was, to say the least, paradoxical. He recognized the foolishness of having two utility companies compete for the business of an area that could support only one such enterprise. He noted that the case was unique in that "plaintiff resists defendant's order to raise its rates." However, "there is method in it, the object, cut-throat competition to a finish anticipated of a rival so lost to ethics as to poach upon plaintiff's preserves and underbid it, its attitude that, in a restricted field wherein both cannot survive, if it must perish, it will die fighting rather than by slow starvation; and that it has an inalienable right of self-preservation to lay on until the other first cries, 'Hold, enough,' and flees the field whether or not damned."[25]

Rather than focus on the "madness," as Bourquin perceived it, he preferred to emphasize the deadly struggle of the Great Northern with an unethical competitor. The judge seemed to enjoy the fighting spirit of the company, and he embellished its struggle in flowery metaphor. Indeed, Bourquin may have resorted to such rhetorical flourishes particularly when he felt the strong pull of competing values. In this case, the idea of free enterprise seemed to clash with Bourquin's notion of practical business sense.

Bourquin first charged the state—"the remedy is in that state's hands"—with restricting "the number of utilities to the need of the field."[26] The interest of the public would have to be maintained without the government interfering with the right of the company to survive. On the other hand, Bourquin found no benefit to the public interest in the state commission forcing that company to sell its gas at higher rates than it wished, writing that the "power to regulate is not the power to destroy useful and harmless enterprise, but is to protect, foster, promote, preserve, control with due regard to the present and future interests of the utility, its patrons, and the public."[27] After describing the "cut-throat" battle in bloody terms, Bourquin found the utility company engaged in "harmless enterprise." If the state raising gas rates infringed on the company's Fourteenth Amendment property rights, how did Bourquin expect the regulatory commission to "remedy" the situation without infringing on the property rights of the Great Northern competitor? Could not the competition sue the state for its right to free enterprise? Bourquin stated that the power of the people preceded common law. If the people wished to have regulatory agencies, it was their right. Yet, the Fifth and Fourteenth Amendments prevailed over the state's right to regulate. Because the lower rates were clearly a matter of the public good, and because the Great Northern cut its rates in order to survive, Bourquin upheld its claim. In addition, Bourquin recognized the legitimacy of the company's "right of necessity to fight to a finish for financial life."[28]

Intellectually, Bourquin recognized the futility of such a situation in which two companies were competing over a business that could support only one. As a product of his culture, however, he reaffirmed the basic premise of social Darwinism, "the survival of the fittest," though he added the twist of the "common good."

Bourquin also closely examined the role of regulatory agencies. He acknowledged that the commission sought to encourage reduction of rates in order to benefit the public. Indeed, for him this was the sole object of regulation. In addition, each company was guaranteed the liberty of contract and property by the Fourteenth Amendment. Preventing a company from lowering its rates would deprive it of an important constitutional guarantee. Furthermore, the fact that the United States fixed minimum rates for interstate carriers did not violate the Fifth Amendment, for "the federal power is derived from the commerce clause of the Constitution to which the Fifth Amendment yields."[29]

Bourquin sought to justify his constitutional understanding of the public's rights with an historical overview:

> In the beginning the people had all, unlimited and absolute power. To its exercise was no barrier save their will. For purposes of administration, by the Federal Constitution in the United States they vested all power to

regulate interstate carriers and therein to fix minimum rates; and by State Constitutions in the states they vested like power in respect to intrastate utilities. That this power had not been exercised in respect to minimum rates during the reign of the common law imports only that for it was then no occasion. The common law did not create it, nor could it destroy it. It is an inherent right of the people, superior and prior to the common law. Moreover, the common law is not so conservative that it forbids anything should be done for the first time; it does not prevent growth, progress, extension of principles to apply to new subjects and conditions. . . . All power was the people's before and despite the common law by them ordained, and it is theirs today, though to some extent by Federal and State Constitutions they have limited its exercise by themselves or their legislative bodies until said Constitutions are duly changed. So it is that both federal and state sovereignties, in exercise of these their powers of rate regulation, by the people have been alike limited, viz., by the principle of due process of law in the Fifth and Fourteenth Amendments contained.[30]

In the name of the public good, the public had imposed limitations on itself. It had to obey the Constitution or change it. Yet Bourquin found it unreasonable for the state to insist on minimum rates when these rates would cause bankruptcy to the company providing the service. Above all, Bourquin—in this instance proving to be a devout legal formalist— viewed courts as responsible for deciding whether the regulatory powers were exercised legally. He stressed that just as "constitutional laws may be administered unconstitutionally, the lawful power to regulate may be abused and result in unlawful orders."[31] When that happened, courts had to annul such action. Furthermore, Bourquin felt that the power to regulate was not the power to destroy "useful and harmless" enterprises but was "to protect, foster, promote, preserve, control with due regard to the present and future interests of the utility, its patrons and the public."[32]

For Bourquin there was no safer way to ensure the public good than to protect the authority of the Constitution and the courts. In relation to the concept of the public good, the maverick Montana judge thus earned the right to be known as a civil libertarian of the highest degree. In granting the farmers of Sanders County the right to a conciliation commissioner under the Bankruptcy Act of 1933, Bourquin again revealed his curious stance as an independent liberal/conservative jurist who was not a slave of ideology. In Bourquin's decision in *In re Conciliation Commissioner for Sanders County, Montana* (1933), he granted a farmers' petition to combat the "tyranny" of federal usurpation of power at the expense of the

judiciary and legislature despite his evident misgivings about the constitutionality and effectiveness of conciliation commissioners.

Initially, Bourquin demeaned the notion of a referee to be known as
a conciliation commissioner, viewing such commissioners' status as akin
to being a "dry-nurse." He feared that creditors might be in ever more
precarious circumstances than the farmer/debtors. The conciliation
commissioners might have the power to "coerce creditors to enter into
new contracts with their debtor [who may be solvent and in less distress
than his creditors], and without consideration to extend or reduce their
just claims."[33] And Bourquin questioned the very constitutionality of the
conciliation commissioners under the Bankruptcy Act because "even as
in respect to any power by the Constitution granted to Congress, the
power to legislate 'on the subject of Bankruptcies' is not power to embrace therein by mere label, characterization, form, or forum what is not
of, or is foreign to, bankruptcy. Labels, names, go for nothing."[34]

For a farmer to have his debt rescheduled by a conciliation commissioner had nothing to do with bankruptcy at all. The question of constitutionality, however, "may properly be left until made an issue in some
adversary proceeding."[35] Why, in light of his obvious displeasure with the
notion of conciliatory commissioners on both moral and constitutional
grounds, did Bourquin perform a liberal about-face?

Apparently, though he did not say so directly, there was a constitutional issue that could not be left to a future decision, and that issue was
the basis for the judge's decision to grant the farmers' petition. The idea
that the extension of the Bankruptcy Act prohibited the appointment of
conciliation commissioners without the specific consent of the president
was intolerable for Bourquin. This was because the order was entirely in
keeping with government in defiance of the Constitution, "but it is a futile
brutum fulmen [empty noise] impotent to deprive the farmer of any just
benefit the statute may afford, or to bring the judiciary to heel at executive command."[36]

To defend farmers was not the focus of Bourquin's decision. He sought
to limit what he called the arrogance and tyranny of the executive branch
of government. "Incidentally, the author of the circular is not the first Attorney General to be obsessed by a delusion that federal courts are little
more than appendages of his and the executive office," Bourquin tartly
noted.[37] Because of his Jeffersonian approach, Bourquin doubted the effi-
cacy and justice of appointing a conciliation commissioner, yet his moral
outrage at the executive's invasion of the court's domain suggested his
ongoing progressive attitude toward preservation of the constitutional
division of governmental powers.

"Corner Park & Main," Business College on third floor, Butte, Montana. Photograph by Owsley Block, ca. 1900, 946-089. Reprinted by permission of the Montana Historical Society Research Center—Photograph Archives, Helena, Montana.

Bourquin was clearly considerably distressed by what he viewed as a usurpation of executive power. "Abuse of executive power was notorious," he wrote. "It tended to dominate both legislative and judicial . . . little by little it will supersede and both undermine and overthrow the Constitution." However, he assured all that "the Constitution like the flag is 'still there,'" and that the court existed to protect against the arrogance of the executive. Bourquin concluded by defining the role of the courts as a balance against those "obsessed with the delusion that federal courts are little more than appendages of . . . executive office." Though Bourquin ruled in favor of protecting the public good, in this case he clearly was also motivated by a deep desire to protect the judiciary from the executive.

For Bourquin, there also was an inherent connection between the right of property and the law. In some respects, the law seemed to be created in Bourquin's mind for no other purpose or reason than to uphold the property rights inherent in the Fourteenth Amendment. Yet Bourquin could also show considerable flexibility. In some of his cases involving property, it seemed that "justice" had equal footing with his legal interpretations.[38]

In *United States v. Rockefeller* (1919), for example, Bourquin upheld the right of the federal government to enter into treaties, while at the same time he revealed himself to be one of the earliest conservationists. One Howard Rockefeller had taken possession of wild ducks protected by the Migratory Bird Treaty concluded by the United States with Great Britain in 1918. Rockefeller demurred, claiming that the regulatory power of the treaty was unconstitutional.

Bourquin rejected Rockefeller's claim because the treaty concluded with Great Britain was nothing more than the valid exercise of the federal power granted by "the states themselves [in the sense of their people] . . . in the federal Constitution ordained and established by them."[39] The federal power to engage in treaties takes precedence over the state regulatory power. Bourquin therefore anticipated Justice Oliver Wendell Holmes's US Supreme Court decision in *Missouri v. Holland* (1923).

However, beyond the matter of the constitutionality of the law was Bourquin's strong belief in the protection of wildlife and other natural resources, something that he described as part of the foundation of civilized behavior. Anything less than an international treaty could not prevent the extinction of various animal species: "Not otherwise can migratory birds be preserved from extinction. . . . Their continued existence is beyond the power of separate states and nations. It can be accomplished only by treaty to that end between nations."[40]

Bourquin saw no abuse of authority in the exercise of federal power to control resources that belonged within the realm of the common good. Such an endeavor by the federal government was both legal and, perhaps more important, moral:

> Fisheries have for the subject of treaties always and the principles and objects thereof are equally applicable and desirable in relation to migratory birds and other game. So doubtless of air and water, their protection from pollution, their conservation, apportionment, and their use. The object of all thereof is to peacefully share those natural resources which are the property of no one till reduced to possession, from which all may take when within their territory, which are alternately found within the territory of several nations and in places common to all as the high seas, which

may be wholly seized and exterminated by one to the great detriment and irreparable damage of all, which in accord may be persevered and enjoyed as a blessing to all, which in discord may be annihilated to the injury of all, and which may become legitimate causes for war, to obviate which is the most ancient and important object of the treaties.[41]

Bourquin thus tied his three main concerns into one knot. Civilized nations had to protect those resources that belonged to all but were the possession of none. Nations had long concluded similar treaties to the one in question, and, finally, disregard for the well-being of natural resources could result in war. Bourquin again demonstrated that he defied traditional political ideological characterizations and ruled independently in a clear manner. Bourquin appreciated the civilizing influence of properly utilizing the world's treasures. Some properties were universal in nature and needed legal protection.

Bourquin's penultimate remark was once again an affirmation of the authority he held dearest—that of the law. He observed that the Migratory Bird Treaty "neither barters away nor divests any property right of state or Citizen, but only regulates their control and exercise of rights of the chase, duly subordinates the valid exercise of federal authority to enter into treaties to promote national and international objects, welfare, and peace."[42] Utmost in Bourquin's legal concerns was the valid exercise of authority, which he quite often applied to uphold the legitimate control of property rights.

Decades before the US Supreme Court required the suppression of all illegally obtained evidence, Bourquin, like most judges, measured the public interest in weighing evidence obtained illegally against the accused. In *Nan v. Rasmusson, Collector of Internal Revenue* (1932), Bourquin refused to interpret the Fourth Amendment to serve the interests of a known criminal. Though federal narcotics officers had seized Nan's bankbooks and statements in a raid without specific coverage by warrant, their action did not authorize a later suit to restrain collection of income taxes subsequently assessed. The income tax assessed was based on the information contained in Nan's bankbooks and statements, yet for Bourquin the two illegal actions did not neutralize one another. Nan was, in Bourquin's view, still liable for the taxes assessed, even if the evidence had been seized illegally. Bourquin had no desire to protect the property rights of a criminal, especially at the expense of the federal government.

Bourquin believed that Nan did not have the right to sue to enjoin collection of taxes because there were no "extraordinary and exceptional circumstances." Only in such circumstances did the Supreme Court allow a suit to enjoin collection of taxes to take place. Under no circumstance would Bourquin be implicated in a situation in which, he claimed, the Fourth Amendment was amended in order to protect a crime "until no longer the intended shield for the innocent."[43] For Bourquin, Nan's obvious criminality was the crux of the matter at hand. Because he was so earnest about constitutional liberties, Bourquin was unwilling to allow their "perversions" in the service of society's outcasts. It seemed that Nan's constitutional rights simply held little interest for him.

In *United States v. Butte, A. & P. Ry. Co.* (1930), Bourquin explored the double-edged sword of entrepreneurial initiatives and the demands from a railroad company for "sound morals and good conscience."[44] The argument between the company and the government centered on a governmental provision to make up any "red ink" losses incurred by the company after the temporary period of government subsidization had expired. Not only did the United States grant land to the railroad companies, it also subsidized their first few years of operating expenses and guaranteed a minimum income. After the trial period expired, the railroad sought and received from the Interstate Commerce Commission reimbursement commensurate with loss of operating income rather than a return for income less than outlay by the railroad. Quite simply, the railroads refused to part with their subsidy. Bourquin was unwilling to allow the railroad to increase their income at the expense of the public.

Bourquin reminded the railroad company that the "defendant's road earned a substantial net railway operating income."[45] Bourquin thus insisted that the entrepreneur be held responsible for his speculation: "Those who claim to be of the class of beneficiaries must find their warrant in express languages of grant making, and not at all in strained, ingenious, and unusual interpretations and inferences."[46]

That the company was now earning less money than it had during the war did not, Bourquin thought, entitle it to subsidized profit at the expense of the federal government. Moreover, though the Interstate Commerce Commission reimbursed the railroad company for its "loss," Bourquin did not find that decision binding. He argued that "if the special tribunal's decision involves no dispute of fact, and is inspired by and rests upon sheer erroneous construction of the statute," it was beyond the tribunal's authority, and thus the government could act "to recover any money paid by reason of the mistake."[47]

If anything disturbed Bourquin as much as the greed of the railroad companies, it was that the government exceeded its authority, wittingly or unwittingly. However, what Bourquin mainly objected to was any attempt by the railroad to live in and profit by the "laissez-faire" capitalist world and yet simultaneously demand a governmental guarantee of high profitability. Those who speculated must live with the consequences. Nothing incensed Bourquin more than corporate greed at the expense of an innocent public. The very idea of a hardworking individual exploited by a corporation was anathema to Bourquin. To safeguard the property of the little man was a necessary prerequisite for a law-abiding society.

In *Shoemaker v. Merrill* (1933) Bourquin protected the shareholders of a company from corporate raiders within its directorate. Bourquin despised "the conscienceless betrayal of trust" inherent in the manipulations of the corporation's directors. He abhorred their pretensions of respectability, most especially when those "highwaymen" preyed upon the "thrifty." The "modern pirates" had attacked the Puritan value of thrift.[48] Indeed, Bourquin accused the corporate world of "crimes" against the people and held them responsible "for the desperate condition of the nation and its people, and for the very real revolution now upon them."[49] Bourquin framed the class struggle in the bleakest and most extreme terms. As Bourquin had always suspected, should corporate business abuse the trust and property of the common citizen, "socialism" would not be far behind.

Invoking the spirit as well as the rage of Cato, Bourquin revealed his familiarity with the world of antiquity. He despised the "arrogantly assume[d] . . . pose of experts and advisers" who did no more than bleed the people dry. And returning to Christian imagery, Bourquin painted a picture of wolves shepherding lambs "until again fat and toothsome."[50] The "lambs" had been taken advantage of mercilessly by ruthless stock-jugglers.

Though Bourquin could be quite flexible in his legal opinions, his ideological foundation remained unshaken. Whether deciding for or against big business, Bourquin firmly believed that property must be protected to ensure that American society remained free of socialism, anarchy, and chaos. The federal Constitution afforded every citizen the opportunity to live the American dream. In Bourquin's court, that right was close to sacrosanct.

Chapter VI

BOURQUIN ON NATIVE AMERICAN HISTORY AND RIGHTS

ourquin's concern for rights was not limited to those of the white majority. Being a federal district judge in the post-frontier West, he heard several cases that directly involved Native American rights. In his rulings, Bourquin demonstrated an unusual sensitivity to Native American traditions and customs, including a dedication to the communal tribal ownership of resources. This was particularly striking, as he saw himself as a westerner and a pioneer. People in these categories usually were not defenders of Native American rights.

In 1831, Chief Justice John Marshall in *Cherokee Nation v. State of Georgia* concluded that the Indian nations, though "nations," and even "states," could not be considered "foreign states." He defined their status as "domestic dependent nations."[1] Thus based on Article 3, Section 2 of the US Constitution the Native Americans tribes that were not defined as foreign nations or as states could not sue a state of the Union as a foreign state. A year later, in *Samuel Worcester, Plaintiff in Error v. State of Georgia*, Marshall expanded the legal definition of Indian nations and ruled that "the Indian nations had always been considered as distinct, independent political communities."[2]

The legal and political history of relations between the federal government and Native Americans continues to be reinterpreted. The historical debate is more than academic and continues to have important consequences in the judicial and legislative treatment of contemporary Indian claims. In *United States v. Sioux Nation of Indians* (1980), for example, US Supreme Court justices engaged in a bitter dispute about the history of the Sioux Nation and how it was treated by the federal government more than a century earlier. In his dissenting opinion, Justice

William H. Rehnquist vehemently attacked what he termed the "bleeding heart" historical revisionism of the majority opinion that tried to make amends for what it viewed as the past exploitation of the Indians. Indeed, the majority attempted to evaluate the entire scope of historical relations between Native Americans and the federal government in its decision.[3]

Yet judges who carefully consider the history of Native American–federal government relations are rare today. It is even more surprising to discover a judge nine decades ago who incorporated the Indians' tragic history within his legal reasoning as part of his effort to aid Native Americans. Bourquin's decisions anticipated the debates that followed the fundamental changes in national Indian policy that began with the Wheeler-Howard Act of 1934—the first act that recognized Native American tribal communal ownership.[4]

Some of the most intriguing parts of his legal career occur in Bourquin's decisions regarding Native Americans. His written opinions showed him to be a strikingly versatile person—historian, cultural commentator, philosopher, and Jeffersonian democrat. His stance on civil liberties was remarkable. His decisions on the subject of the plight of Native Americans were, in many respects, an even more impressive aspect of his legal legacy.

Bourquin was sensitive to the injustice that characterized Native American–white relations. As in his civil rights decisions, Bourquin responded forcefully to what he perceived as governmental excesses in the treatment of Native Americans. In the early 1930s, Bourquin already was interpreting and using American history in a manner that since has become the norm for important decisions in recent American jurisprudence.[5]

In his decisions, Bourquin relied on an analysis of the treaties and laws that provided the legal basis for the tragic Native American–white relationship. The first official treaty, between the federal government and the Flathead Kootenai and Upper Pend d'Oreilles tribes, was concluded at Hell Gate in the Bitterroot Valley, not far from the present location of Missoula, Montana. On March 8, 1859, the Senate ratified the treaty, which set aside some land for Native American use and gave the United States rights to the rest of the land,[6] and President James Buchanan signed it on April 19 of that year. Isaac I. Stevens, governor and superintendent of Indian affairs for the Territory of Washington, which at that time included Montana, negotiated with "chiefs, headmen and delegates" of the confederated tribes. The treaty left the Indians with approximately one-eighth of the land they had occupied in the Montana area.

In one ruling (discussed below), Bourquin referred to the document produced by Stevens as a "treaty," using quotation marks to signify his doubts about the validity of the agreement. He underscored its dubious nature by describing the events preceding the negotiations, and he referred to the document's contents with biting sarcasm, noting that in order to "promote a favorable atmosphere, Stevens gave to the few Indians assembled a small quantity of brilliant beads, gaudy calicoes, and other gewgaws of the 'trade goods' of the time, and to insure the chiefs' complacency promised each of them $500 yearly for 20 years, house, furniture, and garden."

Bourquin believed that the Indian delegates were much like the biblical Esau: the first case in recorded history of disinheritance by contract.[7] Like Esau, Bourquin wrote, the Indians relinquished unconditionally to the United States "this extensive empire, their tribal birthright." In evaluating the true value of this piece of real estate, Bourquin declared that the deal "cast into the shade Manhattan's famous bargain," though it was not unusual because it had "many counterparts the country over." The result of the treaty was that the Indians were "cribbed, cabined, and confined."

Bourquin did not stop with the Esau and Jacob analogy. He proceeded to an even more extreme example of biblical disinheritance. He likened most treaties with Indians to the story of King Ahab and the theft of Naboth's vineyard.[8] The Naboth comparison revealed a good deal about Bourquin's mindset. Bourquin considered the Bible a living guide. Just as King Ahab coveted the beautiful vineyard of his neighbor Naboth, "the whites exceedingly coveted these fragments of the Indian empire," he wrote. Naboth refused to sell his vineyard, claiming that God forbade the transfer to outsiders of the inheritance he had received from his fathers. King Ahab and Queen Jezebel conspired to have Naboth murdered. False witnesses accused Naboth of disloyalty and disrespect toward the king. Naboth was found guilty and was executed. The king then confiscated his property. Bourquin found little difference between the legal methods employed by the United States and those employed by Ahab to exterminate his neighbors in order to seize their lands. America had its indefatigable lobby [Jezebel], he wrote, determined to besiege Congress [Ahab's kangaroo court], "which . . . often capitulated."[9] In both cases, the appetite of the wrongdoers "grew by what it fed upon."

Bourquin noted that in 1871 the United States had enacted a law that destroyed the last vestiges of Indian rights by repudiating the Indians' right to negotiate treaties.[10] By statute, Congress had assumed control of the Indian nations. For his part, Bourquin, though generally a great believer in the literal interpretation of law and the Constitution, did not believe that Congress could seize control of another nation simply by means of appending one sentence to an appropriation bill.[11]

Bourquin also analyzed the General Allotment, or Dawes, Act of February 8, 1887.[12] The Dawes Act held part of the Indian land in trust for a period of twenty-five years, in theory, so Indians could acquire the ability to manage their own affairs successfully and avoid selling land for a handful of trinkets or a paltry sum of money. The act provided that allotments were to be selected by the Indians individually. An Indian entitled to an allotment had to make his choice within four years or the government agent would make it for him. The federal government would hold the land in trust for him for twenty-five years. After allotment, those parcels of land that remained were the subject of negotiations between the secretary of the interior and the Indian tribes and were sold to white settlers. The main purpose of the Dawes Act was said to be to assimilate the Indians. It was the logical result of white insistence that Native Americans adopt the white man's concepts, principles, and values, particularly in terms of individual ownership of land. The Indian practice of communal ownership of land was neither recognized nor respected. The Dawes Act has been characterized as "the most important, and to the tribes, the most disastrous piece of Indian legislation in United States history."[13]

Senator Henry M. Teller of Colorado was an outspoken critic of this policy. In 1881, Teller dramatically and prophetically declared: "I want it put upon the record my prophecy on this matter, that when thirty or forty years shall have passed and these Indians shall have parted with their title, they will curse the hand that was raised professedly . . . to secure this kind of legislation."[14]

In 1886, after three years as secretary of the interior, Teller still opposed the bill, but now he did so because it did not go far enough. If assimilation was the goal, it should be all encompassing, he later argued.[15] In 1887, about 130 million acres of land were held in trust by the government for the Indians; by 1933, the figure was 52 million acres of marginal lands.[16]

By 1904, Congress had decided that the land of the Flathead reservation would be allotted according to the Dawes Act and that the "excess" land would be sold at prices fixed by a commission, of which fifty-two members would be of "tribal relations."[17] This act was amended in 1906 so that no Indian would be deprived of "water appropriated and used" by him.[18]

Also in 1906, an act was passed authorizing the secretary to issue a fee patent when "satisfied" of the Indians' ability to manage their own affairs.[19] Bourquin was cynically realistic when he evaluated this policy. Clearly, there was no altruism in the ideal of setting the Indian "free." The "evil climax" could only be the continuing degradation of a "dependent and unhappy people" in complete poverty.[20] Indirectly, Bourquin attacked the free market theory that prevailed at the expense of the Indian, just as he had earlier assaulted "state socialism." In addition, Bourquin despised the insidious notion that one must inquire as to the Indian's competence before purchasing his land. He noted the double standard in the matter, as the white purchaser did not have his competence examined by anyone.

The first case that dealt with these issues was *Scheer v. Moody*, in 1931, which combined ten cases that ostensibly dealt with water rights of non-Indian plaintiffs who had purchased Indian land. The plaintiffs had purchased what had been allotted lands of American Indians.[21] In order to irrigate their lands, the plaintiffs claimed water rights and demanded that the government pay the cost of constructing irrigation ditches. C. J. Moody, manager of the Flathead Reclamation Project, not only refused to comply with the plaintiffs' demands but also insisted that the government be paid for the water and for construction of ditches. He conceded, however, that plaintiffs held rights to the water. Moody claimed to be immune from prosecution because he was acting as a government official.

On the other hand, the plaintiffs sought an injunction against the government and demanded that their titles to the former Indian land be confirmed. The farmers who sued had obtained the land at extremely low prices at the expense of the Indians. The lands had either been bought from the government after being expropriated from the Indians or "bought" from the Indians in exchange for "a small quantity of brilliant beads, gaudy calicoes, and other gewgaws of the 'trade goods' of the times." The plaintiffs were not satisfied with having acquired Indian land at ridiculously low prices. They also insisted that the government pay for the building of irrigation ditches on the land, just as the government had provided that service to the Indian owners before them.

In this case, Bourquin did more than rule on the legitimacy of the effort by the manager of a reclamation project to charge farmers for use of water. He reviewed the "disgraceful" Indian policy of the US government, criticized a government agent for interfering in the affairs of private business, and emphasized the importance of the "public good" while projecting a deep suspicion of the "socialist" attitude regarding governmental regulation of natural resources. He believed that private enterprise was the most efficient instrument for exploiting natural resources, though he deplored the greed of private citizens. His most powerful statement, however, had little to do with his actual ruling in these cases: Bourquin offered a remarkable review of US Indian policy, which confirmed his innate legal conservatism.[22]

The irony of the plaintiffs' suit against a government official who attempted to limit their control over the land was not lost on Bourquin. He argued that the Indians had been exploited in as severe a manner as that of the first victim of stolen birthright, the biblical Esau. Unlike the majority of his predecessors and contemporaries, Bourquin refused to subscribe to a mythical, nostalgic recollection of America as a "virgin land." Indeed, Bourquin's vision of America's origin was strikingly different. It was all too clear to him that at the time of the so-called golden age in America's history, the Indians already were on the land, and they were its "natural owners."[23]

Bourquin made it abundantly clear that he had little sympathy for the advocates on both sides. He characterized their pleadings as "far from models" and their arguments as "scandalously verbose."[24] Bourquin was unwilling to overlook the fact that the farmer plaintiffs and the federal government shared the blame for the tragedy of the American Indian. In his extended analysis of the "history" of the Indians' plight and of the "policy" of the US government toward Native Americans, he emphasized that the case stemmed from what he called "the humiliating record of our oppression, expropriation, dispersion, and destruction of the Indian nations that formerly exercised dominion over all this broad land."[25]

In a classic understatement, Bourquin, who often tended to describe the Native American experience in an idyllic manner, sardonically added that the advance of this frontier did not benefit the Indians. Specifically, the lands of the Flatheads had been seized immorally, if not illegally, in the 1859 treaty. To Bourquin, Indian rights could be traced back to "time immemorial," and the lands certainly were in their possession in 1859 when they signed the first "treaty" giving up land west of the Continental Divide. Until that time, Indians lived the life they had known for countless centuries, described by Bourquin as follows:

In 1855, the Flathead and other Indians, many, many, thousands, free, content, and happy, were natural owners, occupants, and overlords of all the vast domain west of the Continental Divide and within what is now Montana. Rich and lovely as that region was and is, as always, it excited white avarice and intrigue to oust the red; as always, the alibi, uplift, and civilization. Thereupon was invoked the established policy, "buy when you can, cheap, fight when you must."[26]

Bourquin was not only concerned about the government's unfair practices in Indian affairs. He also objected to "the rather state socialistic policy of governmental irrigation of private as well as public lands, initiated in [the Reclamation Act of] 1902."[27] According to the law dealing with the appropriation of Indian lands, those who had purchased former Indian lands from the government were to pay for the construction of irrigation projects at subsidized rates, while the Indians were to receive those same services without additional charge for irrigating the lands they still held. The Indians already had funded these projects, albeit indirectly, by forfeiting most of their land to the government. Bourquin objected to government subsidization of the water projects and of the land for white purchasers, and he noted that the defendant—the federal government agent—had refrained from attempting to collect water fees until 1917. This was well after the United States had spent money on the construction of various water projects on the properties of the new white owners. In essence, Bourquin believed that the government no longer could demand payment for services rendered so many years earlier. Moreover, Bourquin maintained that the government agent, in trying to collect fees, acted improperly and exceeded his and the government's authority. Ironically, Bourquin decided to exonerate the government and to protect it from its overly zealous employees. He found the government agent guilty of overstepping the bounds of his authority in a situation in which the government had no jurisdiction. Bourquin believed that the individual in the case before him, the government agent, must be held accountable for his actions. Because of sovereign immunity, it probably was possible to obtain a remedy only from the government agent and not from the government itself. Based on the "fiction" that the agent was acting ultra vires (outside the law), a principle of the "noble lie" established in *Ex parte Young* (1908), Bourquin found that "unless justified by some constitutional statute, a governmental officer or employee acts at his peril and personally pays for his wrongs—a salutary principle necessary to discourage abuse of power, that official power, which the great Marshall declared, would be abused wherever authority was reposed." Furthermore, Bourquin argued that "suits against any such trespasser are not against the government," but rather against the United States itself.[28]

Bourquin condemned the abuse of power by the water project manager and held him accountable only as a private citizen rather than as a government official, a capacity in which he would be immune. The government had "to discipline its derelict agent whose excesses tend to defeat its obligations and to bring it into disrepute."[29] The government had agreed to grant water rights and irrigation ditches for the land in question. Forty years after the fact, the white owners now wanted to receive the construction costs of the ditches and sued the government agent for refusing to honor government policy. The agent believed that Indian rights did not transfer to the white owners. Bourquin thought Indian rights were valid throughout the trust period, regardless of who previously owned the land. It was clear that the secretary of the interior had great discretion in the matter.[30] Only the acts of August 1, 1911,[31] and May 18, 1916, subjected land of Indian allotters to construction costs in proportion to benefits received.

Therefore, Bourquin granted injunctive relief to the plaintiffs—"white owners" of the former Indian land allotments—and he enjoined C. J. Moody, project manager of the Flathead Reclamation Project, from assessing or charging plaintiffs for the construction, operation, and maintenance of the water project and from determining the amount of water to which the plaintiffs' lands were entitled.

Bourquin attacked the government on the issue of the suit itself. He emphasized the unfair advantage a government official had over those who would litigate against him. This offended Bourquin because it was contrary to "a fundamental principle that in court and before the law all are equal, the humblest with the greats or even with the government itself."[32] However, he noted that, to his regret, this principle was celebrated in theory but not honored in practice. Bourquin had no doubt that Congress disregarded its treaty obligations to the Indians. Yet his Jeffersonian view led him to claim that the law had created valuable property rights that deserved protection under the Fifth Amendment. In rejecting the attempt to combine tribal liability and individual liability, Bourquin was trying to help individual Indians, though the implications of his stark separation, "as night from day," were dangerous for tribal sovereignty. Bourquin failed to recognize and accept the communal nature of the Indian concept of ownership. He is dedicated to the concept of individual ownership in American capitalism. Bourquin entered the debate because the government was raising additional technical claims about waiving rights or receiving benefits adequate to compensate for any intrusion on protected property. Bourquin scolded the government for trying to use its role as guardian and administrator to hide its own violation of fundamental rights.[33] This helps explain his desire to ensure that the government agent could not hide behind the cloak of governmental immunity.

Bourquin went so far as to argue that Congress, in effect, had explicitly imposed all the conditions that could be imposed. Therefore, as a matter of lawyers' logic, no other conditions might be implied. Bourquin underscored this in his forceful rejection of a statute of limitations claim. He called this "a defense as mean as it is invalid."[34] Thus he was able to weave his way through or around a vast number of technical defenses. He was innovative in the remedy he granted. He apparently wished to do justice after reviewing the tragic history of what a "too easily satisfied secretary" and an unjust Congress had done or could otherwise do. In this sense, and in his willingness to believe the arguments of the Indians as to events that had occurred so many years ago, Bourquin sought to deal with much more than the specific case before him.[35] Alloters in later property disputes and numerous Indian claimants in other contexts might have used this case had Bourquin not been overruled on technical grounds.[36] Bourquin's concern for the ordinary individual was paramount because of his legal conservatism. He believed that individuals needed to be protected both from themselves and from governmental excess.

Clearly, Bourquin's complex opinion expressed dissatisfaction with all the parties involved except possibly the Indians. The government expropriated land immorally and had acted in a "socialistic" manner by its excessive subsidization of the expropriated land. Yet the government was immune from suit and theoretically had to be protected from agents who exceeded their authority and would be held personally responsible. The government had the right to charge the plaintiffs for public works that enlarged their water supply, but after the government failed to impose those charges, it had no right to charge for water obtained through private ditches and water rights and had no right to charge the plaintiffs for water given originally to the Indians. To the degree that the United States spent money on constructing these ditches, "it was of the ordinary appropriations in support of a people whose original sources of livelihood had by government been appropriated, and whether to pay a debt or to appease uneasy conscience was not to be reimbursed."[37]

If additional justifications were necessary for finding in favor of the plaintiffs, Bourquin was not hard-pressed to discover them. He said of the plaintiffs' water rights: "any such right is limited to water in equality with all other like users and to the extent reasonably necessary."[38] By limiting the use of water necessary to the "public good," Bourquin in effect legitimized the water rights of the plaintiffs. They could not have a monopoly on the water rights, but they were entitled to reasonable use of the water without governmental interference. Moreover, the Indians, and through them the vendees of their lands, enjoyed valuable property rights in the ditches they had created. Bourquin viewed this right as property protected by the Fifth Amendment and therefore beyond any acts of government "which assume to destroy it."

Bourquin also used the *Scheer v. Moody* cases to criticize the government's decision to shorten the trust period for Indians originally stipulated by the Dawes Act of 1887. The commissioner of Indian affairs had shortened the twenty-five-year trust period, conveniently satisfied that Indians had become able to control their destiny long before the waiting period expired. Bourquin viewed this reduction in the government's fiduciary obligations as particularly unfair. He claimed that white "covetousness" was the key motivation for the decision, leaving the Indian landowners "hopelessly cast adrift on a strange competitive sea which threaten[ed] their wreck upon the reefs of pauperism."[39] Despite his evident disgust for all those involved in reducing the Indian to poverty and total disenfranchisement, Bourquin remained loyal to the principles of law as he understood them.

Bourquin bitterly attacked the reality and the spirit of the Dawes Act. With a rhetorical flare he wrote that the "care-free rovers of forests and plains were perforce to be transformed into toiling agriculturists, and yielding to the inevitable, these unfortunate peoples sought to accommodate themselves to bureaucratic fashioning."[40]

Apparently, the government feared the potential ramifications of Bourquin's decision in *Scheer v. Moody*. The decision could have led to a state of affairs in which the Indians would be allowed to protect their valuable property and to manage their own affairs. On July 27, 1933, in the case of *Moody, Project Manager v. Johnston*, and four companion cases, the Ninth Circuit Court of Appeals reversed Bourquin's decree, with directions to dismiss the complaint for want of necessary party or parties.[41] The Ninth Circuit Court stated that the secretary of the interior, or the United States, or both, should have been party to the lawsuit. Moody, as an employee of the US government, had performed all his acts under the authority of the secretary of the interior and not in his capacity as a private individual. Bourquin had denied Moody's motion to dismiss the plaintiffs' complaint on these grounds, stating that Moody was a trespasser acting outside the scope of his authority and that suits against trespassers could not be filed against the US government. The Ninth Circuit Court strongly disagreed. One suspects that the appellate court reversed Bourquin on a technicality because upholding his decision could cost the federal government an enormous amount of money.

Scheer v. Moody marked a departure in two basic ways that might have greatly aided the rationale for Indian claims; these were Bourquin's sense of tragic history and his anticipation of the need both to redress and to amend injustice toward the Indian perpetuated by the government. As both a legal realist and a moralist, he sought to overcome a range of technical defenses in order to do justice. Well ahead of his time, Bourquin attempted to use history to redefine the relationship between Native Americans and the federal government.

The paternalistic attitude toward Native Americans that had been subtly suggested in Bourquin's ruling in *Scheer v. Moody* became quite evident in the judge's later decisions. For example, in *United States v. Trinden* (1932), Bourquin found that "infant" Indians who had taken a federal government automobile and wrecked it were not guilty of "stealing." Stealing, Bourquin reasoned, both in common law and under Criminal Code no. 35, imports concepts of "larceny," or felonious taking, and intent to permanently deprive an owner of his property.[42] He went so far as to reject the plea of guilty, and he dismissed the case.[43] Bourquin wrote his decision in an ironic mode, seeming not willing to take the issue seriously. The defendants were minors, "Indians, wards of the government," and they took the car for "temporary local use." Unfortunately, their "joy riding terminated against a telegraph pole." Bourquin viewed the indictment as "a lesson to them and other young braves disposed to infringe their guardian's rights of property."[44] Thus at the very moment Bourquin upheld the rights of Indians, he deflated the notion that they could be held truly responsible for their actions under the law. "Wards of the government" enjoyed privileges that need not be granted to adult, responsible citizens.

In *United States v. Healy* (1913), Bourquin had previously exhibited a judicial double standard when the rights of Native Americans directly opposed the rights of the white man. Dennis Healy, a Caucasian, was convicted of selling intoxicants to a Native American. Bourquin, on his own motion, set aside the verdict and discharged the defendant. It was true that Healy had sold liquor to a Native American, but Healy was ignorant of that fact. To convict a man for such an infraction, in Bourquin's view, would be "contrary to public policy."[45] Of course, ignorance of the law was not an excuse if the violation was committed voluntarily. However, the Native American, who was actually working as a government decoy, had taken Healy in. He was selected for that role precisely because he did not look or dress like a Native American. Bourquin remarked: "Many of the government's Indian wards are not distinguishable from Caucasians."[46] The issue in the case, however, was precisely that the law perpetuated the otherness of the Native American, who did not en-

"Indian Encampment on the Flathead." Photograph by N. A. Forsyth, n.d. Stereograph Collection, ST 001.368. Reprinted by permission of the Montana Historical Society Research Center—Photograph Archives, Helena, Montana.

joy equal opportunity under government auspices. Essentially, Bourquin based his legal opinion on the fact that Native Americans could not be distinguished from whites. Yet Bourquin, who considered himself to be an ever-diligent guardian of constitutional liberties, still found nothing unusual about the fact that the law prohibited the Native American from enjoying the same privileges as a white person: specifically, in this case, the right to purchase and consume alcoholic beverages. Healy's liberties were safe in Bourquin's hands because the judge struck out against governmental "over zealousness" in pursuing those who broke the law and sold whiskey to Native Americans. He did not, however, concern himself with the violation of Native Americans rights.

Bourquin's paternalism was most evident in his decision in *United States v. Twelve Bottles of Whiskey*. In this case, Bourquin differentiated between strict adherence to the law and the possibility of congressional intervention to create a more protective law for the Native Americans. Therefore, in the matter before him, Bourquin ruled that land that had formerly been an active part of an Indian reservation yet later was acquired by whites was not included in the ban on the sale and use of liquor in accordance with the rules that governed Native American territory: "It is settled law that, when the Indian title to lands is extinguished, such lands are no longer 'Indian country.'"[47] Bourquin noted, however, that Congress had the right to make treaties with the Native Americans and regulate commerce with them. Congress could have enforced such a ban had it stipulated such a condition in a law regulating Native American commerce. He called this "omission" unfortunate but something that "might be cured" in the future. Clearly, he would have supported such a measure "in view of the evils visited upon the Indian by intoxicants, and of the century-old policy to protect the Indian there from."[48]

Thus, Bourquin was protecting Native Americans from themselves, just as he paternalistically objected to Native Americans being allowed to govern their own affairs before the trust period had expired, as demonstrated in *Scheer v. Moody*. There was no doubt that his intentions were honorable and charitable, but he offered no remedy for the plight of Native Americans outside the scope of white paternalism.

Bourquin's sense of tragic history and his anticipation of the need to redress and amend the injustice toward Native Americans perpetrated by the government were ever present in rulings. So there was some irony to the fact that three years after this decision, Bourquin was thrashed in his bid for the US Senate in Montana by Burton K. Wheeler. Wheeler, the incumbent, was coauthor of the Wheeler-Howard Act, which attempted to reverse much of the misfortune perpetrated by the Dawes Act by recognizing the communal nature of Indian land ownership.[49]

Chapter VII
BOURQUIN ON ETHICS

Today, the realm of legal ethics is receiving considerable written attention, hand-wringing, and litigation.[1] The professional responsibility of lawyers is currently a subject of great controversy. At the same time, the method of choosing jurors and their perceived role in the legal system has been fundamentally altered.[2] In the early part of the twentieth century, it was unusual for a judge to comment extensively about professional ethics. But running throughout Bourquin's judicial decisions was an attention to ethics within the legal profession. He had very clear and forceful opinions on the subject and, in his usual direct manner, did not hesitate to express and act on them.

One of the most basic and also most controversial issues centers on the counsel-client relationship. To whom does counsel owe his/her "highest duty"? In addition, how isolated from public attention and influence should the legal system be? In a remarkable series of decisions, Judge Bourquin highlighted and sought to establish a legal standard to resolve these sensitive issues.

In a case called *In re Kelly* of 1917, for example, Bourquin forcefully presented his views on lawyers, law, and the jury system.[3] Bourquin repeatedly commented on such issues throughout his career. In this case, the evidence seemed to establish that two prominent Montana attorneys, D. M. Kelly and A. J. Galen, went to a local bar to converse with a juror who was to decide the fate of their client. In addition, Galen had spoken with another juror and promised him an introduction to state legislators who could facilitate passage of a bill that would help the juror in his business affairs. Supposedly, Galen met a number of times with that juror.[4]

Burton K. Wheeler, the US district attorney, headed the prosecution, while Lewis O. Evans, who was chief counsel of the mighty Anaconda Copper Mining Company, headed the battery of defense attorneys in the Kelly and Galen contempt trial.[5] The juror, Brown, was described as a "substantial rancher" from Helena. A number of jurors, including Brown and another named Warner, were promised various things, such as introductions to members of the Montana legislature. Kelly and Galen claimed that their meetings with the jurors were spontaneous; they had not entered the bar with the jurors nor had they planned to meet them. They said they did not discuss the case with the jurors, nor did they attempt to influence them in any way concerning the case.[6]

Bourquin acknowledged that Brown and Kelly were old friends, accustomed to "mak[ing] libation at the shrine of Bacchus."[7] But after analyzing the evidence at great length, he found both attorneys guilty of contempt, obstruction of justice, and improper professional conduct. Indeed, Bourquin severely criticized the conduct of lawyers in general.[8]

That Bourquin found Kelly and Galen guilty of obstruction of justice and fined each five hundred dollars, the cost of trial, was not unusual —the evidence clearly demanded such a decision. What was particularly noteworthy was the passion that Bourquin brought to his decision. He considered the legal system the barrier between persons who follow their base instincts and those who "reconcile" themselves to the law. He explained that society depends on juries for protection. He noted that though "the jury system is not perfect," and that "society is not yet ready to accept any substitute." He explained that "jurors, even as judges, are officers of courts and administrators of justice. Indeed, they are judges obligated to impartiality, fairness, and justice. Their oath and duty are to 'true verdict render in accordance with the law and in the case.'" He concluded by affirming that the "law and safety of man and property demand that oath be kept, that duty be performed."[9]

Apparently, Bourquin's passion was that of the civil libertarian who upheld the right of citizens to be tried by a fair jury. A close examination of his decision, however, shows that Bourquin undermined that liberal spirit with his deep-seated pessimism. The "philosophical writer" in Bourquin suggested that persons became "civilized" when they began to obey the law. The jury system would act as a deterrent to crime. Ironically, however, Bourquin also suggested the opposite. He wondered whether the jury system did not encourage "sometime violat[ors] of [the] law" to believe they had a reasonable chance to escape punishment because a jury was fallible and could sometimes be persuaded to find a guilty person innocent. The paradox, then, was that at the very moment Bourquin presented an uncompromising demand for the integrity of the jury system, he also suggested that the system could tempt "the individual man" to perform criminal acts.

In his typical stern fashion, Bourquin demanded that being part of a community limits the person as an individual. However, the community was far from exemplifying perfect justice. Tampering with juries was intolerable because it resulted in decreased respect for the law, and "incites violation of law, and encourages primitive force to avenge or remedy wrongs, endangers persons and property, breeds mobs, riots, and lynch law, and makes for disorder, crime and anarchy."[10] Because of his innate suspicion of humanity, Bourquin envisioned "herd" justice if the integrity of the legal system were tarnished by improper behavior on the part of jurors. One of Bourquin's primary concerns was the preservation of property. While Bourquin's interests seemed to be in line with those of any civil libertarian, in effect he also viewed the legal system as capitalist society's primary defense against the inherent irrationality of human behavior.

Precisely because Bourquin perceived humans and their legal system as inherently fragile, he believed that jurors should not be subjected to any sort of influence outside the jury box. Any suspicion that jurors were unduly influenced or tampered with was intolerable because "it impairs public confidence in juries and verdicts, creates doubts of the court's ability to do justice, lessens respect for law, incites violation of law." In such an anarchic state, the darker side of humanity gained ascendancy, encouraging "primitive force" such as "lynch law" to replace the organized legal system. Bourquin considered it especially insidious to abuse friendship to affect a jury's verdict. Friendship was part of a human's "finer nature," but it had a powerful potential for abuse should friendly relations be developed or maintained between counsel and jurors. Viewing the world "through a glass darkly," as he often did, Bourquin distrusted any bond among people that might impair the legal process. Should counsel solicit friendship among jurors, a trial might be converted "into a tragedy, and transform juries from administrators of justice to purveyors of injustice."[11] Bourquin also used the term "tragedy" to call attention to the theatrical aspects of trial by jury. In such a setting, any suspicion that jurors were not completely impartial had a devastating effect on justice. Because the human condition was so fragile, it followed for Bourquin that the legal system was every bit as ethereal. He poetically described the situation in this way: the "scales of justice are of delicate poise, and in a jury's hands may be affected by improper trifles as light as air."[12] Human law, unlike the law of God, was always in the hands of inherently flawed beings, and thus has to be upheld as precisely as possible.

Bourquin repeatedly emphasized that it was the counsel's duty to be on guard when friends or acquaintances served on a jury. The counsel had to avoid appealing to friendship. Bourquin differentiated between chance meetings between jurors and lawyers, which he viewed as inevitable, and lengthy conversations, planned or unplanned, as well as drinks and amenities. Those, according to him, were not acceptable methods to influence jurors.

Bourquin was particularly disturbed by the flagrant disregard of legal principles by the attorneys in the Kelly case. Immediately after the verdict to acquit in the felony trial, the juror named Warner met with Kelly and Galen to discuss the favors he desired, while juror Brown renewed his old friendship with Kelly during the trial. The attorneys claimed they did not intend to influence the jurors, and the jurors claimed they were not influenced by their relationship with counsel. Kelly and Galen conceded that their behavior might have been indiscreet, but they claimed it clearly was not contemptuous. Bourquin thundered back: "Lack of evil intent goes only in mitigation."[13] Bourquin believed that the counsels' intentions would determine the severity of their punishment but not their guilt. As lawyers, Kelly and Galen should have acted more responsibly.

Indeed, Bourquin was enraged by the counsels' denials of "evil" intent. Clearly, he did not believe them. Kelly and Galen had adopted "conduct forbidden by law" under those circumstances. Bourquin observed that "they intentionally violated law in the only sense in which the law considers intent."[14] And Bourquin expressed skepticism of the jurors' ability to decline to reciprocate counsels' favorable treatment and to remain impartial in their judgment:

> It is not alone a question of ultimate intent, or of mere courtesy, or little monetary value, but it is also a question of the impression the conduct may make upon jurors. Friendship, courtesy, favors, are the great and enduring forces. In the long run, they are stronger than mere money. Ends are often gained by good impressions created, where direct solicitation would fail. To reciprocate courtesies, hospitality, and favors is a natural impulse. A generous man remembers and responds in some kind. Only the base receives favors and returns none. Inexperienced jurors might hastily conclude that by their verdict alone could they timely reciprocate counsels' attentions.[15]

The "dangerous" tendencies of human nature dictated that this type of conduct on the part of jurors and counsels be entirely avoided. Admittedly, probable injuries to the legal system because of "social" behavior were difficult to prove. Bourquin warned that one could not account for mental or emotional processes affecting a juror. One might never know what had or had not influenced him because "his [the juror's] mental state is not accessible to other testimony." For this reason, Bourquin believed that "it is what respondents intentionally did, and its probable effect, not its intended or actual effects, that is the gist of their offending."[16]

In American criminal law, once a jury acquits a defendant, no further criminal action can be undertaken because of double jeopardy. Bourquin insisted that in this particular case, should he ignore the theoretical if not practical damage to the legal system's integrity, the example set by Kelly and Galen might lead to significant evil. In civil cases there was always recourse, but in a criminal case, Bourquin felt the need to interpret the law strictly. He believed that "the government in behalf of society is entitled to fair jury trials, even as persons are," though in criminal cases "the law forbids it to have a new trial." Thus, the government "has no remedy, and can only discipline the offender and discourage imitators, by proceedings for contempt as here."[17]

The people deserved equal opportunity at the "temple of justice." Because double jeopardy prevented the retrial of a case in which jury tampering was committed, Bourquin did his utmost to shame and punish the "sinning" counsels and to censure them. Five hundred dollars might not have been a prohibitive fine for the defendants, but the taint upon their reputations from Bourquin's jeremiad might have a lasting effect.

In writing his Kelly decision, Bourquin noted that "crime, its repression and punishment is a grave problem." Some publicists already were calling crime a "national disgrace." According to Bourquin, the reasons for the rise of crime were that "ancient rules based on vanished reasons make more to protect criminals against society, than to protect society against criminals."[18] Yet in the Kelly case, Bourquin found further potential for the destruction of rule of law in the unethical behavior of the counsel: "Counsel and juror gravitated toward each other, like drifting ships upon a calm sea, or steel and magnet, or perhaps like men not averse to reciprocal favors."[19] The "continuing journey" of immorality by counsel and jurors "must be either into the bar or down to a basement toilet."[20] The counsels had dared to celebrate publicly the acquittal of their clients with members of the jury, which led Bourquin to lament that "such celebrations are not uncommon in this country."[21] In his desire to preserve the sanctity of the courts, Bourquin had little doubt that justice, law, and the preservation of the entire legal system were the first and foremost responsibility of lawyers, superior to counsels' duty to their clients. He warned that "counsel must remember they, too, are officers of the courts, administrators of justice, oath-bound servants of society; that their first duty is not to their clients, as many suppose, but is to the administration of justice." Furthermore, he wrote, counsel must abide "scrupulously" by the codes of law and ethics, and if they fail to do so "they injure themselves, wrong their brothers at the bar, bring reproach upon an honorable profession, betray the courts, and defeat justice."[22] For Bourquin the issue was simple: those within the system of justice who became derelict in their obligations to preserve the law ought to be forced to take their places with the base representatives of society—those forced to "respond at the bar of the court." The "treasonous" behavior of immoral emissaries of the law was intolerable in Bourquin's court.

In *Jackson v. Genzberger* (1933), Bourquin had another opportunity to comment on counsels' conduct and role in the legal system. Bourquin denied the defendant, attorney Earle N. Genzberger, a new trial after finding for the plaintiff, attorney B. M. Jackson.[23] Jackson, an attorney for an executor of a California estate, hired Genzberger to procure the services of an administrator to handle all estate matters in Montana. Plaintiff and defendant agreed that all legal fees received for the Montana estate would be divided equally between them. However, Genzberger and the administrator he hired, Hugo Kenck, then agreed that Kenck would dismiss Jackson. Safely entrenched as executor for the estate in Montana, Kenck fired Jackson, claiming that his services were no longer needed. Subsequently, Genzberger refused to divide the fees with Jackson. Genzberger apparently had made a superceding arrangement with Kenck.[24]

Bourquin, it seems, had to choose between two unpleasant alternatives: whether to vindicate the behavior of Jackson or that of Genzberger. Bourquin was disgusted by the shallow, avaricious practices of both. Bourquin as much as accused both plaintiff and defendant of bad faith. Perhaps even more disturbing to the judge was the attorneys' apparently correct belief that the courts of Montana were more "liberal with other people's money." Bourquin did manage to refute that belief by citing the Montana court ruling lowering the value of the estate for tax purposes. Bourquin was clearly enraged by the defendant's contention that Jackson was merely a "runner" to secure business for the defendant and had received his "commission" for services rendered. Bourquin interpreted that contention as implying that "the court sanctions a variety of so-called ambulance chasing."[25] In Bourquin's view, Jackson and Genzberger had a contractual agreement that was not affected by Kenck's action. The entire problem was summed up sardonically by Bourquin as "a rift in the lute of harmony."[26] Despite his evident distaste for the pursuit of inflationary fees by lawyers whom he branded as no better than ambulance chasers, Bourquin insisted that Genzberger honor his contract. Bourquin was so taken with the persistent theme of greed in this case that he entered a protest poem of the "ancients" in his decision: "All sense of honor, men and nations, in decay, Repudiation is the order of the day. The idler and the wastrel of the thrifty make a prey; their substances beg and borrow, whine and welsh and not repay."[27]

The defendant, through no more than "transparent subterfuge, pretext, and alibi," sullied his honor and denied his obligation to Jackson, but Bourquin was concerned with a much larger dilemma. It seemed to him to be part of the modern human condition that people, in their "lust for gold," abandoned "honor" and obedience to the law. In Bourquin's view, a society without laws was nothing more than an anthropomorphic "herd." Attorneys, as officers of the courts, had a greater responsibility to the law than did ordinary citizens; Bourquin categorized lawyers as those "enrolled in the great office of trust and confidence."[28]

Those "enrolled in the great office of trust and confidence" that attempted to manipulate the judicial process unscrupulously could not expect cooperation from the judge. Bourquin was most unsympathetic to motions of the "catch-all" variety requesting new trials. In *United States v. Noble* (1923), for example, the defendants Noble and Peters claimed misconduct on the part of jurors. Specifically, they alleged that juror Woolman "had expressed hatred and enmity towards Noble."[29] Noble and Peters also claimed "accident and surprise" when a codefendant, Funk, though promising to testify in a manner consistent with theirs, "shielded himself" by implicating Noble in his testimony. Finally, the defendants claimed "irregularity" in the court proceedings because the judge gave supplementary instructions to the jury without notice to and in the absence of the defendants.

On the issue of the tainted juror, Bourquin ruled that there was no evidence to support such a claim. The fact that Funk reneged on his private pledge to Noble to present his testimony in a manner consistent with Noble's position had no bearing on the legality of the trial itself. The most interesting legal issue, however, involved the obligation of a court to defendants, such as Noble and Peters, who had been released on bail. Bourquin reviewed the court's longstanding position on that issue, which was that

it is the rule and practice of this court for more than 12 years that defendants on bail be not taken into custody at and during trial; that, present when trial for felony begins, defendants and counsel thereafter control their own movements . . . ; that at any reasonable time the court will sit to grant any of the jury's request for refreshment of recollection or for supplementary instructions; that therein the court neither searches nor waits for defendants or counsel.[30]

According to Bourquin, bail was a privilege that called for responsibility on the part of its recipients. If defendants voluntarily absented themselves from judicial proceedings, the court was not responsible for locating and informing them of supplementary instructions to the jury. This view was the "correlative" of the right of bail. Though the law did demand that all proceedings of a trial take place with accused or counsel present, that rule "fails when they [defendants] are voluntarily absent, and the rule fails with it."[31] To be sure, Bourquin indirectly criticized the attorneys for the defense. Based on their advice, Noble and the other defendants thought they could subvert the legal process by not appearing in court at the proper times. Irresponsible behavior by or on behalf of anyone connected to the legal process, however, was not tolerated in Bourquin's court.

Bourquin had little patience for those who viewed the law in a one-sided fashion, without considering the defendants' responsibilities. Bourquin would not have "judge and jury . . . cool their heels about the corridors until accused and counsel condescend to come into court; nor is there any obligation upon the court to dispatch messengers to the four quarters of the compass to search out and solicit them to do so."[32] Despite Bourquin's somewhat humorous tone, he would not have his court submit to the disrespect he saw in the defendants' cavalier attitude. The law was much too serious a concern for that kind of attitude.

Ethical behavior, moreover, was not something Bourquin demanded only from professional representatives of the legal system. The same demand was placed upon plaintiff, defendant, and witness in Bourquin's courtroom. Should a defendant be found to have committed an illegal act that offended Bourquin's ethical values, he/she would be foolish to rely on his mercy. In *United States v. Meagher* (1929), for instance, Bourquin argued for strict interpretation of the law when applied to someone who committed a crime in the hope that "mitigating" circumstances would soften if not eliminate his punishment.[33]

A seventy-six-year-old embezzler, C. E. Meagher, sought probation in place of a six-month sentence on grounds of ill health and insolvency.

This may be Sidney Leonard "Buster" Smith's bar at 5 or 7 South Wyoming in Butte near Finlen Hotel. N.d. PAc 96-45.23. Reprinted by permission of the Montana Historical Society Research Center—Photograph Archives, Helena, Montana.

Bourquin denied probation, handing down his judgment in strict adherence to the law. Bourquin often displayed flexibility, legal maneuverability, and even compassion for a variety of defendants. Why, then, was Bourquin so strict with a seventy-six-year-old, of obvious ill health and with only a short sentence to serve? Bourquin fully played the role of angry Old Testament judge. His guiding philosophy in the case before him seemed to be: "probation has its uses, but no less its abuses." Bourquin believed that criminals must take responsibility for their actions and that the criminal must be prepared to pay the price for breaking the social contract. In his dark view of human nature, Bourquin claimed that the "terrors of penalties" were commonly what kept citizens from going astray. If probation was the norm, those "terrors" would lose their deterrent effect. In addition, Bourquin assumed that a first offender such as Meagher had no special claim to probation because "first offender too often means first detected, and shall every man be licensed to one crime even as every dog to one bite?"[34]

In Bourquin's worldview, a person had no "natural" right to crime, despite humanity's inherently depraved nature. Instead, Bourquin subscribed to the idea of the contract as a foundation of society. A person living in society agrees to obey the rules or to pay the price for disobedience. Bourquin believed strongly in "repentance, reformation, and rehabilitation following payment." He especially preferred "rehabilitation" after serving sentence, to avoid attempts to subvert the law by criminals whose high-priced lawyers encouraged their clients to "welsh and avoid payment" for their crimes.[35] In a near rage full of fire and brimstone, Bourquin argued that should "the sanctions of the law fail . . . the example encourages crime." He railed against convicts, urging "treatment appropriate to their offenses, rather than that to more or less favored guests will go far to solve the problem of crime, farther than ought else save inculcation of good morals from youth to age."[36]

Bourquin preferred moral fortitude to serve as a deterrent to crime. Yet should one's morality be found lacking, an offender would have to learn his lesson through incarceration. Bourquin was not swayed by age or by illness when sentencing violators of the law. He showed little mercy, because "those not too old and ill to plan and execute crime likewise are not too old to pay the price . . . he alone is at fault and responsible."[37] Bourquin's motto was: "To every man according to his works."[38] Anything less and the foundations of civilized behavior, the law and its sanctions, would crumble.

In *United States v. Herrig* (1913), the "letter" and the "spirit" of the law were central issues.[39] A. L. Herrig was indicted for making false entries in a report of a national banking association to the federal comptroller. Bourquin found him innocent for two reasons: Herrig had submitted an incomplete rather than inaccurate report, and he was not personally responsible for the "false" entry. Herrig had completed the entry "Notes and bills rediscounted . . ." with ellipsis points rather than a specific number. The report should have specified $5,000. The government contended that by leaving said entry "blank," Herrig implied that there were no notes and bills rediscounted. Bourquin decided that the government's indictment lacked substance. In explaining his legal reasoning, he relied partly on grammatical principles. As far as Bourquin was concerned, Herrig had fulfilled his duties by not leaving the entry blank. Ellipsis was used to indicate the completion of a grammatical construct or idea by relying on the reader's "comprehension." In order for the entry to be false, Bourquin argued that the insert be "none" or a number other than $5,000. Ellipsis invited the reader to imagine the writer's conclusion. Clearly, in a financial report, where a specific number was required and expected, the use of ellipsis undermined the reader's expectations. Bourquin, excellent reader that he was, understood that Herrig's report was calling attention to someone's financial impropriety, though not Herrig's own.

In this case, Bourquin had greater concerns than proper English usage, however. In a statutory offense, he wrote, "the statute must be strictly construed, not to defeat the legislative will, but to effectuate it, to the end that no case not by Congress brought within the letter of the statute shall be included by construction."[40] Bourquin demanded that the "letter" of the law be obeyed. In doing so, Bourquin believed he was reinforcing the right of Congress to make laws. Indeed, the "legislative will" was not to be "defeated" by flexible interpretation of cases outside "the letter of the statute." Judging by other Bourquin decisions, one might conclude that Bourquin himself often found the need to interpret the "spirit" rather than the "letter" of the law.

Perhaps greater than his concern for the "legislative will" was his desire to protect the rights of the individual. No one should be indicted for "sins" of omission in place of "sins" of commission. At worst, Herrig's entry was ambiguous. Because of the "presumption of innocence," he should not be held accountable for irregularities committed by others. "Men's guilt or innocence depends on their own acts and their aspect when performed," he wrote, "not on the alternative inferences of other persons thereafter." Should guilt be established on the basis of inference, "prosecution is persecution." In Bourquin's court, the latter was not to be allowed.[41]

One of the attorneys appearing for the government in the Herrig case was Assistant District Attorney Sam C. Ford, who served as Montana's attorney general from 1916 to 1920. Ironically, in 1925, twelve years after the Herrig decision, Bourquin found Ford guilty of contempt in *United States v. Ford*.[42] Bourquin fined Ford $300 because he had falsified a bill of exceptions and amended assignments while representing one Gordon Campbell in Bourquin's court. Wellington Rankin, one of the most important leaders of Montana's Republican Party, represented Ford. In his decision, Bourquin remained unmoved by the powerful counsel hired to defend Ford. Ford was charged with filing a bill of exceptions containing fifty-five exceptions to rulings of the court, of which twenty-seven had no existence in fact. Ford also "expanded" his fifteen original assignments of error to thirty-eight. In the most flagrant falsification of the assignments Ford submitted, assignment thirty-four claimed "that the trial court erred in denying defendant's motion for a directed verdict made by the defendant at the close of the government's case,' for no such motion was at any time made."[43]

Bourquin's decision seemed to find Ford guilty for two major reasons. First, Bourquin was not convinced that Ford had, as the defendant claimed, no actual knowledge of the "fictitious" assignments presented in the proceedings in error. Second, in regard to counsel, Bourquin believed that presenting improper or untrue documents without knowledge was still a "voluntary and intentional" act that therefore was culpable and contemptuous. Yet, in other decisions Bourquin had been much more tolerant of "unintentional" error, which suggests that the motivation for Bourquin's harsh treatment of Ford may be found in a closer reading of the text.

In *United States v. Herrig*, as noted above, Bourquin differentiated between sins of "commission" and sins of "omission." Herrig, a comptroller, had filled a critical entry in a financial report with ellipsis only, and Bourquin found him not guilty of falsifying a report based on the work of another accountant.[44] Why, then, was Bourquin so concerned with protecting the individual rights of Herrig, while in the Ford case he held the defendant responsible for sins of "omission"? Indeed, it was a court reporter, Rose, acting in his private capacity, who had prepared the bill of exceptions in skeletal form for the defendant and had admitted to inserting the fictitious exceptions. Why should Ford be held responsible for Rose's actions?

Freely admitting the application of a "double standard," Bourquin contended that counsel had a greater responsibility to the court than any "ordinary" defendant. He argued that if "counsel presents improper or untrue documents without knowledge thereof, it is his voluntary and intentional act, and is so far culpable and contemptuous that his other labors, haste, carelessness, neglect, or consequent ignorance is no defense thereto, but may go in mitigation."[45] Indeed, in the Ford case, Bourquin was unwilling to accept that the defendant had been "duped" into presenting false evidence. Once again, he embraced a double standard: "Falsification of judicial proceedings or records, or attempted falsification, intentionally in fact, or its equivalent, is contempt of authority of the court, and when done by an attorney of the court, it is more reprehensible than by others."[46] Bourquin found the defendant's testimony of a nature more commonly presented to juries than to courts—"some variety of mental irresponsibility, a 'split personality,' or other psychic infirmity, somnambulism, or other unconsciousness, amnesia, or the like, with subsequent recovery."[47]

The type of defense to which Bourquin sarcastically referred was acceptable to him, even if ludicrous, when an "outsider" was brought before the court and was doing his/her utmost to escape conviction. However, Bourquin insisted that counsels be held to a more demanding standard of conduct; for attorneys to abuse their position as officers of the court was intolerable to him. They had a special duty to uphold the integrity of court proceedings. Should they fail to do so it was "more reprehensible" than in other instances because the integrity of the court itself became the issue. Despite what most attorneys believed to be the case, Bourquin insisted that an attorney's first loyalty was to the court rather than to his/her client. An attorney who "betrayed" the court in his client's interest undermined the high ideal of justice. Justice was not an abstract concept in Bourquin's court; it was the very foundation of his legal reasoning. He plainly emphasized that falsification of judicial proceedings and records "obstructs and defeats justice. In consequence, if falsification be done or attempted intentionally in fact or equivalent as aforesaid, it is contempt of the authority of the court, and usually also a crime." Such a crime committed by an attorney is even more "reprehensible . . . ; for it is an abuse of his office, a betrayal of his trust, a violation of his oath, infidelity to the court to which, and not to his client, is counsel's first duty always, and a profanation of the temple of justice."[48]

Bourquin did more than place the concept of justice on a pedestal. He deified it. He insisted that to subvert justice was a "profanation." The "temple of justice" Bourquin envisioned was nothing other than the courtroom, especially one where he presided. A close rereading of his Ford decision eliminates the mystery of Bourquin's "double standard." Bourquin believed that Ford had decided to take a "sporting chance" that "opposing counsel [would be] as busy or negligent as defendant assumes [him] to have been." [49] Bourquin would not permit his courtroom to function in such a manner. Justice was on a higher plane, and Bourquin would allow no one to debase his exalted "temple," especially not an officer of the court.

Attorneys and juries were not the only "institutions" to come under Bourquin's scrutiny. The role of judges in the legal system did not escape his observations. Indeed, Bourquin probably demanded more of judges than he did of anyone else. In *Great Falls Gas Co. v. Public Service Commission of Montana* (1930), for example, Bourquin focused on judges and their role in jurisprudence.[50]

Bourquin was willing to confront the government whenever he believed it had overstepped its legal or moral boundaries. In *United States v. Freund* (1923), a Prohibition-related case, Bourquin upheld the right of Congress to enforce Prohibition by enacting reasonable laws. He took special care to note that courts had no concern with the "wisdom or necessity" of laws, lest the judicial branch impinge on the "supremacy" of Congress within its proper prerogatives. Bourquin's ruling in the Freund case was based on his interpretation of the adjective "reasonable," which suggested that he was far from content with the idea of Prohibition and with Congress's limitations upon the liberties of citizens. In addition, the case raised a basic question of medical ethics. The government sought to interfere with the legal practice of medicine through what Bourquin saw as an unreasonable interpretation of what constituted "ethical" behavior by a physician.

Dr. J. B. Freund was accused of violating the National Prohibition Act by prescribing alcohol as a remedial agent in more than a hundred prescriptions within a ninety-day period. Bourquin found it unreasonable for Congress to limit the scope and nature of a physician's activity after it had accepted, in principle, his/her right to prescribe alcohol legally. The other violation of the act that Bourquin rejected was the supposed illegality of prescribing more than half a pint of alcohol within any given ten-day period for an individual patient. Bourquin's decision rested on his view that there was an irreconcilable contradiction between congressional interpretations of the National Prohibition Act—in effect, the Eighteenth Amendment—and the property rights guaranteed by the Constitution and regulated by the states: namely that

> to practice medicine is a property right, subject to no police power of regulation but that of the states, that the statutory provisions aforesaid are prohibitory of what the Eighteenth Amendment does not denounce, that they unduly interfere with the judgment of physicians, supplant the latter by an arbitrary, unreasonable, and futile mandate of Congress, impair the liberty of physician and patient, and withhold means and remedies for and jeopardize the health of the people.[51]

Rather than alluding to the futility of the Prohibition legislation, he focused on its constitutionality. By depriving Freund and his patients of the right of the physician to give the best possible medical care he could,

Congress violated Freund's and his patients' property and liberty rights without due process of law.

That Bourquin did perceive the Eighteenth Amendment as futile was suggested by his "advice" to Congress:

> With the wisdom or necessity of laws and means that measure up to these requirements, courts have no concern. If unwise, the remedy is in appeal to Congress to change them, and not to the courts to nullify them. Otherwise would subject the judgment of Congress, supreme. Within its own powers, to review by the courts, and would overrule it by the judgment of the latter, impossible in constitutional government like America's.[52]

Though Bourquin seemed to reiterate his strict interpretation of separation of powers, in effect he was advising Congress of the futility of the Prohibition Act. As a representative of the courts, Bourquin was unable to nullify laws, but he took pleasure in exposing the illegality of this specific and ultimately unwise and fruitless imposition on civil liberties. As a final twist, Bourquin found Congress to be in violation of perhaps the ultimate liberty: the right to be treated as an individual. Bourquin was especially disturbed by the "10 day" restriction: "If therapeutics were an exact science, if diseases and their courses were of determined diagnosis and invariable prognosis, if patients were constituted alike and affected alike, if remedies could be admeasured by fixed rule, this provision would be valid."[53] Because Bourquin was concerned with the patient as an individual, however, the act constituted "an extravagant and unreasonable attempt to subordinate the judgment of the attending physician to that of Congress."[54] The physician himself was an individual due the trust and respect inherent in his having received a license from the state to practice medicine. Therefore, Bourquin demanded that "if a physician cannot be trusted wholly, he should not be trusted partially."[55] And so a "trusted" and licensed physician should not be stymied by congressional interference in the professional aspects of medicine. Bourquin was unwilling to tolerate such an egregious violation of liberty without due process of law.

Though Bourquin did not say so specifically, he perceived an inherent connection between ethics and the legal system. Congress had no right to limit the "ethical" practice of medicine by abusing its legislative privilege. Bourquin may or may not have believed this particular physician was acting in an ethical manner. However, his inherent suspicion of humanity led him to view darkly the imposition of frivolous laws to regulate the practices of legally licensed professionals.

Bourquin interpreted the Constitution literally, but he was also guided by his pessimism. The courts and the law were the sole defense of civilization in the face of ever-threatening barbarism. Bourquin therefore demanded a higher standard of ethics from anyone associated with the legal system. He demanded an even greater standard from those learned in the law. In Bourquin's worldview, attorneys were the high priests who served in a holy shrine that entailed responsibility for the entire future of civilization. Bourquin was committed to the idea that the first and foremost responsibility of lawyers was to the law and the legal system, rather than to their clients. However, each member of the legal system had his/her crucial part to play. Regardless of whether a person was a defendant or a plaintiff, lawyer or juror, judge or witness, Bourquin constantly demanded a strict adherence to the highest standards of legal and ethical behavior for the future good of civilization.

Chapter VIII
THE JUDGE AS POLITICIAN: THE 1934 MONTANA SENATE CAMPAIGN

n 1934, George M. Bourquin, at seventy-one, decided to retire from the bench and to run for the US Senate as a Republican. In a sense, the 1934 Montana election was a referendum on the New Deal. As was the case in the entire nation, Montanans were directly affected by the nation's severe economic crisis. Hunger and poverty were particularly acute in Montana's agricultural sector. Declining demand, lack of capital, shortage of markets, and a decrease in purchasing power resulted in the deterioration of the copper and wood markets, which created large unemployment and serious economic crises in mining towns and lumber camps. In turn, this had a marked effect on the railroad industry and resulted in still more unemployment.

This domino effect left tens of thousands of Montanans in such dire need of help that traditional voluntary social services and the churches could not begin to provide. The state did not have the means or the machinery to provide assistance. Constrained by political and economic ideology, President Herbert Hoover and the federal government also could not provide adequate relief. Numerous Montanans, like a majority of the nation, turned to Franklin D. Roosevelt and the Democratic Party for help.[1]

By mid-1934, after more than a year of intensive activity under New Deal programs, there was a noticeable improvement in Montana's economic situation. The political climate of opinion also changed significantly. The Roosevelt administration invested large amounts of federal aid in Montana. Between 1933 and 1939, federal aid to Montana totaled $3,815,822,693. This sum was not exceptional compared to the amount spent by the federal government in other western states. However, Mon-

Judge George M. Bourquin. Associated Press photo, December 13, 1927. PAc 2003-72.4. Reprinted by permission of the Montana Historical Society Research Center —Photograph Archives, Helena, Montana.

tana received $510 per resident, a sum much greater than the amount received by any western state except Nevada.[2]

However, Bourquin presented clear ideological opposition to the New Deal, its concepts, policies, and programs, and he stressed his own libertarian dislike of "big government" and popular appeals. Bourquin ran on a platform that was a direct continuation of the ideologies that he had supported in his career as a judge. Immediately after the campaign ended, with a great loss for the judge, the *Great Falls Tribune* speculated that Bourquin had received the nomination through manipulations of Republican Party leaders, who knew that they did not have the slightest chance to unseat Wheeler and therefore agreed to permit Bourquin to run a hopeless race against him.

The building of the Fort Peck Dam, a huge federal project, provides a good example of the type of popular New Deal policy that Bourquin opposed. As soon as building commenced in 1934, the project provided work for seven thousand Montanans. By 1939, it represented an enormous project. The dam became a symbol of the essence of the New Deal: jobs for the unemployed, vast federal investment in the economy of a suffering state, and extensive use of natural resources.[3] Beyond the debate over the dam's long-range value and merit, opposition to any large-scale project that provided numerous job opportunities supported by federal funds was tantamount to political suicide during the Depression. Bourquin characterized the project as a "duck pond" that would cause Montana much more harm than good.[4] By opposing the project Bourquin doomed his chances for election.[5]

In the election, the Democratic candidate, incumbent Burton K. Wheeler, captured all fifty-six counties of the state and decisively vanquished Bourquin by 142,823 to 55,519 votes.[6] The results mirrored Wheeler's strength, not only among Democrats but among Republicans. The traditional conservative base crumbled, and a rare consensus existed between the Republican ranchers and farmers of eastern Montana and the laborers in the towns of the western section of the state.

Wheeler's triumph stretched beyond economic and political issues; beyond the unity of the Democrats compared to the Republicans' split; beyond the contributions of the New Deal and the senator's own effectiveness on behalf of his constituents in Washington. The results could be attributed to the ideologies and worldviews of the candidates. In a sense, it was the clash between modernism and tradition. Bourquin's speeches are an excellent source for analysis of his political ideology.

They also highlight the difference between the judge as a legal ideologue and as a politician.

A cartoon in the *Daily Missoulian* a few weeks before the elections summed up brilliantly the reasons for Bourquin's political failure (see page 121). The cartoon was titled "Pastime for Autumn Leisure." It depicts a scoreboard surrounded by figures such as Presidents Jefferson, Lincoln, and Washington; the score marks the number of times each was quoted by Bourquin in the campaign: Jefferson led with 17,942, just edging out Lincoln.[7] In other words, although Montana's problems were extremely real and pressing, Bourquin conducted a learned seminar in history, law, political science, and the sacred values of the Founding Fathers. His speeches revealed a conservative approach in which the study of history provided solutions to contemporary questions. Bourquin assigned an almost sacred quality to social institutions developed by the march of civilization. Therefore, he sought to honor the contractual agreements arrived at by the citizenry of the Republic. In the United States, he believed, the essence of this sacred covenant was represented by a strict interpretation of the Constitution of 1787.

Bourquin had faith that the problems of the present could be solved through knowledge and the experience of the past. He analyzed the story of mankind using the experiences, trials, and tribulations of antiquity, the feudal society of the Middle Ages, the Elizabethan period, Cromwell's England, the formation of the United States, World War I, the stock market crash, and the Depression. In the background were the Hebrews, the apostles, and the teachings of the New Testament. All were ever-present to Bourquin as he lashed out against the frailties of mankind. For him all these periods and characters had clear direct lessons for contemporary affairs. Aristotle, for example, became a witness for the importance of the American Constitution: "Men should live according to the role of the Constitution for it is their salvation, says Aristotle."[8]

In addition, King Solomon, Plato, Cato, Washington, Jefferson, and numerous other figures provided guidance on subjects such as the importance of honesty and honor in public service, the dangers of central government, dictatorship, and the sanctity of the Constitution.[9] One of the conclusions Bourquin drew from history was that civilization progressed naturally along evolutionary lines. This, he insisted, was the basis for the process mankind had undergone since creation, through antiquity, the Middle Ages, and into the modern era. It was a natural and harmonious process that should not be tampered with or disturbed.

Nonetheless, Bourquin was not entirely oblivious to the severity of the situation during the Depression, and his campaign speeches included recognition of its seriousness. America was in the grip of a grave economic crisis, and for that reason the social system was undergoing severe strains. The Democrats in power were attempting to change a part of society's mechanisms in response to crisis, and Bourquin was afraid that the entire system would change as a result and would lose its special meaning. According to Bourquin, the ills of the sociopolitical system had to be addressed. Under no circumstance, however, should the system be drastically changed or replaced.

Bourquin reviewed the major tenets of the New Deal and criticized them vehemently. He was dubious about the capacity of such measures to improve the situation, and he expressed great concern about their long-range ramifications for the country's economic, political, social, and legal institutions. He viewed the New Deal as a serious threat to the contractual covenant, the Constitution. Tampering with basics could lead to the destruction of the sacred liberties so deeply embedded in the foundation of the American system and its way of life. Such alteration could lead to the country becoming a dictatorship, with institutions and systems similar to those characteristic of other parts of the world, such as Soviet collectivism. For these reasons, Bourquin claimed that the Republicans were correct in supporting the policies of laissez-faire economics. He believed that "New Deal" was a "misnomer," in that it was not new but rather rooted in history. He characterized it as having "a theory in it [that] has been tried and discarded in failure. . . . Always their regimentation enslaved and pauperized the people. It halts improvement, paralyzes progress, breeds unrest, resentment and poverty, and destroys liberty."[10]

His conclusions were clear and simple: The New Deal had no solutions or remedies for current exigencies. Moreover, its programs constituted direct threats to the American way of life, to its ethos, and especially to its inherent principles of liberty. Bourquin expressed deep concern while responding to a message sent to Congress by the president, proposing to unify the three branches of government under one executive. He accused Roosevelt of initiating a process that would lead to a dictatorship.[11] In fact, Bourquin believed that Roosevelt was purposely laying the foundations for a dictatorship in the United States.[12] When the outlines for the National Recovery Administration (NRA), a major piece of New Deal legislation, were presented to the House of Representatives, many there believed that the plan gave the president extraordinary powers and influence and labeled him a "benign dictator." Bourquin protested: "There is no such animal as a benign dictator. The experience of 4,000 years proves that dictatorship always ends in tyranny and chaos. . . . By gradual encroachment are the liberties of the people destroyed."[13]

Bourquin believed that in addition to sowing seeds of dictatorship, New Deal principles injured the US Constitution. The Constitution was the contractual manifestation of the social covenant that the American people had endorsed for the past one hundred fifty years. It was the foundation of institutions and values that had served the American people so well throughout their history. Bourquin believed that the government was the people, and the people elected representatives to labor on their behalf. The administration was the public's servant. It was meant to protect and ensure the well-being of the voters and their dependents and to guarantee the rights promised them by the Constitution. However, the officials of the newly elected Democratic administration usurped the authority delegated to them through suffrage. Bourquin insisted they disregarded their pledges, denied legal protections, and disregarded the Constitution they had taken an oath to uphold. In fact, he argued, New Deal agencies and programs such as the Agricultural Adjustment Act (AAA), the NRA, the administration's gold policy, and the excessive authority awarded to the executive branch all represented a usurpation and illegal extension of the authority bestowed by the people upon their representatives.[14] Historical experience dictated that, above all, the Constitution must be preserved. Writing in the *Montana Record Herald*, Bourquin argued that the "Constitution is the very flower and fruit of the wisdom of all the ages; it is the price of the sacrifice of treasure, tears, blood and lives of our forefathers to free our country from England's arbitrary and despotic rule."[15] The Constitution, written by such men as Hamilton and Madison, had served the people well for more than a century, caused them to prosper, and gave them good government.[16] He continued:

> the Constitution, the noblest instrument of government conceived by man, the wonder and admiration of states-men everywhere, the model of all free peoples, the Ark of the Covenant and the charter of all our rights and liberties, is being destroyed.[17]

> The Constitution has, in all our national existence, been all-embracing and quite benevolent in carrying this great country through emergencies far worse than the present crisis. Why junk it now?[18]

In New Deal activities there were, according to Bourquin, grave distortions of the fundamental laws of the land that were dangerous to American democracy. The NRA granted its officials the authority to act as judges for alleged code violations without the need to resort to the courts. This, he said, was a conclusive demonstration of the New Deal's assault on the judicial branch, whose duty it was to provide the ultimate protection of the Constitution. The attempts of the New Deal to intimidate the Supreme Court of the United States were deplored by Bourquin, who described "visionaries in high offices [as] apprehensive the courts will not uphold many matters of legislation desired by presidential advisors, and it is openly whispered in the national capital that in order to override the integrity of our national judicial group, the membership of the Supreme Court may be increased by four new appointees, sufficient to control the court."[19] Bourquin was prophetic, forecasting in 1934 Roosevelt's "court-packing plan" in 1937.

In order to prevent injury to the courts, to avoid impairment of the laws and the rights of the people, to avert the ascendancy of dictatorship, and to ensure the return to sanity and normalcy, Bourquin urged the populace to elect Republicans. Once more, he found the lessons of history instructive, recalling that eighty years prior the Republican Party had been organized with a platform to "maintain and defend the Constitution, its guarantee of life, liberty, property and the pursuit of happiness, and to preserve a government of laws instead of men, to the end that 'government of the people, by the people, and for the people' shall not perish from the earth."[20]

According to Bourquin, the just tenets, humanistic ends, and patriotism of the Republican Party fit the needs of the hour. Republican concepts guaranteed hope, courage, and loyalty, and the response, he believed, would be immediate. Bourquin thought that Americanism and the Republican Party were one and the same entity. Bourquin meditated on the ideologies of the Founding Fathers—Washington, Madison, and Jefferson—who identified routes in the fields through which the United States must march. Bourquin believed that the founders and their basic principles had led the United States to flourish. What was true and right during their era was still correct in the 1930s. Adherence to those notions was what sustained the Union during times of severe crisis. Bourquin kept on reminding his listeners of 1860 and the Civil War, in which one sector did not keep faith and broke the covenant. In the name of sacred constitutional tenets, the other section launched a bloody defense of the

Constitution and preserved the Union. In the same way that the terrible crisis of the Civil War was overcome, so other difficulties, including the present one, would also be.

Like Jefferson, Bourquin believed that a government that governed least governed best. He conveniently forgot other ideas raised by Jefferson, such as the need to update the Constitution to the special needs and exigencies of each generation. Jefferson supported the strict construction of the Constitution as long as it corresponded well to changing needs. However, Jefferson did not hesitate to diverge from his "Jeffersonian ideas" when he became president and found it necessary to broaden presidential prerogatives. Bourquin thus was more Jeffersonian than Jefferson himself. As a politician, he allowed no room for a more elastic interpretation of the Constitution under any circumstances, not even during a world war, or during a deep national economic and social crisis.

Two schools of thought, liberal and conservative, thus faced each other directly against the background of the stock market crash and the Depression, though adapted to the specific circumstances of the western states. The election results came as no surprise. The New Deal clearly triumphed, as the *Great Falls Tribune* stated a day after the election. Montana opted for Roosevelt and his policies.[21] The newspaper explained that the Republican debacle stemmed from their inability to present a positive program. Bourquin and his allies had no chance, as they had no ammunition in their arsenal. The results were inevitable because, the newspaper claimed, the reactionaries and conservatives were in control of the Republican Party, and they refused to modify their economic and financial stances. They continued to lecture the voters using nineteenth-century language and concepts, and they failed completely to find common ground with the electorate or to present a coherent plan of action.[22]

Bourquin either was not wise enough to understand or simply refused to accept a basic fact adopted by a major portion of the American people:

> There are some political beliefs, which no longer can be rejected by any party. The country has put behind it some of the old deal ideas most definitely and no manner of propaganda can revive them. The right of labor to organize, protection for the farmers, increased security for the mass of people and some measure of control by the government of industry and finance in the public welfare are permanent principles in American political belief.[23]

An inevitable question is how was it possible for George M. Bourquin, who had been an exceptional judge, was well versed in the intricacies of politics and government, and was extremely knowledgeable about his environment, not to foresee the futility of his Senate venture. Did he really think that he could prevail in the 1934 contest with his conservative philosophical rhetoric? Bourquin must have realized before the campaign ever began that his chances were slim, regardless of his platform rhetoric. Even if Bourquin were to embrace some progressive elements or endorse some of Roosevelt's programs, Wheeler, directly responsible for acquiring large sums of money for the state, would triumph. Perhaps Bourquin, tired of his long judicial experience, desired one last opportunity to express his ideas, philosophy, and visions of the world to a much wider forum. In that sense, the 1934 election campaign was a golden opportunity. Even though he attracted much opposition, his message was heard across Montana. Although his ideas were not widely supported, they could not be ignored. Thus, through his energetic speechmaking, Bourquin was, at the very least, heard.[24] Nevertheless, his political campaign was certainly not easy, and it is hard to credit one newspaper's assessment: "Former Federal Judge George M. Bourquin concluded his campaign for the United States Senate with the observation it had been one of the most enjoyable experiences of his long career in public life."[25]

Bourquin's political worldview paralleled his legal one. Both were characterized by classical conservative themes: resistance to any expansion of federal governmental authority; a limited, strict interpretation of the Constitution; and an almost pedantic adherence to what he perceived to be the Constitution's basic ideas. In a sense, he practiced his legal thought through his political agenda. A legislator, he knew, should employ instruments of thought and action that were different from those used by a judge; the former could initiate and institute procedures, while the latter commented on and evaluated actions that had already taken place. Ignoring this basic fact made much of his election campaign an ongoing anachronism. Bourquin's dedication to the lessons of historical experience, protection of the status quo, and belief in the certain slow process of the development of civilization mirrored his legal thought. But these convictions did not translate easily into Montana's political world in 1934.

Bourquin's legal positions contained a unique mixture of classical conservatism, emanating from his suspicion of the evil nature of humanity, and liberal-progressive "civil libertarianism." His political vision was composed only of the conservative strains. On the bench, Bourquin often employed what seemed to be liberal ideas to further the fundamental goals of his conservative thought. He defended ideologies he abhorred, such as socialism, because he believed that a government that was not subjected to a "rule of law" and did not protect unpopular opinions would descend rapidly into tyranny. As a judge, Bourquin could say, "I find you not guilty, but don't do it again." As a politician, however, he could not do anything like that because he found it necessary to be much more doctrinaire. Bourquin was never a "liberal," but some elements of his legal thought could be described as "liberal." Bourquin sustained his belief in protecting the individual from the evils of the ever-encroaching government octopus and championed individualism and "real free enterprise," the basic principles of the "old liberalism" that dominated until the end of the nineteenth century. However, in the 1930s those were not considered liberal principles anymore.

In fact, the core of the meaning of the term "liberal" remained, but a deep change occurred in the principles called upon to transfer the ideal into reality. Because the focus—the essence of liberalism—was not an idealistic dedication to absolute liberty, political or economic, but rather a focus on the individual and his needs, principles of liberty were only guidelines for action designed to reach that goal. There was a key difference between the old liberalism's plan of action that emphasized liberty and the plan of action of the "new liberalism." The new liberalism emphasized governmental responsibility for the well-being of the citizenry. This was achieved by regulation and control over the economy and numerous other facets of the daily life of the populace. This involvement could lead to interference in, limitations on, and damages to individual rights. The post-New Deal version of the welfare state that put great emphasis on the interests of the majority of Americans clashed with the traditional policy that concentrated on advancing the interests of the economic elites.[26]

Actually, the debate among various aspects of liberalism had been present in American political thought and tradition from the earliest days of the Republic. Jefferson focused on the individual and on ensuring his capacity to pursue happiness. There were many concepts of what the proper tools and methods might be to carry out and reach this goal. A certain measure of governmental involvement in the economic sphere always existed in US history, but the old methods and principles of governmental action reigned until the "constitutional revolution" of 1937. The transformation in the meaning of liberalism, which involved new modes and forms of action, accompanied the Progressive ascendancy at the beginning of the twentieth century and peaked with New Deal policies when the principles of the "new liberalism" became hegemonic.

The disappearance of the liberal element from Bourquin's political thought can be explained by the simple fact that liberal expressions did not necessarily indicate liberal beliefs. Accordingly, Bourquin remained a conservative; as much as his liberal expressions were part of his legal philosophy and emanated from his dedication to liberal thought, they were a direct product of his conservative beliefs. His suspicion of humanity and his concern for safeguarding the individual rights of the citizen against government came directly from his strict doctrinaire interpretation of the law and the Constitution. His view did not stem from optimistic faith in mankind but from the exact opposite. Bourquin thought humans would, if given the opportunity, always demonstrate their worst propensities. Only good laws and their zealous enforcement could protect humanity from itself, from anarchy and from barbarism. Free men might become an uncontrolled mob if not ruled properly. This was the raison d'être for society and its institutions—to guard social order. However, leaders could always be corrupted, and because governmental institutions were constructed by humans, power inevitably resulted in tyranny. Bourquin likened the law to a barricade, a barrier against anarchy on the one hand and tyranny on the other. The basic social concept agreed on by the members of a society produced a system of laws—a constitution—that had to be guarded assiduously because any departure could doom that society.

This was the philosophy at the foundation of Bourquin's political and legal world. However, it found a quite different expression in his legal judgments than in his political discourse during his brief career as a politician. The differences stemmed from the altered social circumstances of the times and from the divergent needs of society. During World War I and the Red Scare that followed, the hysteria that swept the United States caused injury to individuals, their liberties, and rights, and seemed to necessitate strict adherence to constitutional principles such as those contained in the Bill of Rights to ensure individual rights. Conversely, during the period of the stock market crash and the Great Depression, a departure from the strict interpretation of the law and a liberal interpretation of the Constitution assisted in preserving individual rights and liberties that were lost when the individual had no external support available. In the 1930s, the threat to democracy came from both the extreme right and the extreme left. Unlike many of Europe's democracies that opted for authoritarian regimes during times of severe economic dislocations, the United States rejected both poles of the political spectrum and succeeded, by means of applying both flexible constitutional principles and New Deal policy, in preserving its democratic institutions. The federal government now declared that it had a legitimate role to play in the endeavor to guarantee each American an opportunity to succeed.

Bourquin did not stray from his convictions. His lack of faith in humanity caused him to assign central significance to those instruments that would restrain humanity from its own evil. Yet his negative view of humankind and his rejection of "big government" hindered his goals of assisting the weak in society. Bourquin failed to comprehend that very strict interpretations of the Constitution, at times, would not help the very people he wished to protect. If Bourquin had had greater faith in humanity, he might have understood better that the goal is to improve the conditions of human beings. This could and should be achieved through a broader interpretation of the Constitution. A more supple interpretation of the Constitution did not irrevocably result in the destruction of the existing order. Those human skills that created the existing order, as well as the laws protecting it, were also capable of changing that order, including the enactment of new laws.

Faced with ever-changing conditions, Bourquin suppressed the frontiersman's natural inclination toward compromise, flexibility, and dedication to survival and pragmatism. Another frontier characteristic triumphed over his pragmatism; this was Bourquin's bedrock fear of the demonic power of the strange, central, and remote federal system. However, though Bourquin viewed central power as threatening, evil, powerful, and corrupt, the Washington establishment could assist when extreme conditions recommended it. The Republican Party of Montana could not comprehend or accept this, and this failure was the root of its overwhelming defeat.

Bourquin's 1934 Senate campaign was a sad ending to the public life of a talented person. However encyclopedic his knowledge and however encyclopedic his intelligence, his narrow worldview prevented him from grasping the vast changes that his world was undergoing. Bourquin desperately attempted to hold on to the "good old days" and to the "lost world of Thomas Jefferson." He sought to embrace the values of an old-style liberalism that encouraged absolute freedom and free enterprise. He still believed, in 1934, that self-reliance, industry, honesty, and hard work guaranteed success. Such truisms might or might not have been useful during the previous century in a small, developing society with virtually endless resources on an ever-expanding frontier. However, modern, industrial, corporate America needed different values and new instruments of actions. Adherence to the old way of life was not an effective way to tackle modern realities. What social thinkers began to comprehend during the first thirty years of the century was understood by the Roosevelt administration and by many citizens of the United States after the economic crash. Yet Judge Bourquin either did not or could not accept

"The Grand Stairway, Columbia Gardens, Butte, Montana." Photograph by N. A. Forsyth, n.d. Stereograph Collection, ST 001.123. Reprinted by permission of the Montana Historical Society Research Center—Photograph Archives, Helena, Montana.

such new realities. The sad story of the political chapter of his life was common to numerous people in twentieth-century America who were left stranded, grieving over the passing of their "lost world."

The political philosophy Bourquin advocated in his political campaign was echoed somewhat by the newly established conservative American Liberty League.[27] The league brought together conservative Democrats who opposed Roosevelt's policies and were dedicated to the "education" of the public. Bourquin similarly propounded conservative political and economic thought and combined social Darwinism, laissez-faire economics, Old Testament apocalyptic prophecy, devout adoration of the Founding Fathers, and veneration of the Constitution. However, Bourquin the politician, like Bourquin the judge, did not adopt the conservative agenda verbatim. In both capacities, he supported labor unions, defended the rights of workers to organize, found justifications for governmental intrusions into the economic sphere through the use of injunctions, and supported governmental intervention in the economy, especially to regulate areas that, he was convinced, involved the "common good" and the interests of the general public. Although he often expressed his disdain for President Wilson, he rarely attacked Progressivism. His campaign rhetoric was devoid of the demonization of President Franklin D. Roosevelt that characterized the Liberty League's publications and speakers. Thus, though agreeing with much of the Liberty League's platform, Bourquin actually sought to establish his own, distinct public position.

Just as Bourquin was trounced in the 1934 senatorial election in Montana, the Liberty League was defeated in the 1936 presidential election, which was convincingly won by "that man in the White House."[28] Explaining the defeat at the end of his study of the Liberty League, historian George Wolfskill wrote:

> The League could never understand why no one listened. The farther it went the more futile, the more disillusioned it became. It could only conclude that Roosevelt and the New Deal had completely debauched the people, bought them off with bread and circuses, sown the seeds of class consciousness, lulled and beguiled them into a passive servitude with promises of security from crib to crypt. This was hardly the case. The League failed because the people, rightly or wrongly, regarded it as the executor of a bankrupted estate, the medicine man selling worthless stump water. The League failed because it represented economic and political conservatism at a time when both were out of style.[29]

The same description might apply to the Bourquin campaign. In summarizing the 1936 presidential elections, John D. M. Hamilton, chairman of the Republican National Committee, exclaimed: "The Lord couldn't have beaten Roosevelt in 1936, much less the Liberty League."[30] This, too, could be said of Bourquin's campaign, albeit with a slight twist. Even with the Lord's direct assistance, Bourquin had very little chance to win, given his political stance.

The rest of Bourquin's life was not unhappy or tragic. He retired, returned to Pennsylvania, and spent his time traveling extensively until his death in 1958. His brief, sad foray into politics certainly did not overshadow his twenty-two years as an innovative and courageous federal judge. He ranks as one of the finest and ablest federal judges ever to occupy the bench in the American West. After Bourquin's death, his colleagues eulogized him aptly: "There was only one Judge Bourquin in the world. He was an individualist in thought and action; none was more original, none sounder or more realistic. There will never be another like him."[31]

Daily Missoulian cartoon, October 16, 1934.

APPENDIX 1: UNITED STATES V. HALL, 248 F. 150

This was Bourquin's most important judicial decision and is discussed in most histories of civil liberties in the United States. During the days of mass fear and hysteria during World War I, Bourquin defended the rights of free expression. His ruling was an important precedent that diminished the clout of the infamous National Espionage Act of 1917 and led the attorney general to ask Congress to correct Bourquin's "mistake." This resulted in the passage in Congress of the much more draconian National Sedition Act of 1918.

Following the Alien and Sedition Act of 1798, Congress avoided passing laws that directly suppressed criticism of the government. Yet very few judges had the courage to oppose the pressures for suppression, and First Amendment rights were often disregarded. Bourquin courageously opposed this trend and construed the National Espionage Act narrowly. Bourquin ruled that Congress did not intend to suppress "criticism, denunciation, truth or slander, oratory or gossip, argument or loose talk." Bourquin made a clear distinction between "opinions" and "disloyal acts," while the great majority of judges ruled that opinions, thoughts, and statements were disloyal acts and participated in the "patriotic" orgy that greatly weakened constitutional rights during crisis times.

District Court, D. Montana, January 27, 1918

BOURQUIN, District Judge. On yesterday, granting defendant's motion for a directed verdict, the court stated that, because of the grave issues involved and the necessity for interpretation of the Espionage Act, to the end that a precedent be established, it would incorporate its reasons and views in a written decision and opinion, made a part of the records of the case and of the court. It accordingly does so as follows:

The indictment charges that defendant violated section 3 of the Espionage Act, in that (1) he did "make and convey false reports and false statement with intent to interfere with the operation and success of the military and naval forces of the United States and to promote the success of its enemies"; and (2) that he did "cause and attempt to cause insubordination, disloyalty, mutiny, and refusal of duty in the military and naval forces of the United States, and to obstruct the recruiting and enlistment service of the United States, to the injury of the service of the United States." Specifically as follows: At divers times, in the presence of sundry persons, some of whom had registered for the draft, defendant declared that he would flee to avoid going to the war, that Germany would whip the United States, and he hoped so, that the President was a Wall Street tool, using the United States forces in the war because he was a British tool, that the President was the crookedest ——— ever President, that he was the richest man in the United States, that the President brought us into the war by British dictation, that Germany had right to sink ships and kill Americans without warning, and that the United States was only fighting for Wall Street millionaires and to protect Morgan's interests in England.

Having in mind the rule applicable to this motion for a directed verdict, the evidence would justify a finding that defendant did so make the declarations charged. But it would not support a verdict of guilty of any of the crimes charged. It appears the declarations were made at a Montana village of some 60 people, 60 miles from the railway, and none of the armies or navies within hundreds of miles, so far as appears. The declarations were oral; some in badinage with the landlady in a hotel kitchen; some at a picnic; some on the street; some in hot and furious saloon argument.

[1-3] Adverting to the crimes designated (1), false reports and false statements import reports and statements of facts, and not accused's opinions, beliefs, intentions, and arguments. Hence defendant's beliefs, opinions, and hopes are not within the statute. But his slanders of the President and nation are false reports and false statements, and are within the Espionage Act. While the act makes the (1) offenses substantive, they are of the nature of attempts, like in principle, and largely and to the extent indicated governed by the law of attempts. It is settled law that attempts are efforts with specific intent to commit specific crimes, which efforts fail, are apparently adapted to accomplish the intended crimes, and are of sufficient magnitude and proximity to the object of their operation that they are reasonably calculated to excite public fear and alarm that such efforts will accomplish the specific crimes if they do not fail. These slanders by defendant satisfy magnitude and apparent adaptation, but, in view of all the facts and circumstances in proof, neither the specif-

ic intent to interfere with, nor proximity to the military and naval forces appears.

When facts and circumstances will justify a finding that accused intended the natural and ordinary consequences of his acts, the intent may be inferred. There are two fatal objections to such inference here, viz.: Interference with the operation or success of the military or naval forces is not the natural and ordinary consequences of said slanders, but rather breach of the peace and a broken head for the slanderer are, and the facts and circumstances, times and places, oral kitchen gossip and saloon debate, the impossibility of far-distance military and naval forces hearing or being affected by the slanders, and all else, render the inference unjustified, absurd, and without support in the evidence. Military and naval forces, in the Espionage Act, mean the same as in the declarations of war, the ordinary meaning, viz. those organized and in service, not persons merely registered and subject to future organization and service. Furthermore, even if the slanders with the specific intent denounced by the Espionage Act, they fail of the required proximity to constitute attempts and the said (1) offenses. Under the circumstances they were not reasonably calculated to create public fear and alarm that they would interfere with the operation and success of far-distant armies and navy. Rather would they create anger, disgust, and desire to publish the slanderer. It is as if A. shot with a .22 pistol with intent to kill B. two or three miles away. The impossibility would prevent public fear and alarm of homicide, and A. could not be convicted of attempted murder.

There is now no claim of intent to promote enemy success. Otherwise, the foregoing also applies to those crimes charged. It is admitted no insubordination, disloyalty, mutiny, or refusal of duty by the military or naval forces was caused by the slanders, and, in view of the law and reasoning aforesaid, the charges of attempts thereto likewise are not sustained by the evidence.

[4] Nor does the evidence sustain the charge of "willfully obstructing the recruiting or enlistment service of the United States, to the injury of the service of the United States." To sustain the charge, actual obstruction and injury must be proven, not mere attempts to obstruct. The Espionage Act does not create the crime of attempting to obstruct, but only the crime of actual obstruction, and when causing injury to the service. Whenever Congress intended that attempted obstructions should be a crime, it plainly said so, as may be seen in the statute making it a crime to attempt to obstruct the due administration of justice. Section 135, Penal Code.

[5] The Espionage Act is not intended to suppress criticism or denunciation, truth or slander, oratory or gossip, argument or loose talk, but only false acts, willfully put forward as true, and broadly, with the specific intent to interfere with army or navy operations. The more or less public impression that for any slanderous or disloyal remark the utterer can be prosecuted by the United States is a mistake. The United States can prosecute only for acts that Congress has denounced as crimes. Congress has not denounced as crimes any mere disloyal utterances, not any slander or libel of the President or any other officer of the United States.

United States attorneys throughout the country have been unjustly criticized because they do not prosecute where they cannot. In instances their proper failure to prosecute has been made subject of complaint to the Department of Justice to oust them or to defeat reappointment. The patriotism that inspires such criticism and complaints is less a passion than passionate. In the main, the government attorneys are of good judgment, and will not be coerced by such criticism and complaints to futile prosecutions or persecutions.

[6] In so far as disloyal slanders or libels cause or tend to cause breaches of the peace, they are offenses against the state of Montana, and can be prosecuted only in the courts of the state, by the state's prosecutors. Slanders like those herein are unspeakable. (Incidentally, the defendant denies them.) They should be made crimes against the United States, at times like these, at least. But, since the sedition law had its share in the overthrow of the Federalists and in the elevation of Jefferson to the Presidency and his party to power, Congress has not ventured to denounce as crimes slanders and libels of government and its officers. The genius of democracy and the spirit of our people and times seem yet unable to avoid greater evils than benefits from laws to that end.

Any attempt to define all that will or will not constitute the crimes denounced by said section 3 would be difficult—yes, impossible. Every case will depend on its own facts and circumstances, as various as human conduct.

The motion to direct a verdict of acquittal of defendant is granted, and the clerk will enter such a verdict of record.

APPENDIX 2: EX PARTE STARR, 263 F. 145

During World War I the Montana legislature passed a series of laws designed to crush dissent and criticisms of Wilson administration policies. Under these laws, in 1918, E. V. Starr was convicted and sentenced to ten to twenty years in Montana state prison for stating the following about the American flag: "What is this thing anyway? Nothing but a piece of cotton with a little paint on it and some other marks in the corner there. I will not kiss it. It might be covered with microbes." Starr was convicted of sedition and appealed to the federal court.

During the height of the hysteria that engulfed Montana and the nation during the Red Scare, Bourquin rendered his decision in Starr's appeal. It was a brilliant treatise on patriotism and free speech. Bourquin abhorred Starr's comments but ruled that he broke no law. He added that Starr was "more sinned against than sinning" and that he was "in the hands of one of those too common mobs vindicating its peculiar standard of patriotism and odd concept of respect for the flag." Bourquin believed that forcing a person to kiss the flag "was a spectacle for the pity as well as the laughter of gods and men." A Bourquin lecture on the true meaning of patriotism followed.

District Court, D. Montana, January 31, 1920
No. 704

BOURQUIN, District Judge. In this habeas corpus it appears that in February, 1918, the Montana Legislature enacted a statute "defining the crime of sedition." Which in so far as it relates to the flag, is like the federal Espionage Law of May, 1918. In August, 1918, an information was filed in the state court, charging that in March, 1918, the petitioner had "committed the crime of sedition," by uttering and publishing contemptuous and slurring language about the flag and language calculated to bring the flag into contempt and disrepute, as follows:

"What is this thing anyway? Nothing but a piece of cotton with a little paint on it and some other marks in the corner there. I will not kiss that thing. It might be covered with microbes."

Tried and convicted, he was sentenced to the state penitentiary for not less than 10 years nor more than 20 years at hard labor, and to pay a fine of $500 and costs. Not apparent whether he appealed; in November, 1919, he applied to the state Supreme Court for habeas corpus, was denied, and thereupon made this application.

His principal contention is that the state law is repugnant to the federal Constitution, in that it assumes powers vested in the United States alone and by it exercised, and hence that he is imprisoned in violation of the Thirteenth and Fourteenth Amendments. Despite Urquhart v. Brown, 205 U.S. 181, 27 Sup. Ct. 459, 51 L. Ed. 760, Frank's Case, 237 U.S. 328, 35 Sup. Ct. 582, 59 L. Ed. 969, warrants consideration of the merits of petitioner's application. That the state may legislate in protection of the flag is settled by Halter v. Nebraska, 205 U.S. 41, 27 Sup. Ct. 419, 51 L. Ed. 696, 10 Ann. Cas. 525. Although that case leaves open whether such state legislation will be superseded by later like federal legislation, the issue is not involved herein, for that petitioner's offense against the state is prior to the federal law, which latter neither pardons the offense nor draws it within federal jurisdiction.

In the matter of his offense and sentence, obviously petitioner was more sinned against than sinning. It is clear that he was in the hands of one of those too common mobs, bent upon vindicating its peculiar standard of patriotism and its odd concept of respect for the flag by compelling him to kiss the latter—a spectacle for the pity as well as the laughter of gods and men! Its unlawful and disorderly conduct, not his just resistance, nor the trivial and innocuous retort into which they goaded him, was calculated to degrade the sacred banner and to bring it into contempt. Its members, not he, should have been punished.

Patriotism is the cement that binds the foundation and the superstructure of the state. The safety of the latter depends upon the integrity of the former. Like religion, patriotism is a virtue so indispensable and exalted, its excesses pass with little censure. But when, as here, it descends to fanaticism, it is of the reprehensible quality of the religion that incited the massacre of St. Bartholomew, the tortures of the Inquisition, the fires of Smithfield, the scaffolds of Salem, and is equally cruel and murderous. In its name, as in that of Liberty, what crimes have been committed! In every age it, too, furnishes its heresy hunters and its witch burners, and it, too, is a favorite mask for hypocrisy, assuming a virtue which it haveth not. So the mobs mentioned were generally the chosen and last resort of the slacker, military and civil, the profiteer, and the enemy sympathizer, masquerading as superpatriots to divert attention from their real character. Incidentally, it is deserving of mention here that in the records of this court is a report of its grand jury that before it attempts had been made to prostitute the federal Espionage Law to wreak private vengeance and to work private ends.

As for the horrifying sentence itself, it is of those criticized by Mr. Justice Holmes in Abrams' Case, 250 U.S. 616, 40 Sup. Ct. 17, 63 L. Ed. 1173, in that, if it be conceded trial and conviction are warranted, so frivolous is the charge that a nominal fine would serve every end of justice. And it, with too many like, goes far to give color, if not justification, to the bitter comment of George Bernard Shaw, satirist and cynic, that during the war the courts in France, bleeding under German guns, were very severe; the courts in England, hearing but the echoes of those guns, were grossly unjust; but the courts of the United State, knowing naught save censored news of those guns, were stark, staring, raving mad. All this, however, cannot affect habeas corpus. It can appeal to the pardoning power alone.

The state law is valid, petitioner's imprisonment is not repugnant to the federal Constitution, this court cannot relieve him, and the writ is denied.

APPENDIX 3: EX PARTE JACKSON, 263 F. 110

ourquin was dedicated to the idea that a true democratic system is judged not only by its protection of the rights of the majority but also by the ways it protects the rights of unpopular minorities and dissenters. He strongly believed that if a dissenter's right of free speech was abridged, eventually one's own rights would be curtailed. In the Jackson case the government wished to deport an immigrant Wobbly-"Red." Bourquin found that in this case, during the height of the Red Scare, the government exceeded its authority and lashed out against what he considered government despotism. Bourquin ruled that it was overzealous government officials that disregarded "due process" and that it was the government and not Jackson that broke the law. Jackson's sole transgression was his lack of enthusiasm for the war effort, and for that "crime" Bourquin did not allow his deportation. A fierce attack on what Bourquin termed "lynch law" followed.

District Court, D. Montana, February 12, 1920

BOURQUIN, District Judge. Petitioner, held for deportation as an alien "found advocating or teaching the unlawful destruction of property," and who at time of entry "was a person likely to become a public charge," seeks habeas corpus, for that the evidence against him in the deportation proceedings was unlawfully secured, that proceedings were unfair, and the findings quoted without support. Respondent returns the record of said proceedings. Therefrom it appears that from August, 1918, to February, 1919, the Butte Union of the Industrial Workers of the World was dissatisfied with working places, conditions, and wages in the mining industry, and to remedy them was discussing ways and means, including strike if necessary. In consequence, its hall and orderly meetings were several times raided and mobbed by the employers' agents, and federal agents and soldiers duly officered, acting by federal authority and without warrant or process. The union members, men and women, many of them citizens, limited themselves to oral protests, though in the circumstances, the inalienable right and law of self-defense justified resistance to the last dread extremity. There was no disorder save that of the raiders. These, mainly uniformed and armed, overawed, intimidated, and forcibly entered, broke, and destroyed property, searched persons, effects, and papers, arrested persons, seized papers and documents, cursed, insulted, beat, dispersed, and bayoneted union members by order of the commanding officer. They likewise entered petitioner's adjacent living apartment, insulted his wife, searched his person and effects, arrested him and seized his papers and documents, and in general, in a populous and orderly city, perpetrated a reign of terror, violence, and crime against citizen and alien alike, and whose only offense seems to have been peaceable insistence upon and exercise of a legal right.

The raid of February, 1919, three months after practical end of the war, was upon a union meeting in discussion of the condition created by a reduction of $1 per day made in miners' wages. Petitioner, arrested, for several days was imprisoned and denied bail and counsel. He was then taken before an immigration inspector, flanked by a policeman and a soldier, and, these four alone present, was interrogated. He objected generally, but finally answered, and also in respect to pamphlets seized as aforesaid and introduced in evidence against him. At later appearances, before the inspector, petitioner was permitted to have counsel. At these, statements made by raiders, without petitioner's presence, identifying papers and pamphlets so seized, and somewhat in respect to petitioner's conduct of a union meeting, were introduced in evidence against him. Some of these raiders were produced for petitioner's cross-examination, but one, Sergeant Ambord, was not. Petitioner demanded his production, and was denied, because he would not comply with a condition that he state what he expected to prove by Ambord and that he deposit costs. Objections by petitioner throughout the proceedings are excluded from the record and are now forgotten.

The facts in respect to the condition and objections aforesaid appear ex necessitate by oral testimony in the instant proceeding. The record further discloses that petitioner is a young, able bodied man, and was when in 1915 he entered with his wife; that since entry he has supported his family, including a child here born, by ordinary mining and other labor; that in 1917 he joined the aforesaid organization, and, for the latter half of 1918 was assistant secretary of the Butte union, and also janitor of the hall for a Finnish society, its owner. He disclaims advocacy, teaching, or belief in unlawful destruction of property, admits having seen some of the pamphlets in the hall and for sale, admits having sold any thereof asked for and on hand for sale, admits having read some thereof, but, disremembering contents cannot say he indorses them. These pamphlets are assumed to advocate and teach sabotage, and because thereof, and of petitioner's status and relation to them as aforesaid, in the deportation proceedings it is inferred and found that he advocated and taught unlawful destruction of property. Without these pamphlets, and brought home to petitioner, there is no evidence against him.

[1,2] Pretermitting review of these pamphlets, and having in mind the political control over aliens, the summary character of deportation proceedings, and the limited jurisdiction of courts in respect thereto, it is believed the deportation proceedings are unfair and invalid, in that they are based upon evidence and procedure that violate the search and seizure and due process clauses of the Constitution. The situation is not one wherein the mode of procurement of evidence cannot be collaterally raised and determined at a trial (see Silverthorne's Case [Jan. 26, 1920] 251 U.S. 385, 40 Sup. Ct. 182, 64 L. Ed.——), but is one wherein the government in both the deportation proceeding and this at bar freely discloses its own wrong by which it secured the evidence. The law and courts no more sanction such evidence than such methods, and no more approve either than the thumbscrew and the rack. Otherwise, the vicious circle of age-old tyranny—to subject to and convict by unlawful means because guilty, and to condemn as guilty because subjected to and convicted by unlawful means, to which both alien and citizen fall victim. The Declaration of Independence, the writings of the fathers, the Revolution, the Constitution, and the Union, all were inspired to overthrow and prevent like governmental despotism. They are yet living, vital, and potential forces to those ends, to safeguard all domiciled in the country, alien as well as citizen.

[3] For the inalienable rights of personal security and safety, orderly and due process of law, are the fundamentals of the social compact, the basis of organized society, the essence and justification of government, the foundation, key, and capstones of the Constitution. They are limited to no man, race, or nation, to no time, place, or occasion, but belong to man, always, everywhere, and in all circumstances. Every nation demands them for its people from all other nations. No emergency in war or peace warrants their violation, for in emergency, real or assumed, tyrants in all ages have found excuse for their destruction. Without them, democracy perishes, autocracy reigns, and the innocent suffer with the guilty.

Without them is no safety, peace, content, happiness, and they must be vindicated, defended, and maintained in the face of every assault by government or otherwise. All judgments based upon their violation must be set aside.

Assuming petitioner is of the so-called "Reds" and of the evil practice charged against him he and his kind are less a danger to America than are those who indorse or use the methods that brought him to deportation. These latter are the mob and the spirit of violence and intolerance incarnate, the most alarming manifestation in America today. Far worse than the immediate wrongs to individuals that they do, they undermine the morale of the people, excite the latter's fears, distrust of our institutions, doubts of the sufficiency of law and authority; they incline the people toward arbitrary power, which for protection cowards too often seek, and knaves too readily grant, and subject to which the people cease to be courageous and free, and become timid and enslaved. They advocate and teach, not only unlawful destruction of property, but in addition unlawful destruction of persons, and they engage in the practice of both. They lay the ax to the root of all government. Doubtless some of those, of some variety of prestige, who horrify the thoughtful lovers of America by their loose suggestion and advocacy of stone walls, shootings at sunrise, and other lynch law, are animated by sincere, but mistaken, concern for national welfare; but equally doubtless many of them are incited by unholy desire for personal advantage—money profit, popular approval, or political preferment. They are breeders of suspicion, fear, anger, revenge, riot, crime, class hatred, "Reds," despotism, threatening, if aught can, civil anarchy and revolution, and they and the government by hysteria that they stimulate are more to be feared than all the miserable, baited, bedeviled "Reds" that are their ostensible occasion and whose sins they exaggerate.

The application of the principle that convicted the Haymarket anarchists may hold guilty these advocates of lynch law, if their recommendations be followed, unless, indeed, there are distinctions in administration of criminal law. They are no new thing, these present excesses. They are the reactions of all great wars, and in due time run their course. In his Constitutional History of England, Freeman describes much the same following the Napoleonic wars, viz. that in England those who ventured to raise their voice to reform corrupt politics and oppressive government, or to improve conditions for the working class, were bitterly denounced as pro-French, charged and tried for treason, popular clamor and violence directed against them, and the bar intimidated from defending them. How history doth repeat itself! The situation vindicates the wisdom of the philosopher who observed that in war the belligerents tend to exchange of national characteristics. It is said that Prussia approaches ultra democracy, and it seems that America verges upon Prussian autocracy. And yet confidence in the Constitution and national sanity is justified. All extremists will fail to overthrow them. Even as the "Reds," the advocates of arbitrary power, whether within or without law, will in due time pass away. It is for the courts to restrain both, when brought within jurisdiction.

[4.5] In so far as petitioner asserts unfairness, in that his objections are excluded from the record, the rules permit objections to be made in briefs. Whether fair or not in ordinary cases, in a case wherein the alien's rights have been infringed to the extent here, the court will take note of it, whether or not objections have been made with technical precision, and hold the proceedings unfair. So were the proceedings unfair for failure to produce Ambord for cross-examination. The rules require his production. The condition the inspector imposed is unwarranted. It is authorized only in respect to petitioner's witnesses, and not in respect to government's witnesses and their cross-examination. Ambord was a vital witness. He identified pamphlets as those seized, an essential link in the chain of circumstances. Although there was another witness to the same matter, none the less was the alien entitled to the benefit of the rule, and to cross-examine Ambord; and failure to produce Ambord denied the alien the due process of the rule, and is fatal to fairness of the proceedings. It cannot be said that in any event the decision would have been the same, unless it also be said that in any event the alien was to be deported. There is indication of the latter. It is found in the finding that he "was a person likely to become a public charge" when he entered. This is a make-weight precaution, without a scintilla of evidence to support it. The inspector, who first advanced it, in the next paragraph complained that petitioner "was working and earning a good salary, but never purchased any War Savings Stamps or Liberty Bonds." This and like war references betray some the atmosphere surrounding the proceedings.

The writ is granted.

NOTES

Foreword

1. Roger H. Tuller, *Let No Guilty Man Escape: A Judicial Biography of "Hanging Judge" Isaac C. Parker* (Norman: University of Oklahoma Press, 2001).
2. Christian G. Fritz, *Federal Justice in California: The Court of Ogden Hoffman, 1851–1891* (Lincoln: University of Nebraska Press, 1991).
3. Louise Ann Fisch, *All Rise: Reynaldo G. Garza, the First Mexican American Federal Judge* (College Station: Texas A&M University Press, 1996).
4. Jace Weaver, *Then to the Rock Let Me Fly: Luther Bohanon and Judicial Activism* (Norman: University of Oklahoma Press, 1993).
5. Harry H. Stein, *Gus J. Solomon: Liberal Politics, Jews, and the Federal Courts* (Portland: Oregon Historical Society Press, 2006).
6. Also see Polly Price, *Judge Richard S. Arnold: A Legacy of Justice on the Federal Bench* (New York: Prometheus Books, 2009) and Gerald Gunther, "Learned Hand and the Origins of Modern First Amendment Doctrine: Some Fragments of History," *Stanford Law Review* 27 (1975): 719–73. Federal Judge Morris Arnold, in addition to his work on the bench, is a historian: he authored *Unique Laws unto a Savage Race: European Legal Traditions in Arkansas* (Fayetteville: University of Arkansas Press, 1985) and *Colonial Arkansas, 1686–1804: A Social and Cultural History* (Fayetteville: University of Arkansas Press, 1991). Morris "Buzz" Arnold is a respected legal historian. President George H. W. Bush appointed him to the Western District of Arkansas at Fort Smith. Richard was his older brother and is deceased. Although not about the American West, readers should compare Anna R. Hayes, *Without Precedent: The Life of Susie Marshall Sharp* (Chapel Hill: University of North Carolina Press, 2008). Sharp rose to chief justice of the North Carolina Supreme Court, and her letters and journals reveal a far more complex person than the public record portrayed.
7. D. Kurt Graham, *To Bring Law Home: The Federal Judiciary in Early National Rhode Island* (DeKalb: Northern Illinois University Press, 2010), 137.
8. John Phillip Reid, *Legitimating the Law: The Struggle for Judicial Competency in Early National New Hampshire* (DeKalb: Northern Illinois University Press, 2012), 95.

Introduction

1. Oliver Wendell Holmes, Jr., Papers, Harvard Law School Library, box 29, folder 4, letter from Holmes to Felix Frankfurter, March 27, 1917.
2. *Schenck v. United States*, 249 U.S. 47 (1919); *Frohwerk v. United States*, 249 U.S. 204 (1919); *Debs v. United States*, 249 U.S. 221 (1919). For a discussion of the contradictions in Holmes's views on the free speech subject before his *Schenck* decision, see Sheldon N. Novick, *Honorable Justice: The Life of Oliver Wendell Holmes* (Boston: Little Brown, 1989).
3. *Abrams et al. v. United States*, 250 U.S. 616, 624 (dissenting opinion). See Richard Polenberg, *Fighting Faiths: The Abrams Case, the Supreme Court, and Free Speech* (New York: Viking, 1987).
4. See Anthony W. Gengarelly, *Distinguished Dissenters and Opposition to the 1919–1920 Red Scare* (Lewiston, NY: E. Mellen Press, 1996). Bourquin is overlooked in this fine study and is mentioned only once (on p. 263).
5. Melvin I. Urofsky and Paul Finkelman, *A March of Liberty: A Constitutional History of the United States*, vol. 2, *From 1898 to the Present* (New York: Oxford University Press, 2002), 500–520. Bernard Schwartz, *A History of the Supreme Court* (New York: Oxford University Press, 1993), 233–45.
6. William H. Simon, "The Warren Court, Legalism, and Democracy: Sketch for a Critique in a Style Learned from Morton Horwitz," in *Transformations in American Legal History: Law, Ideology, and Methods*, vol. 2, eds. Daniel W. Hamilton and Alfred L. Brophy (Cambridge, MA: Harvard Law School, 2010), 412–14.
7. Frederick Schauer, "Formalism," *Yale Law Journal* 97, no. 4 (March 1988): 509–48.
8. Morton Horwitz, *The Transformation of American Law, 1870–1960* (New York: Oxford University Press, 1992), 9–32.
9. US Const., art. I, §10 (on contracts); Fifth and Fourteenth Amendments (on property).
10. Horwitz, *Transformation of American Law, 1780–1860*, 253–54.
11. These important decisions included *The Slaughter-House Cases* (1873), *Munn v. Illinois* (1877), *United States v. E.C. Knight Co.* (1895), *In re Debs* (1895), *Plessy v. Ferguson* (1896), *Northern Securities Co. v. United States* (1904), *Lochner v. New York* (1905), *Adair v. United States* (1908), *Standard Oil Co. of New Jersey v. United States* (1911), *Adkins v. Children's Hospital* (1923).
12. See Arnold M. Paul, "Traditional Legal Conservatism," 54–62; Michael Les Benedict, "The Libertarian Foundations of Laissez Faire Constitutionalism," 62–79; Judith Baer, "Women Workers and Liberty to Contract," 118–29; Melvin I. Urofsky, "The Courts and the Limits to Liberty of Contract," 129–41; all in Kermit L. Hall, ed., *Major Problems in American Constitutional History*, vol. 1, (Lexington, MA: Cengage Learning, 1992). See also John E. Semonche, *Charting the Future: The Supreme Court Responds to a Changing Society, 1890–1920* (Westport, CT: Greenwood Press, 1978); Melvin I. Urofsky, *A Mind of One Piece: Brandeis and American Reform* (New York: Scribner, 1971); Melvin I. Urofsky, *Louis D. Brandeis: A Life* (New York: Pantheon Books, 2009).

13. Melvin I. Urofsky, "Myth and Reality: The Supreme Court and Protective Legislation during the Progressive Era," *Yearbook of the Supreme Court Historical Society* (1983): 53–72. Melvin I. Urofsky, "State Courts and Protective Legislation during the Progressive Era: A Reevaluation," *Journal of American History* 72 (1985): 63–91. See also Aviam Soifer, "The Paradox of Paternalism and Laissez Faire Constitutionalism: The United States Supreme Court, 1888–1921," *Law and History Review* 5 (1987): 249–79.

14. Horwitz, *Transformation of American Law, 1870–1960*, 131.

15. Federalist 78.

16. David M. Kennedy, *Freedom from Fear: The American People in Depression and War, 1929–1945* (New York: Oxford University Press, 1999), 334–37; William E. Leuchtenburg, *The Supreme Court Reborn: The Constitutional Revolution of the Age of Roosevelt* (New York: Oxford University Press, 1995), 82–162, 213–36; Marian C. McKenna, *Franklin Roosevelt and the Great Constitutional War: The Court Packing Crisis of 1937* (New York: Fordham University Press, 2002); Peter Irons, *New Deal Lawyers* (Princeton, NJ: Princeton University Press, 1982), 272–89.

17. John Philip Reid, "The Layers of Western Legal History," in *Law in the Western United States*, ed. Gordon Morris Bakken (Norman: University of Oklahoma Press, 2000), 3–42.

18. Ibid.

19. Ibid., 7. On debts, see *Clark v. Crosland*, 17 Arkansas 43 (1856). On railroads, see *Briscoe v. Southern Kansas Company*, 40 F. 273.

20. Tuller, *Let No Guilty Man Escape*.

21. Paul Kens, *Justice Stephen Field: Shaping Liberty from the Gold Rush to the Gilded Age* (Lawrence: University Press of Kansas, 1997).

22. Fritz, *Federal Justice in California*.

23. Michael J. Brodhead, *David J. Brewer: The Life of a Supreme Court Justice, 1837–1910* (Carbondale: Southern Illinois University Press, 1994).

24. Arnon Gutfeld, *Montana's Agony: Years of War and Hysteria, 1917–1921* (Gainesville: University Press of Florida, 1979); Clemens P. Work, *Darkest Before Dawn: Sedition and Free Speech in the American West* (Albuquerque: University of New Mexico Press, 2005).

Chapter 1

1. Transcript of interview with attorney Dennis Bourquin and his sister Marilyn Bourquin, (grandchildren of Judge Bourquin), Redwood City, California, August 7, 1993 (65 pages), 41–42. (In possession of the author. Copy also available in Montana Historical Society Library.)

2. Interview with Federal District Attorney and Judge Russell Smith, Missoula, Montana, June 30, 1967, and with Attorney E. C. Mulrony, Missoula, Montana, July 13, 1967; letter from Wheeler to Patrick Sherlock, April 12, 1967. (Copy of letter in possession of author.)

3. Transcript of interview with Dennis and Marilyn Bourquin, 51.

4. *Montana Standard* (Butte), January 6, 1959.

5. Ibid.

6. Ibid. Attorney Dennis Bourquin was very suspicious about those two quotations. About the first he commented: "I've heard it in every court I've ever been in my life, and I have been a lawyer for 31 years . . . I rather suspect he did not [say it]." About the second quotation he said: "I've heard that quoted almost seventeen different ways." Transcript of interview with Dennis and Marilyn Bourquin, 44.

7. Bourquin's decisions can be found in the *Federal Reporter*, vols. 195–300; *Federal Reporter*, 1st series, vols. 1–60; *Federal Reporter*, 2nd series, vols. 1–10; and in the *Federal Supplements*.

8. Transcript of interview with Dennis and Marilyn Bourquin, 3–4.

9. Ibid., 51–52.

10. Ibid., 53.

11. The materials on the fascinating genealogy of the Bourquin family, 1340–1732, can be studied in the New York Public Library in the Irma and Paul Milstein Division of United States History, Local History, and Genealogy. See especially Harry Alexander Davis, comp., *Some Huguenot Families of South Carolina and Georgia*, 2nd ed., rev., (Washington DC: 1940), i–iv, 1–2. In vol. 1, published in 1926, it says, "well known family in Canton Neuchatel, Switzerland."

The name Bourgoing, alias Bourgoin and Bourquin, had been known in France since the fourteenth century. The family possessed a coat of arms, which belonged to Jean Bourgoing, a public prosecutor at the bailiwick of Saint Pierre de Montiers. Their arms are at the Cabinet des Titres and were registered at the Armorial General de France as an ordinance issued on June 8, 1698. The first items of the genealogy of the family are found on a brass tablet sealed in the wall of Saint Martin's Church in Nevers. The first record is by Jean Bourgoing, or Bourgoin, husband of Marie N. Bourgony, who in 1340 took part in the defense of Nevers against the English. The record at the Archives of the "Armorial General de France," manuscripts of the Cabinet of Titres in Paris, Archives of the Department de Nevers, and the Library of the Chamber of Deputies in Paris show that in the early 1690s Jean Francois Bourquin, a Huguenot, was banished from France and migrated to Switzerland. Further evidence demonstrated that part of the family immigrated to Colonel John Pury's colony and settled in Purysburg, South Carolina, in 1732. Between the 1340s and the 1690s, Bourquins were found to be public prosecutors, lieutenants of the king, protonotary of the Holy See, and high-ranking military men. Dissent and practice of law were an important part of the family's history. In the late sixteenth century, Ennemond Bourgoin, a Jacobite monk, was put on the rack at Rours because of a sermon that he had preached. Another Bourquin moved to Geneva, Switzerland, in the early 1600s. His son, Florimund, became a barrister at the parliament there.

12. Transcript of interview with Dennis and Marilyn Bourquin, 10–11.

13. Helen Fitzgerald Sanders, *A History of Montana* (Chicago: Lewis Publishing, 1913), 2:12; transcript of interview with Dennis and Marilyn Bourquin, 19.

14. Transcript of interview with Dennis and Marilyn Bourquin, 29.
15. Ibid.,17–18.
16. Ibid., 16.
17. Ibid., 34.
18. Ibid., 11–12. On Butte's ethnic makeup, see Emmons, *The Butte Irish*.
19. Ibid., 25.
20. Ibid.
21. Ibid., 19.
22. Sanders, *A History of Montana*, 2:1270.
23. On Progressivism in generals and on the 1912 elections in particular, see M. J. Heale, *Twentieth Century America: Politics and Power in the United States, 1900–1920* (London: Hodder Arnold, 2004), 1–80.
24. Transcript of interview with Dennis and Marilyn Bourquin, 31.
25. *Montana Standard* (Butte), June 6, 1959.
26. Ibid.
27. Ibid.
28. Transcript of interview with Dennis and Marilyn Bourquin, 45.
29. *Montana Standard* (Butte), June 6, 1959.
30. Kenneth Ross Toole, *Montana: An Uncommon Land* (Norman: University of Oklahoma Press, 1959), 139–210.
31. See chapter 7, on ethics.
32. Burton K. Wheeler, *Yankee from the West: The Candid, Turbulent Life Story of the Yankee-Born U.S. Senator from Montana* (Garden City, NY: Doubleday, 1962), 159–60.
33. Ibid., 46–47.
34. Transcript of interview with Dennis and Marilyn Bourquin, 5.
35. Ibid., 4.
36. Ibid., 47–48.

Chapter 2

1. Horace C. Peterson and Gilbert C. Fite, *Opponents of War, 1917–1918* (Madison: University of Wisconsin Press, 1957); Zechariah Chafee, Jr., "Freedom of Speech in Wartime," *Harvard Law Review* 32 (1919): 932–73; Zechariah Chafee, Jr., *Free Speech in the United States* (Cambridge, MA: Harvard University Press, 1941); Robert Justin Goldstein, *Political Repression in Modern America from 1870 to 1976* (Urbana: University of Illinois Press, 2001); Stanley Coben, *A. Mitchell Palmer: Politician* (New York: Columbia University Press, 1963); Frank L. Grubbs, Jr., *The Struggle for Labor Loyalty: Gompers, the A.F. of L., and the Pacifists, 1917–1920* (Durham, NC: Duke University Press, 1968); John Higham, *Strangers in the Land: Patterns of American Nativism, 1860–1925* (New York: Atheneum, 1963); Robert K. Murray, *Red Scare: A Study in National Hysteria, 1919–1920* (1955; Minneapolis: University of

Minnesota Press, 1964); Polenberg, *Fighting Faiths*; Harry N. Scheiber, *The Wilson Administration and Civil Liberties, 1917–1921* (Ithaca, NY: Cornell University Press, 1960).

2. Wheeler, *Yankee from the West*, 136–50.

3. Arnon Gutfeld, "The Speculator Disaster in 1917: Labor Resurgence in Butte, Montana," *Arizona and the West* 11 (1969): 27–38; Michael P. Malone, Richard B. Roeder, and William L. Lang, *Montana: A History of Two Centuries* (Seattle: University of Washington Press, 1991), 274; Wheeler, *Yankee from the West*, 137; Daniel Harrington, *Lessons from the Granite Mountain Shaft Fire, Butte* (Washington DC: Government Printing Office, 1922).

4. Wheeler, *Yankee from the West*, 137.

5. Richard T. Ruetten, "Anaconda Journalism: The End of an Era," *Journalism Quarterly* 37 (1960): 3–12, 104; John M. Schlitz, "Montana's Captive Press," *Montana Opinion* 1 (1956): 1–11.

6. The best work on this subject remains Vernon H. Jensen, *Heritage of Conflict: Labor Relations in the Nonferrous Metals Industry Up to 1930* (Ithaca, NY: Cornell University Press, 1950). See also Jerry Calvert, *The Gibraltar: Socialism and Labor in Butte, Montana, 1895–1920* (Helena, MT: Montana Historical Society Press, 1988). Specifically on World War I conditions, see Arnon Gutfeld, "The Murder of Frank Little: Radical Labor Agitation in Butte, Montana, 1917," *Labor History* 10 (Spring 1969): 177–92.
Gutfeld, "Murder of Frank Little."

7. Wheeler, *Yankee from the West*, 142.

8. The best study of IWW is Melvyn Dubofsky, *We Shall Be All: A History of the Industrial Workers of the World* (Chicago: Quadrangle Books, 1969). For the conditions in Montana, see Gutfeld, *Montana's Agony*, 23–92.

9. Gutfeld, "Murder of Frank Little," 188.

10. Wheeler, *Yankee from the West*, 142.

11. Ibid., 143.

12. Ibid., 144.

13. Ibid.

14. Ibid.

15. Ibid., 147–48.

16. Ibid., 150.

17. *United States v. Butte*, 38 F.2d 871, 872 (D. Mont. 1930).

18. *Ex parte Starr*, 263 F. 146 (D. Mont. 1920).

19. See Gutfeld, *Montana's Agony*, chaps. 3–5; Kenneth Ross Toole, *Twentieth Century Montana: A State of Extremes*, (Norman: University of Oklahoma Press, 1972), 175–93; Nancy Rice Fritz, "The Montana Council of Defense," MA thesis, (University of Montana, 1966); and Malone, Roeder, and Lang, *Montana*, 274–79.

20. Toole, *Twentieth Century Montana*, 172–73.

21. Ibid.

22. Ibid.

23. Ibid., 173; Wheeler, *Yankee from the West*, 159–60.

24. See chapter 4.

25. Toole, *Twentieth Century Montana*, 175–93, and Fritz, "Montana Council of Defense."

26. Malone, Roeder, and Lang, *Montana*, 275–76.

27. Memorandum to Mr. Bettman, February 13, 1918, DJ file 189730-2.

28. James H. Rowe to John Speed Smith, Chief Naturalization Examiner, Seattle, WA, January 31, 1918, DJ file 189730-1.5; also Rowe to Senator Henry L. Myers, January 31, 1918. Myers sent the letter to the Department of Justice on February 9, 1919, ibid.

29. U.S. Stat. Espionage Law of 1917, vol. 40, part 1, 217.

30. Stenographer's copy of Bourquin's oral decision, attached to Wheeler to Attorney General Thomas Gregory, March 11, 1918, DJ file, 189730-9; also in *United States v. Ves Hall*, 248 F. 150–51 (D. Mont. 1918).

31. 248 F. 150–54 (D. Mont. 1918).

32. Wheeler, *Yankee from the West*, 152; Wheeler to Attorney General Gregory, January 14, 1918, DJ file 189730-1.

33. *United States v. Ves Hall*, 248 F. 154 (D. Mont. 1918).

34. Ibid., 153.

35. Ibid., 151, 153.

36. *Great Falls Tribune*, February 4, 1918; Governor Stewart to Senator Myers, January 28, 1918, DJ file 189730-2.

37. Campbell to Myers, January 27, 1918, DJ file 189730-2.

38. LaFollette to Attorney General, February 2, 1918, ibid.

39. *House Journal of the Extraordinary Session of the Fifteenth Legislative Assembly of the State of Montana*, February 14–25, 1918, 1–2.

40. *Laws Passed by the Extraordinary Session of the Fifteenth Legislative Assembly*, 14.

41. *House Journal*, 15, 50, 72.

42. *Congressional Record* 55, 6039; *Congressional Record* 56, 4714. See also *Senate Journal of the Extraordinary Session of the Fifteenth Legislative Assembly of the State of Montana*, February 14–25, 1918, 50.

43. *Congressional Record* 56, 4695.

44. U.S. Stat. Sedition Law of 1918, vol. 40, part 1, 553.

45. *Anaconda Standard*, February 23, 24, 26, 1918.

46. See chapter 4, which deals with the impeachment of Judge Crum.

47. Syndicalists including the IWW advocated bringing industry and government under the control of federations of labor unions by the use of direct action, violence, strikes, and sabotage. The IWW called for direct action by the labor class to abolish the capitalist order, including the state, and replace it with the *syndicat*, a free association of self-governing producers. Under the criminal syndicalism acts, advocating these ideas and actions became a criminal offense.

48. O'Brian to Gregory, February 27, 1918; memorandum to O'Brian, February 18, 1918; memorandum to Bettman, February 13, 1918; all in DJ file 189730-2.

49. Attached to Captain J. T. Jones to Justice Department and reply, May 22, 1918; O'Brian to Lt. Colonel Churchill, Military Intelligence Section, June 19, 1918, National Archives, DJ record group 60, Glasser file.

50. Gregory to Walsh, March 13, 1918, DJ file 189730-8, answer to letter of March 9, 1918; O'Brian to Walsh, March 6, 1918, DJ file 189730-7, answer to letter of March 5, 1918.

51. *Congressional Record* 56, 900, 4559–72.

52. Ibid., 4623–39.

53. Ibid., 4715.

54. Ibid., 7054.

55. Wheeler to author, July 12, 1967.

56. See Geoffrey R. Stone, *Perilous Times: Free Speech in Wartime* (New York: Norton, 2004), 135–233.

57. See Peterson and Fite, *Opponents of War*, chap. 19, and Donald Johnson, *The Challenge to American Freedoms: World War I and the Rise of the American Civil Liberties Union* (Lexington: University of Kentucky Press, 1963), chap. 3.

58. US Department of Labor, "Report of President's Mediation Commission to the President of the United States," *Report of the Department of Labor*, pp. 4, 6, 14. See also Harold M. Hyman, *Soldiers and Spruce: Origins of the Loyal Legion of Loggers and Lumbermen* (Los Angeles: Institute of Industrial Relations, University of California, 1963).

59. *Annual Report of the Attorney General of the United States for the Year 1918*, circular no. 838: 674. See also Alexis J. Anderson, "New England's Experience with Punishing Political Speech during World War I: A Study in Prosecutional Discretion," *Massachusetts Legal History* 4 (1998): 83–135.

60. *New York Times*, May 3, 2006; *Washington Post*, May 4, 2006. See chap. 4 on Judge Crum. See also Work, *Darkest before Dawn*, 180–259.

Chapter 3

1. *Ex parte Starr*, 263 F. 146 (D. Mont. 1920).

2. Numerous studies support this point; see especially Peterson and Fite, *Opponents of War*; William Preston, *Aliens and Dissenters: Federal Suppression of the Radicals in the United States* (Cambridge, MA: Harvard University Press, 1941); Chafee, *Free Speech in the United States*; Johnson, *Challenge to American Freedoms*; Paul L. Murphy, *World War I and the Origins of Civil Liberties in the United States* (New York: Norton, 1979); Murray, *Red Scare*; and Coben, *A. Mitchell Palmer*.

3. *Ex parte Beck*, 245 F. 967 (D. Mont. 1917).

4. Ibid., 971.

5. Ibid., 969.

6. Ibid., 970.

7. Ibid., 972, relying on *Wise v. Withers*, 3 Cranch (7 U.S.) 331 (1806).

8. *Ex parte Beck*, 245 F. 972–73 (D. Mont. 1917).

9. U.S. Stat. Sedition Law of 1918, vol. 40, part 1, 553.

10. *Ex parte Starr*, 263 F. 145 (D. Mont. 1920).

11. Ibid., 146.

12. Ibid.

13. Ibid.

14. *Abrams v. United States*, 250 U.S. 616 (1919). In *Schenck v. United States* (1919) Justice Oliver Wendell Holmes wrote the unanimous majority opinion that devised one of the great metaphors of constitutional interpretation—the "clear and present danger" test that limited free expression. A few months later in his famous dissent in the *Abrams* case Holmes produced one of the most important statements of free speech in American history. He called the anti-war leaflets that Abrams distributed, and was convicted for under the terms of the Espionage Act of 1917, "silly" and found that they did not interfere with the conduct of the war. Holmes concluded that unless there is real danger that imminent injury will occur, the First Amendment prohibits the government from punishing people for what they say, and added "Congress cannot forbid all efforts to change the mind of the country." In 1969, for example, the Court held that speech may not be punished unless it incites to "imminent lawless action." *Brandenburg v. Ohio*, 895 U.S. 444 (1969). Bourquin expressed this stance in the *Ves Hall* case in 1918.

15. *Ex parte Starr*, 263 F. 146 (D. Mont. 1920).

16. Ibid.

17. *In re Siem*, 284 F. 868 (D. Mont. 1922).

18. Ibid., 872.

19. Ibid., 872–73.

20. Ibid., 872.

21. Ibid., 869. Bourquin cited *Hilton v. Guyot*, 159 U.S. 163, and de Vattel, *Law of Nations*, 294–98.

22. *In re Siem*, 284 F. 870 (D. Mont. 1922).

23. Ibid., 869. Bourquin cited de Vattel, *Law of Nations*, 294; *Luria v. United States*, 231 U.S. 9 (1913); *Selective Draft Law Cases*, 245 U.S. 366, 378 (1918); and two annotated case reporters.

24. *In re Siem*, 284 F. 873 (D. Mont. 1922). See *Temple v. United States*, 248 U.S. 121, 129 (1918).

25. *Ex parte Radivoeff*, 278 F. 227 (D. Mont. 1922).

26. In *Fong Yue Ting v. United States*, 149 U.S. 698 (1893) and *Yamataya v. Fisher*, 189 U.S. 86 (1903), the Supreme Court held that Congress could delegate decisions about deportation exclusively to executive officers, without judicial intervention. Therefore, in a series of laws culminating in the sweeping Immigration Act of February 5, 1917, chap. 29, 39 Stat. 874, Congress allowed immigration authorities virtually unlimited discretion to deport aliens, and the federal courts generally deferred. They held, for example, that "the constitutional power to exclude to deport does not depend upon whether the alien is or is not a criminal, or the advocacy of

lawless ideas." *Lopez v. Howe*, 259 F. 401, 405 (2 Cir. 1919), dismissed for want of jurisdiction, 254 U.S. 613 (1920) (denying writ of habeas corpus sought to halt the deportation of an anarchist who believed in peaceful change).

27. *Ex parte Radivoeff*, 278 F. 227–28 (D. Mont. 1922).

28. Ibid., 229.

29. Ibid., quoting *In re Tam Chung*, 223 F. 802 (D. Mont. 1915).

30. *Ex parte Radivoeff*, 278 F. 229 (D. Mont. 1922), quoting *Kwack Jan Fat v. White*, 253 U.S. 454 (1920).

31. Ibid.

32. Ibid., 230.

33. Ibid.

34. Ibid., 231.

35. *In re Tam Chung*, 223 F. 802 (D. Mont. 1915).

36. Ibid.

37. Chinese Exclusion Act, chap. 1015, 25 Stat. 478.

38. *In re Tam Chung*, 223 F. 802 (D. Mont. 1915).

39. Ibid., 803.

40. *In re Norman*, 256 F. 543, 544 (D. Mont. 1919).

41. Res judicata is a final judgment decided between two parties by a legally con-stituted court having jurisdiction and is conclusive between the parties; the issue cannot be raised again. Bourquin had to acknowledge the litigation should end, although he did not agree with the previous decision.

42. *Ex parte Jackson*, 263 F. 110 (D. Mont. 1920).

43. Murray, *Red Scare*; Preston, *Aliens and Dissenters*.

44. *Ex parte Jackson*, 263 F. 111 (D. Mont. 1920).

45. Ibid.

46. Ibid., 111–12.

47. "Institutions reply: But you have nothing to fear from launching out: we're here to show you discourse is within the established order of things, that we've waited a long time for its arrival, that a place has been set aside for it—a place which both honours and disarms it; and if it should happen to have a certain power, then it is we, and we alone, who give it that power." What Foucault had overlooked was that institutions might fall victim to the disarming power of other institutions—even in-stitutions of the people—thus allowing for the possibility of democratic change in society. See Michel Foucault, "Discourse on Language," *Archaeology of Knowledge*, (New York: Pantheon Books, 1972), 216.

48. *Ex parte Jackson*, 263 F. 112–13 (D. Mont. 1920).

49. Ibid., 113.

50. Ibid.

51. Ibid.

52. Ibid., 114. Bourquin refers here to Edward A. Freeman, *The Growth of the English Constitution from the Earliest Times* (London: Macmillan, 1872).

53. Ibid., 113.

54. Ibid.

55. Ibid., 115.
56. Wheeler, *Yankee from the West*, 136.

Chapter 4

1. *Laws and Resolutions of the State of Montana*, Montana Legislative Council, Denver, CO, 1991.
2. Dave Walter, "Casualties of War: The Tragedy of Judge C. L. Crum," *Montana Magazine* 104 (1990): 56–63. For a study focusing on German-Americans during the period, see Frederick C. Luebke, *Bonds of Loyalty: German-Americans and World War I* (Dekalb: Northern Illinois University Press, 1974).
3. Ibid., 106.
4. *Helena Independent*, February 20, 1918. The impeachment process is outlined in the US Constitution in article 1, section 3. It consists of the lower house of the legislature bringing charges, similar to a grand jury indictment, against a public official. Once articles of impeachment are presented, the upper house prosecutes the offender and must reach a two-thirds majority in order to convict.

In the case of a federal process of impeachment, the chief justice of the US Supreme Court presides. In a state process of impeachment, the chief justice of the state Supreme Court presides. In state impeachments, the legal process is based on the state constitutions, which are patterned on the model of the US Constitution. The US Constitution, in article 2, section 4, defines impeachable acts as "Treason, bribery, or other high Crimes and Misdemeanors." A precise definition of "high Crimes and Misdemeanors" has yet to be reached. Historically, it is clear that political enemies of the various impeached officials have interpreted this ambiguous phrase very loosely.

Throughout American history there have been only thirteen federal impeachments, twelve of which went to trial. Eight of the officials, most of them judges, were acquitted. State impeachment trials have also been infrequent and have usually been politically inspired.

For a thorough discussion of the impeachment process, see Raoul Berger, *Impeachment: The Constitutional Problems* (Cambridge, MA: Harvard University Press, 1973). President Bill Clinton's impeachment brought about numerous studies of the process: Peter Baker, *The Breach: Inside the Impeachment and Trial of William Jefferson Clinton* (New York: Scribner, 2000); Charles L. Black, Jr., *Impeachment: A Handbook* (New Haven, CT: Yale University Press, 1998); Michael J. Gerhardt, *The Federal Impeachment Process: A Constitutional and Historical Analysis*, 2nd ed. (Chicago: University of Chicago Press, 2000); Richard A. Posner, *An Affair of State: The Investigation, Impeachment, and Trial of President Clinton* (Cambridge: Harvard University Press, 1999); Mark J. Rozell and Clyde Wilcox, eds. *The Clinton Scandal and the Future of American Government* (Washington DC: Georgetown University Press, 2000).
5. *Helena Independent*, February 20, 1918.

6. Ibid., February 24, 1918.

7. Wheeler, *Yankee from the West*, 152–62.

8. Burton K. Wheeler to author, July 12, 1967.

9. Wheeler, *Yankee from the West*, 154–55.

10. Ibid., 155. Though not the focus of this inquiry, Crum indeed was an "honorable man." Moreover, his personal history during this trying period can certainly be categorized as tragic.

 Crum was born January 9, 1874, in Underwood, Indiana, to James W. and Sarah Houghland Crum. After two years of college, Crum secured a job as a court reporter in El Reno, Oklahoma Territory. He began to study law in his free time, passed the bar, and opened his own law office.

 In 1896, he married Jessie Helen Mitts of El Reno. Because of his wife's poor health, Crum moved his family to Montana in 1906. He combined work on his homestead with a small legal practice. In 1909, Crum undertook the practice of law on a full-time basis in the county of Rosebud. He was known as an efficient, diligent, and conscientious attorney. Crum was elected county attorney as a Republican in 1910. In 1912, he won a four-year judgeship in Montana's Thirteenth Judicial District. Despite his personal misfortunes—his wife Jessie died at the age of thirty-one, leaving Crum with five children to raise on his own—Crum enjoyed an excellent reputation in his first term as a judge.

 He ran unopposed for his second term in 1916. However, as war hysteria spread in Montana in 1917, Crum began to come under heavy criticism for his so-called anti-American or pro-German sympathies. His life thereafter became a long series of disappointments. Although he lived until 1948, Crum was never the same man after his impeachment and conviction. From the time of the events leading to the impeachment until the end of his life, Crum suffered from alcoholism and depression. For a more detailed biographical sketch, see Walter, "Casualties of War," 56–63.

11. *Proceedings of the Court for the Trial of Impeachments*, 10.

12. Ibid., 142.

13. Ibid., 11.

14. Ibid., 12.

15. Ibid., 160.

16. Ibid., 15.

17. Ibid., 54.

18. Ibid., 16.

19. Ibid., 180.

20. Ibid.

21. Ibid., 171.

22. Ibid., 17.

23. Ibid., 18.

24. Ibid., 50.

25. Ibid., 25.

26. Ibid., 26.
27. Ibid., 29.
28. Ibid., 33.
29. Ibid., 36.
30. Ibid., 38.
31. Ibid., 117.
32. Ibid., 120.
33. Ibid., 43.
34. Ibid., 54.
35. Ibid., 70.
36. Ibid., 76.
37. Ibid., 83.
38. Ibid., 85.
39. Ibid., 133.
40. Ibid., 142.
41. Ibid., 139.
42. Ibid., 144.
43. Ibid., 147.
44. Ibid., 147, 151.
45. *Ex parte Starr v. United States*, 263 F.145 (D. Mont. 1920).

Chapter 5

1. *A. M. Holter Hardware Co. v. Boyle*, 263 F.135 (D. Mont. 1920).
2. Ibid., 137.
3. Ibid.
4. *American Bonding Co. v. Reynolds*, 203 F. 357 (D. Mont.1913).
5. Ibid.
6. *A. M. Holter Hardware Co. v. Boyle*, 263 F. 134–135 (D. Mont.1920).
7. Ibid., 134.
8. *United States v. Smith*, 282 F. 340 (D. Mont. 1922).
9. Ibid.
10. Ibid.
11. Ibid., 341.
12. See Richard Slotkin, *The Fatal Environment: The Myth of the Frontier in the Age of Industrialization, 1800–1890* (New York: Atheneum, 1985). Despite the exhaustion of "virgin land," Slotkin convincingly argued that the myth of the expanding American frontier continued into the twentieth century. Indeed, one could argue, as many have, that the latest version of this myth can be found in America's exploration of outer space. Slotkin suggested that, "Faced with the choice of 'liquidating' the concept of the Frontier or 'renaturalizing' it, Americans chose the latter. By a systematic and highly selective reinterpretation of the language of the Myth,

they adapted it to suit the ideological purposes and needs of the new industrial society" (531).

13. *Yellowstone Park Transportation Co. v. Gallatin Co.*, 27 F.2d 411 (D. Mont. 1928).

14. Ibid., 412.

15. *Yellowstone Park Transportation Co. v. Gallatin Co.*, 27 F. 2d 411 (D. Mont. 1928).

16. *Northern Pac. Ry. Co. v. Board of Railway Commissioners of Montana*, 34 F.2d 296 (D. Mont. 1929).

17. Ibid., 297.

18. Ibid.

19. Ibid.

20. Ibid.

21. *Great Falls Gas Co. v. Public Service Commission of Montana*, 39 F.2d 176 (D. Mont. 1930).

22. Ibid., 178.

23. Ibid., 177.

24. Ibid.

25. *Great Northern Utilities Co. v. Public Services Commission*, 52 F.2d 802–803 (D. Mont. 1931).

26. Ibid., 805.

27. Ibid., 804.

28. Ibid., 805.

29. Ibid., 803.

30. Ibid., 804.

31. Ibid.

32. Ibid.

33. *In re Conciliation Commissioner for Sanders Co. Mont: In re Wilkins*, 5 F. Supp. 131 (D. Mont. 1933).

34. Ibid.

35. Ibid.

36. Ibid., 132.

37. Ibid.

38. On property rights, see John Phillip Reid, *Constitutional History of the American Revolution* (Madison: University of Wisconsin Press, 1995), 3–25. Specifically on the question of property in the West, see Karen R. Merrill, *Public Lands and Political Meaning: Ranchers, the Government, and the Property between Them* (Berkeley: University of California Press, 2002).

39. *United States v. Rockefeller*, 260 F. 347 (D. Mont. 1919).

40. Ibid., 348.

41. Ibid., 347–48.

42. Ibid., 348.

43. *Nan v. Rasmusson*, 1 F. Supp. 446 (D. Mont. 1932).

44. *United States v. Butte*, 38 F.2d 874 (D. Mont. 1930).

45. Ibid., 872.

46. Ibid., 873.
47. Ibid., 874.
48. *Shoemaker v. Merrill Mortuaries*, 2 F. Supp. 672 (D. Mont. 1933).
49. Ibid.
50. Ibid.

Chapter 6

1. 30 U.S. (5 Pet.) 17 (1831).
2. 31 U.S. (6 Pet.) 515 (1832).
3. *United States v. Sioux Nation*, 448 U.S. 371 (1980). The majority opinion affirmed a court of claims holding that the federal government had violated the Fifth Amendment in "taking" Sioux land without compensation in 1877. The court also determined that Congress had not encroached on the judiciary by providing a remedy in the Indian Claims Commission Act of 1978; it thus rejected a constitutional claim that Congress had disturbed the finality of earlier court of claims judgments and thereby violated separation of powers limitations. In his vehement dissent attacking the majority for relying on "revisionist historians," Rehnquist protested that the majority's use of history created a "stereotyped and one-sided impression" of the Black Hills because while there were "less than admirable tactics employed by the Government . . . the Indians did not lack their share of villainy." *United States v. Sioux Nation*, 434–36 U.S. 371 (1980).
4. The Indian Reorganization Act of 1934 (25 U.S.C. 461 et seq., also known by the names of its sponsors in the Senate and House) ended the allotment and sought to enhance the authority of the tribes and to limit the discretion of the Department of the Interior and the Bureau of Indian Affairs. See Janet A. McDonnell, *The Dispossession of the American Indian, 1887–1934* (Bloomington: Indiana University Press, 1991). On the Wheeler-Howard Act, see Vine Deloria, Jr., and Clifford M. Lytle. *American Indians, American Justice* (Austin: University of Texas Press, 1983). Sherry Lynn Smith in her fine study *Reimagining Indians: Native Americans through Anglo Eyes, 1880–1940* (Oxford: Oxford University Press, 2000) focuses on Western intellectuals who in similar fashion to Bourquin were critical of US Indian policy. Some of them were Montanans, contemporaries of Bourquin.
5. See Aviam Soifer, "Objects in Mirror Are Closer Than They Appear," *Georgia Law Review* 28 (1994): 533.
6. Treaty with the Flatheads, July 16, 1855, 12 Stat. 975.
7. Genesis 27.
8. Kings 21.
9. *Scheer v. Moody*, 48 F.2d 327 (D. Mont. 1931).
10. Act of March 3, 1871, Chapter 120 #1, 16 Stat. 566, 25 U.S.C. #71.
11. Milner S. Ball, "Constitution, Court, Indian Tribes," *American Bar Foundation Association Journal* 1 (1987): 52–53.

12. Chapter 119, 24 Stat. 388, codified as amended in various sections of 25 U.S.C.
13. William C. Canby, Jr., *American Indian Law in a Nutshell* (St. Paul, MN: West, 1988), 19. On the Dawes Act and its effects, see McDonnell, *Dispossession of the American Indian.*
14. *Congressional Record*, January 20, 1881, 46th Cong., 3rd sess., 783.
15. Ibid., February 25, 1886, 49th Cong., 1st sess., 1762–1763; see also Brian W. Dippie, *The Vanishing American: White Attitudes and U.S. Indian Policy* (Middletown, CT: Wesleyan University Press, 1982), 161–96; Petra Shattuck and Jill Norgren, *Partial Justice: Federal Indian Law in a Liberal Constitutional System* (New York: Berg, 1991), 57, 91, 97–99, 107, 116, 124, 144; Charles F. Wilkinson, *American Indians, Time, and the Law: Native Societies in a Modern Constitutional Democracy* (New Haven, CT: Yale University Press, 1987), 19, 51; Francis Paul Prucha, *American Indian Policy in Crisis: Christian Reformers and the Indians, 1865–1900* (Norman: University of Oklahoma Press, 1976), 265–92; Wilcomb E. Washburn, *The Assault on Indian Tribalism: The General Allotment Act of 1887* (Philadelphia: Lippincott, 1975).
16. As cited in Wilkinson, *American Indians, Time, and Law*, 151.
17. 33 Stat. 302.
18. 34 Stat. 355
19. 34 Stat. 182, 25 U.S.C.A. #349.
20. *Scheer v. Moody*, 48 F.2d 330 (D. Mont. 1931).
21. *Scheer v. Moody*, 48 F.2d 327 (D. Mont. 1931), 327.
22. Ibid.
23. Ibid., 328.
24. Ibid., 328.
25. Ibid.
26. Ibid.
27. Ibid., 329. Compare with the stances of Judge Isaac C. Parker in an earlier period in Roger Tuller's *Let No Guilty Man Escape*, 106–20.
28. Ibid., 330. *Ex parte Young*, 209 U.S. 123 (1908).
29. Ibid.
30. Ibid., 331 .
31. 33 Stat. 140, 141.
32. *Scheer v. Moody*, 48 F.2d 331 (D. Mont. 1931).
33. Ibid., 331. Also see 276 U.S. 609, 48 S. Ct. 207, 277 U.S. 438, 48 S. Ct. 564.
34. Ibid., 331–33.
35. Ibid.
36. Bourquin's decree in *Scheer v. Moody* granted relief to the plaintiffs, "white owners" of former Indian allotments, and enjoined C. J. Moody from assessing or charging the plaintiffs for the construction, operation, and maintenance of such projects and from determining the amount of water to which these lands were entitled. On July 27, 1933, in the case of *Moody, Project Manager v. Johnston et al., and Four Other Cases* (66 F.2d 999 [1933]), the Ninth Circuit Court of Appeals reversed Bourquin's decision with directions to dismiss the complaint for want of necessary party or parties. The circuit court stated that the secretary of the interi-

or, or the United States, or both, should have been made parties to the lawsuit because Moody, as an employee of the US government, performed all his acts under
the direction and authority of the secretary of the interior and not in his capacity
as a private individual. Bourquin previously had denied Moody's motion to dismiss
the plaintiffs' complaint on these grounds, stating that Moody was a trespasser
acting outside the scope of his authority and that suits against a trespasser are not
against the US government.

37. Ibid.
38. Ibid.
39. Ibid.
40. *Scheer v. Moody*, 48 F.2d 329 (D. Mont. 1931).
41. *Moody, Project Manager v. Johnston et al., and Four Other Cases*, 66 F.2d 999 (1933).
42. Criminal Code #35 (18 U.S.C.A. #82).
43. *United States v. Trinden*, 1 F. Supp. 659 (D. Mont. 1932).
44. Ibid., 659–60.
45. *United States v. Healy*, 202 F. 350 (D. Mont. 1913).
46. Ibid.
47. *United States v. Twelve Bottles of Whiskey*, 210 F.2d 327 (D. Mont. 1912).
48. Ibid.
49. Indian Reorganization Act, 25 U.S.C. #461 et seq.

Chapter 7

1. Perhaps the clearest indicator of this phenomenon is the fact that legal ethics is
now a required course in most, if not all, American law schools. Periodicals on legal ethics, such as the *Georgetown Journal of Legal Ethics*, are extremely successful,
as is the leading textbook by Geoffrey C. Hazard and Susan Koniak, et al., *The Law
and Ethics of Lawyering*, 5th ed. (Foundation Press, 2010). Moreover, legal ethics is
not only an academic concern; it is the focus of much, often costly, litigation, as in
In re Fishbein (OTS AP-92-19-Treasury Dept. 1992), a case involving a prominent
New York law firm. See PLI Corp. Law & Practice Course Handbook, Series No.
B4-7009, Jonathan J. Lerner, *The Attorney-Client Relationship after Kaye, Scholer*
(New York: PLI, 1992); Robert E. O'Malley et al., eds., *The Kaye, Scholer Case and
Other Selected Professional Liability and Ethic Issues* (Attorneys' Liability Assurance
Society, 1992). Other more recent major cases include: *United States v. Goldberger
& Duban*, P.C., 935 F.2d 501 (2d Cir. 1991), holding client identity and amount
of attorneys' fees not privileged and disclosure to the Internal Revenue Service
required under Tax Reform Act of 1984; and *Nix v. Whiteside*, 475 U.S. 157, 174
(1986), holding that attorney's duty of confidentiality does not extend to a client's
announced intention to engage in future criminal conduct.
2. In *Batson v. Kentucky*, 476 U.S. 79 (1986), the US Supreme Court overturned several of its precedents and held that a prosecutor's use of peremptory challenges
to exclude prospective jurors on the basis of race violated the Constitution, no

matter what the race of the defendant. The decision has been extended to peremptory challenges based on race in civil cases, *Edmonson v. Leesville Concrete Co.*, 501 U.S. 614 (1991), and when used by a defense attorney, *Georgia v. McCollum*, 505 U.S. 42 (1992). The court refused, however, to extend *Batson* to exclude potential jurors who acknowledged that because they spoke Spanish, the possibility existed that they would not be strictly bound by the official interpretation of the Spanish-speaking witness's testimony, *Hernandez v. New York*, 500 U.S. 352 (1991). *Batson* was extended to exclusion on the basis of gender in *J.E.B. v. Alabama ex rel. T.B.*, 511 U.S.127 (1994).

3. *In re Kelly*, 243 F. 696 (D. Mont. 1917).

4. Ibid.

5. Ibid.

6. Ibid., 702.

7. Ibid., 703.

8. Ibid., 696–702. On the assorted bag of tricks employed by Anaconda Company lawyers, see Donald MacMillan, *Smoke Wars: Anaconda Copper, Montana Air Pollution, and the Courts, 1890–1924* (Helena: Montana Historical Society, 2000), 125–36, 139, 177–81, 186–88, 200–201, 211, 239–41, 248, 251, 256.

9. Ibid.

10. Ibid., 703.

11. Ibid.

12. Ibid., 704.

13. Ibid., 703–4.

14. Ibid., 704. See *Ellis v. United States*, 206 U.S. 257, 27 Sup. Ct. 660. Bourquin found that the defendants had all the intent he deemed necessary. He cited the Ellis case in a way that actually was much closer to the usual tort standard than to the criminal law approach. In criminal law, specific criminal intent generally must be proven beyond a reasonable doubt. Only in very rare cases is this requirement, mens rea, ignored. For Bourquin, however, dangerous tendencies of probable injury were enough. Bourquin's extremely loose approach in this case was particularly striking in the context of criminal contempt. The rare occasions when specific criminal intent was not required are generally thought to be matters of legislative judgment about some extreme necessity. In effect, Bourquin was playing the role of prosecutor and legislature as well as judge. The reason was his sense of the delicacy of the scales of justice and the fallibility of jurors.

15. Ibid., 704.

16. Ibid. See also *Mattox v. United States*, 146 U.S. 148, 13 Sup. Ct. 50.

17. Ibid., 705. See also *Scott v. Tubbs*, 43 Colo. 221, 95 Pac. 540 (Colo. 1908); *Sandston v. Nav. Co.*, 69 Or. 194, 136 Pac. 878 (Oreg. 1913); *Stockgrowers' Bank of Wheatland v. Gray*, 154 P. 593 (Wyo. 1916); *State v. Snow*, 153 N.W. 526 (Minn. 1915); *George F. Craig & Co. v. Pierson Lumber Co.*, 53 S. 803 (Ala. 1910); *State ex inf. Kimbrell v. Clark*, 114 S.W. 536 (Mo. App. 1908); *Bradshaw v. Degenhart*, 39 P. 90 (Mont. 1895).

18. Ibid., 705.

19. Ibid., 704, 705.

20. Ibid., 704.
21. Ibid., 705. See *Liutz v. Denver City Tramway Co.*, 131 P. 258, 261 (Colo. 1913).
22. Ibid., 705.
23. *Jackson v. Genzberger*, 5 F. Supp. 187 (D. Mont. 1933).
24. According to the ruling: "It is of interest that before plaintiff entrusted the proceedings to defendant, they agreed and Kenck with them, that no contract would be made with Kenck in respect to fees, but the latter would be left to the court; and for that they 'understood' the courts of Montana were very 'liberal' with other people's money in the matter of allowances to attorneys out of estates and other trusts by them administered. Defendant assured plaintiff that contrary to the California rule, they would receive double the administrator's statutory fees. And the device of extraordinary services to swell allowances was by them contemplated. The result vindicated the repute, forecast and strategy aforesaid, for whereas of the California estate fixed at $116,000 administered, the executor and his attorney each received $1980, of the Montana estate inventoried at $130,000 the administrator received $3660, and his attorneys, plaintiff and defendant, $10,000. Whether or not the latter inventory was inflated with an eye to fees, it is a fact that after fees upon that basis were secured, in due hearing in tax proceedings the court determined that the value of the estate in Montana was but $84,000." Ibid., 187–88.
25. Ibid.
26. Ibid.
27. Ibid., 189.
28. *United States v. Herrig*, 204 F. 124 (D. Mont. 1913).
29. *United States v. Noble et al.*, 294 F. 690 (D. Mont. 1923).
30. Ibid., 691.
31. Ibid., 692.
32. Ibid.
33. *United States v. Meagher*, 36 F.2d 824 (D. Mont. 1929).
34. Ibid.
35. Ibid.
36. Ibid., 825.
37. Ibid.
38. Ibid.
39. *United States v. Herrig*, 204 F. 124 (D. Mont. 1913).
40. Ibid., 125.
41. Ibid., 126.
42. *United States v. Ford*, 9 F.2d 990 (D. Mont.1925).
43. Ibid.
44. *United States v. Herrig*, 204 F. 124 (D. Mont. 1913).
45. Ibid., 125.
46. Ibid., 126.
47. Ibid., 992.

48. Ibid., 991.

49. 28 U.S.C.A. #380.

50. 39 F. 176 (D. Mont. 1930).

51. 290 F. 412 (D. Mont. 1923).

52. Ibid.

53. Ibid., 413.

54. Ibid., 414.

55. Ibid.

Chapter 8

1. On the period preceding the stock market crash, the Depression, and the New Deal in Montana, see Malone, Roeder, and Lang, *Montana*, 280–303; Toole, *Montana*, 228–42; Joseph K. Howard, *Montana: High, Wide and Handsome* (New Haven, CT: Yale University Press, 1943), 178–88; Charles Vindex, "Survival on the High Plains, 1929–1934," *Montana: The Magazine of Western History* 28 (1978): 2–11; Leonard Arrington and Don C. Reading, "New Deal Economic Programs in the Northern Tier States, 1933–1939," in *Centennial West: Essays on the History of the Northern Tier States*, ed. William L. Lang (Seattle: University of Washington Press, 1991), 227–43; Leonard Arrington, "The New Deal in the West: A Preliminary Statistical Inquiry," *Pacific Historical Review* 38 (1969): 311–16; James T. Patterson, "The New Deal in the West," *Pacific Historical Review* 38 (1969): 317–27; Michael Malone, "The Montana New Dealers," in *The New Deal*, vol. 2, ed. John Braeman, Robert H. Brenner, and David Brody (Columbus: Ohio State University Press, 1975) 240–68; Michael Malone, "Montana Politics and the New Deal," *Montana: The Magazine of Western History* 21 (1971): 2–11.

2. Arrington, "New Deal in the West."

3. William E. Leuchtenburg, *Franklin Roosevelt and the New Deal: 1932–1940* (New York: Harper and Row, 1963), 157; Malone, Roeder, and Lang, *Montana*, 300–302.

4. *Great Falls Tribune*, October 19, 1934.

5. Wheeler, *Yankee from the West*, 162; Richard T. Ruetten, "Senator Burton K. Wheeler and Insurgency in the 1920s," in *The American West: A Reorientation*, ed. Gene M. Gressley (Laramie: University of Wyoming Publications, 1968), 162; *Great Falls Tribune*, November 2, 1934.

6. Ibid., November 9, 1934.

7. *Daily Missoulian*, October 16, 1934.

8. *Montana Record Herald* (Helena), September 7, 1934.

9. Ibid., September 7, 1934; September 22, 1934.

10. Ibid., September 7, 1934.

11. *Montana Record Herald* (Helena), September 7, 1934; October 19, 1934.

12. Ibid., September 7, 1934.

13. Ibid.

14. *Great Falls Tribune*, September 4, 1934; *Montana Record Herald* (Helena), September 22, 1934.

15. *Montana Record Herald* (Helena), September 7, 1934.

16. *Great Falls Tribune*, October 19, 1934.

17. *Montana Record Herald* (Helena), September 7, 1934.

18. Ibid., September 29, 1934.

19. Ibid., October 7, 1934.

20. Ibid., September 7, 1934.

21. Ibid., November 8, 1934.

22. Ibid.

23. Ibid.

24. It should be noted that Bourquin's grandchildren had no idea why he left the bench and entered a political campaign that he was certain of losing. His granddaughter believed that he felt that he had a chance. The interviewer speculated that when Bourquin was ready to leave the bench, "his values needed someone to stand up for them." Attorney Dennis Bourquin agreed with the interpretation but still questions why a person with limited funds decided on a hopeless run for the US Senate. Transcript of interview with Dennis and Marilyn Bourquin, 52–55.

25. *Great Falls Tribune*, November 7, 1934.

26. Schwartz, *History of the Supreme Court*, 231–45.

27. The American Liberty League was formed in 1934 by a group of conservative Democrats who opposed the economic and fiscal policies of the New Deal. The league was disbanded in 1940, but until then it engaged in extreme attacks on President Franklin D. Roosevelt and his policies. See the following endnote.

28. An excellent study of the Liberty League is George Wolfskill, *The Revolt of the Conservatives: A History of the Liberty League, 1934–1940* (Boston: Houghton Mifflin, 1962). On the league's ideology, see especially pp. 102–41.

29. Ibid., 262.

30. As quoted in ibid., 263.

31. *Montana Standard* (Butte), January 6, 1959.

SELECTED BIBLIOGRAPHY

Documents

Baker, Ray S., and William E. Dodd, eds. *The Public Papers of Woodrow Wilson*. 6 vols. New York: Harper and Brothers, 1925.

Deloria, Vine, Jr., and Raymond J. DeMallie, comp. *Documents of American Indian Diplomacy: Treaties, Agreements, and Conventions, 1775–1979*. Norman: University of Oklahoma Press, 1999

Heckscher, August, ed. *The Politics of Woodrow Wilson, Selections from His Speeches and Writings*. New York: Harper, 1956.

Philip, Kenneth R., ed. *Indian Self-Rule: First Hand Accounts of Indian-White Relations from Roosevelt to Reagan*. Logan: Utah State University Press, 1995.

Roosevelt, Franklin D. *His Personal Letters*. 4 vols. New York: Duell, Sloan, and Pearce, 1947–1950.

Government Documents: State of Montana

Department of Public Instruction. *Minutes of the Meetings of the Board of Education, 1916–1926*. Capitol Building, Helena, MT.

House Journal of the Extraordinary Session of the Fifteenth Legislative Assembly of the State of Montana. Helena, MT: State Publishing Company, 1918.

House Journal of the Sixteenth Legislative Assembly of the State of Montana. Helena, MT: State Publishing Company, 1919.

Laws Passed by the Extraordinary Session of the Fifteenth Legislative Assembly of the State of Montana. Helena, MT: State Publishing Company, 1918.

Montana Department of Labor and Industry. *Third Biennial Report, 1917–1918*. Helena, MT: State Publishing Company, 1918.

Montana Department of Labor and Industry. *Fourth Biennial Report, 1918–1919*. Helena, MT: State Publishing Company, 1919.

Montana Reports, 1919. San Francisco, CA: 1919.

Senate. *Report of the Tax Investigation Committee of the Senate*, 15th Legislative Assembly. Helena, MT: State Publishing Company, 1917

Senate Journal of the Extraordinary Session of the Fifteenth Legislative Assembly of the State of Montana. Helena, MT: State Publishing Company, 1918.

Senate Journal of the Fifteenth Legislative Assembly of the State of Montana. Helena, MT: State Publishing Company, 1917.

Senate Journal of the Sixteenth Legislative Assembly of the State of Montana. Helena, MT: State Publishing Company, 1919.

State of Montana v. William F. Dunne (4411). Helena, MT: State Publishing Company, 1919.

State Agricultural Experiment Station, Bozeman, MT: Report and Letter. 1917–1918.

Resolutions of the State of Montana Legislative Council, Denver, CO: 1991.

Government Documents: United States

[All produced by Government Printing Office]

Congressional Record, 1917–1934.

Department of Interior, Bureau of Mines. *Lessons from the Granite Mountain Shaft Fire, Butte,* by Daniel Harrington. Bulletin 188. Washington DC, 1922.

Annual Report of the Attorney General of the United States for the Year 1918. Washington DC, 1918.

Annual Report of Secretary of Labor 1918. Historical Statistics, Series K 265-7. Washington DC, 1919.

Department of Labor. *Report of the Department of Labor.* Washington, 1919.

US Bureau of Labor Statistics. "Change in the Cost of Living." March 15, 1937. Series N. R555. Washington DC, 1938.

US Bureau of Labor Statistics. Cloice R. Howd. "Industrial Relations in the West Coast Lumber Industry." Bulletin No. 399. Washington DC, 1924.

US Bureau of Labor Statistics. "Wholesale Prices 1890–1919." Bulletin No. 269. Washington, DC, 1920.

US Department of Labor. *Report of the President's Mediation Commission to the President of the United States. Reports of the Department of Labor.* Washington DC, 1919.

Annual Report of the Secretary of the Treasury on the State of Finance, 1918. Washington DC, 1919.

War Department Annual Reports. *Report of the Adjutant General, 1921.* Washington DC, 1923.

Manuscripts Collections
Harvard Law School

Felix Frankfurter Collection

Boxes 50 and 87 dealing with general correspondence; Record File 159, National Popular Government League, 1919–1920.

Zechariah Chafee, Jr., Papers

Boxes 29, 30—Civil Liberties, 1919–1929.
Box 33—Civil Liberties, 1947–1956.

Judson King Collection

Container 2, General Correspondence, 1913–1932; File 70, National Popular Government League Bulletins, 1921–1924.

Library of Congress

William E. Borah Collection
Box 197, General Correspondence, 1919–1920, folder entitled "Espionage."

Montana Historical Society

Hearings Held at the State Capitol, Helena, Montana, May 13, June 1–2, 4–5, 1918 by the Montana Council of Defense in Connection with the Arrest of Von Waldru, alias Charles Stone by Federal Authorities and also in Connection with an Investigation of Charges against Oscar Rohn. A typed manuscript in two volumes (1474 pp.).

Proceedings of the Court for the Trial of Impeachments: The People of the State of Montana by the House of Representatives Thereof Against Charles L. Crum, Judge of the District Court of the Fifteenth District of the State of Montana. Helena MT: State Publishing Company, 1918.

Testimony at Hearings Held at the State Capitol, Helena, Montana, May–June 1918, by the Montana Council of Defense. Typescript, 2 vols. State Historical Society of Montana Library, Helena, MT.

Third Biennial Report of the Department of Labor and Industry, 1917–1918. Helena, MT: State Printing Office, 1919.

University of Montana Investigation Files, Montana State Board of Education Papers, Capitol Building, Helena, MT.

University of Montana, President's Office, Executive Documents, Levine File, Missoula, MT.

National Archives and Records Service

Abraham Glasser File, Records of the Department of Justice, RG 60, National Archives.

Military Intelligence Division G-2 Files 1918–1919. National Archives.

Oliver Wendell Holmes, Jr., Papers, Boxes 20, 29, 30—Correspondence, Frankfurter, Box 40—Correspondence, Croly, Box 48—Correspondence, Pound.

Record Group 60—Justice Department Files.

Record Group 85—Immigration and Naturalization Bureau Files, Files 53244-1D, 54235, 54235–36, and 54235–36F, Deportations, 1919–1920.

Record Group 174—Labor Department Files, 1914–1921.

US Adjutant General's Office, Record Group 94. Records of the AGO. Bulky File 370.6, Butte, Montana, National Archives.

War Department Annual Reports. *Reports of the Adjutant General, 1921.* Washington DC, 1923.

Woodrow Wilson Collection, File 6, Folder 4963, Eugene V. Debs, 1919–1921.

Supreme Court Cases Cited

Abrams et al. v. United States, 250 U.S. 616, 1919.

Adair v. United States, 208 U.S. 161, 1908.

Adkins v. Children's Hospital, 261 U.S. 525, 1923.

Ashton v. Cameron County Dist., 298 U.S. 513, 1936.

Batson v. Kentucky, 476 U.S. 79, 1986.

Brandenburg v. Ohio, 895 U.S. 444, 1969.

Carter v. Carter Coal Co., 298 U.S. 238, 1936.

Cherokee Nation v. State of Georgia, 30 U.S. (5 Pet.) 17, 1831.

Debs v. United States, 249 U.S. 211, 1919.

Edmonson v. Leesville Concrete Co., 500 U.S. 614, 1991.

Ellis v. United States, 206 U.S. 246, 1906.

Ex parte Young, 209 U.S. 123, 1908.

Fong Yue Ting v. United States, 149 U.S. 698, 1893.

Frohwerk v. United States, 249 U.S. 204, 1919.

Georgia v. McCollum, 505 U.S. 42, 1992.

Gilbert v. Minnesota, 254 U.S. 325, 1920.

Gitlow v. New York, 268 U.S. 652, 1925.

Hernandez v. New York, 500 U.S. 352, 1991.

Hilton v. Guyot, 159 U.S. 163, 1893.

In re Fishbein, OTS AP-92-19-Treasury Dept., 1992.

In re Debs, 158 U.S. 564, 1895.

J.E.B. v. Alabama ex rel. T.B., 511 U.S. 127, 1994.

Kwack Jan Fat v. White, 253 U.S. 454, 1920.

Lochner v. New York, 198 U.S. 45, 1905.

Lopez v. Howe, 254 U.S. 613, 1920.

Louisville Joint Stock Land Bank v. Radford, 295 U.S. 555, 1935.

Luria v. United States, 231 U.S. 9, 1913.

Mattox v. United States, 146 U.S. 140, 1892.

Morehead v. New York ex rel. Tipaldo, 298 U.S. 587, 1936.

Munn v. Illinois, 94 U.S 113, 1877.

Nix v. Whiteside, 475 U.S., 157, 1986.

Northern Securities Co. v. United States, 193 U.S. 197, 1904.

Plessy v. Ferguson, 163 U.S. 537, 1896.

Railroad Retirement Board v. Alton, 295 U.S. 30, 1935.

Samuel Worcester, Plaintiff in Error v. State of Georgia, 31 U.S. (6 Pet.) 515, 1832.

Schecter Poultry v. United States, 295 U.S. 495, 1935.

Schenck v. United States, 249 U.S. 47, 1919.

Selective Draft Law Cases, 245 U.S. 366, 1918.
Slaughter-House Cases, 16 Wall 83 U.S. 36, 72, 1873.
Standard Oil of New Jersey v. United States, 221 U.S. 1, 1911.
Temple v. United States, 248 U.S. 121, 1918.
United States v. Butler, 297 U.S. 1, 1936.
United States v. E. C. Knight Co., 156 U.S. 1, 1895.
United States v. Sioux Nation, 448 U.S. 371, 1980.
Weeks v. United States, 232 U.S. 383, 1913.
Whitney v. California, 274 U.S. 357, 1927.
Wise v. Withers, 3 Cranch (7 U.S.), 331, 1806.
Yamataya v. Fisher, 189 U.S. 86, 1903.

Federal District Court Cases Cited

A. M. Holter Hardware Co. v. Boyle, 263 F. 135, D. Mont. 1920.
American Bonding Co. of Baltimore, Md. v. Reynolds, 203 F. 356, D. Mont. 1913.
Andrews, Inspector of Immigration et al. v. Jackson, 267 F. 1022, 9 Cir. 1920.
Bradshaw v. Degenhart, 39 P. 90, Mont. 1895.
Briscoe v. Southern Kansas Co., 40 F. 273, Cir. Ct. W.D. Ark. 1889.
Clark v. Crosland, 17 Ark. 43, 1856.
Eddy's Steam Bakery v. Rasmusson, 47 F.2d 247, D. Mont. 1931.
Ex parte Beck, 245 F. 967, D. Montana, 1917.
Ex parte Jackson, 263 F. 110, D. Mont. 1920.
Ex parte Radivoeff, 278 F. 227, D. Mont. 1922.
Ex parte Starr, 263 F. 145, D. Mont. 1920.
George F. Craig & Co. v. Pierson Lumber Co., 53 S. 803, Ala. 1910.
Great Falls Gas Co. v. Public Service Commission of Montana, 39 F.2d 176, D. Mont. 1930.
Great Northern Utilities Co. v. Public Services Commission, 52 F.2d 802, D. Mont. 1931.
In re Conciliation Commissioner for Sanders Co. Mont: In re Wilkins, 5 F. Supp. 131, D. Mont. 1933.
In re Kelly, 243 F. 696, D. Mont. 1917.
In re Norman, 256 F. 543, D. Mont. 1919.
In re Siem, 284 F. 868, D. Mont. 1922.
In re Tam Chung, 223 F. 802, D. Mont. 1915.
Jackson v. Genzberger, 5 F. Supp. 187, D. Mont. 1933.
Liutz v. Denver City Tramway Co., 131 P. 258, Colo. 1913.
Lopez v. Howe, 259 F. 401, 2 Cir. 1919.
Moody Project Manager v. Johnston et al., and Four Other Cases, 66 F.2d 999, 1933.
Nan v. Rasmusson, 1 F. Supp. 446, D. Mont. 1932.
Northern Pacific Railway Company v. Board of Railway Commissions, 34 F.2d 295, D. Mont. 1929.
Sandston v. Nav. Co., 69 Or. 194, Oreg. 1913.

Scheer v. Moody et al., 48 F.2d 327, D. Mont. 1931.
Scott v. Tubbs, 43 Colo. 221, Colo. 1908.
Shoemaker v. Merrill Mortuaries, 2 F. Supp. 672, D. Mont. 1933.
State ex inf. Kimbrell v. Clark, 114 S.W. 536, Mo. App. 1908.
State v. Snow, 153 N.W. 526, Minn. 1915.
Stockgrowers' Bank of Wheatland v. Gray, 154 P. 593, Wyo. 1916.
United States v. Butte, 38 F.2d 871, D. Mont. 1930.
United States v. Ford, F.2d 990, D. Mont. 1925.
United States v. Goldberger and Duban, P.C., 935 F.2d 501, 2 Cir. 1991.
United States v. Healy, 202 F. 349, D. Mont. 1913.
United States v. Herrig, 204 F.124, D. Mont. 1913.
United States v. Meagher, 36 F.2d 824, D. Mont. 1929.
United States v. Metzdorf, 252 F. 933, D. Mont. 1917.
United States v. Noble et al., 294 F. 690, D. Mont. 1923.
United States v. Premise in Butte, 246 F. 187, D. Mont. 1917.
United States v. Rockefeller, 260 F. 346, D. Mont. 1919.
United States v. Smith, 282 F. 339, D. Mont. 1922.
United States v. Trinder, 1 F. Supp. 659, D. Mont. 1932.
United States v. Twelve Bottles of Whiskey, 204 F. 192, D. Mont. 1912.
United States v. Ves Hall, 248 F. 150, D. Mont. 1918.
United States v. Woods, 224 F. 278, D. Mont. 1915.
Yellowstone Park Transportation Co. v. Gallatin County, 27 F.2d 410, D. Mont. 1928.

Pamphlets

Lewis O. Evans, Chief Council of the Anaconda Copper Mining Company, Before the Chamber of Commerce, Missoula, MT: August 24, 1917. New York Public Library.

Interviews

Lawyer E. C. Mulroney, July 13, 1967.
Jeannette Rankin, August 1, 1967.
Federal District Judge Russel Smith, June 30, 1967.
Transcript of interview with Dennis and Marilyn Bourquin, Redwood City, CA, August 7, 1993 (65 pp.). Copy in author's possession.

Letters

Dennis M. Bourquin to author, undated [June 1995].
Lewis L. Lorwin to author, over fifty letters, 1968–1970.
Burton K. Wheeler to author, August 8, 1967.
Burton K. Wheeler to Patrick Sherlock, August 21, 1967. Letter in author's possession.

Newspapers

Anaconda Standard, 1917–1924.
Billings Gazette, 1917–1924.
Butte Bulletin, 1917–1922.
Butte Daily Post, 1917–1934.
Butte Miner, 1917–1934.
Butte Strike Bulletin, 1917.
Carbon County Journal, 1917–1918.
Chicago Tribune, 1917.
Chinook Opinion, 1917–1918.
Choteau Acantha, 1917–1918.
Cut Bank Pioneer Press, 1917–1918.
Daily Missoulian, 1917–1934.
Dawson County Review (Glendive), 1917–1920.
Fergus County Argosy (Lewistown), 1917–1922.
Great Falls Tribune, 1917–1934.
Hardin Tribune Journal, 1917–1918.
Helena Independent, 1900, 1917–1934.
Helena Record-Herald, 1917–1934.
Jefferson Valley News (Whitehall), 1917–1919.
Livingston Enterprise, 1917–1922.
Madisonian Times (Virginia City), 1917.
Miles City Independent, 1917–1923.
Miles City Star, 1917–1934.
Miners and Electrical Worker Joint Strike Bulletin (Butte), 1917–1918.
Montana Equity News, 1916–1920.
Montana Record Herald (Helena), 1917–1934.
Montana Standard, 1959.
New Northwest (Missoula), 1915–1922.
New York Herald, 1900.
New York Times, 1917–1937, 1959.
Nonpartisan Leader, 1916–1920.
Philipsburg Mail, 1917–1918.
Roundup Tribune, 1917–1922.
Scoby Sentinel, 1917–1919.
Sidney Herald, 1917–1919.
Valley County News (Glasgow), 1917–1952.
Washington Post, 1917–1934.
Western News (Hamilton), 1917–1923.

Books

Auerbach, Jerold S. *Unequal Justice: Lawyers and Social Change in Modern America.*

New York: Oxford University Press, 1976.

Arnold, Morris. *Colonial Arkansas 1686-1804: A Social and Cultural History.* Fayetteville: University of Arkansas Press, 1991.

———. *Unique Laws unto a Savage Race: European Legal Traditions in Arkansas.* Fayetteville: University of Arkansas Press, 1985.

Bailey, Thomas A. *Woodrow Wilson and the Lost Peace.* New York: Macmillan, 1944.

Baker, Peter. *The Breach: Inside the Impeachment and Trial of William Jefferson Clinton.* New York: Scribner, 2000.

Bakken, Gordon Morris, ed. *Law in Western United States.* Norman: University of Oklahoma Press, 2000.

Barth, Alan. *The Loyalty of Free Men.* Hamden, CT: Archer Books, 1951.

Baruch, Bernard M. *American Industry in the War.* New York: Prentice Hall, 1941.

Beaver, Daniel R. *Newton D. Baker and the War Effort, 1917–1919.* Lincoln: University of Nebraska Press, 1966.

Berger, Raoul. *Impeachment: The Constitutional Problems.* Cambridge, MA: Harvard University Press, 1973.

Bing, Alexander M. *War-Time Strikes and Their Adjustment.* New York: E. P. Dutton, 1921.

Black, Charles L., Jr. *Impeachment: A Handbook.* New Haven, CT: Yale University Press, 1998.

Breen, William J. *Uncle Sam at Home: Civilian Mobilization, Wartime Federalism, and the Council of National Defense, 1917–1919.* Westport, CT: Greenwood Press, 1984.

Brissenden, Paul. *The I.W.W.: A Study of Syndicalism.* New York: Columbia University Press, 1919.

Bristow, Nancy K. *Making Men Moral: Social Engineering during the Great War.* New York: New York University Press, 1996.

Brodhead, Michael J. *David J. Brewer: The Life of a Supreme Court Justice, 1837–1910.* Carbondale: Southern Illinois University Press, 1994.

Brooks, John. *American Syndicalism: The I.W.W.* New York: Macmillan, 1913.

Burton, David Henry. *Taft, Holmes, and the 1920's Court: An Appraisal.* Madison, NJ: Fairleigh Dickinson University Press, 1998.

Calvert, Jerry. *The Gibraltar: Socialism and Labor in Butte, Montana, 1895–1920.* Helena, MT: Montana Historical Society Press, 1988.

Canby, William C., Jr. *American Indian Law in a Nutshell.* St. Paul, MN: West, 1988.

Carlson, Leonard A. *Indians, Bureaucrats, and Land: The Dawes Act and the Decline of Indian Farming.* Westport, CT: Greenwood Press, 1981.

Chafee, Zechariah, Jr. *Freedom of Speech.* New York: Harcourt, Brace and Howe, 1920.

———. *Free Speech in the United States.* Cambridge, MA: Harvard University Press, 1941.

Chaplin, Ralph. *Wobbly: The Rough and Tumble Story of an American Radical.* Chicago: University of Chicago Press, 1948.

Churchill, Allen. *Over Here! An Informal Re-creation of the Home Front in World War I.* New York: Dodd, Mead, 1968.

Clark, Jane Perry. *Deportation of Aliens from the United States to Europe.* New York: Columbia University Press, 1931.

Coben, Stanley. *A. Mitchell Palmer: Politician.* New York: Columbia University Press, 1963.

Cohen, Jeremy. *Congress Shall Make No Law: Oliver Wendell Holmes, the First Amendment, and Judicial Decision-Making.* Ames: Iowa State University Press, 1989.

Commager, Henry S. *Freedom, Loyalty, Dissent.* New York: Oxford University Press, 1954.

Corwin, Edward S. *Total War and the Constitution.* New York: Knopf, 1947.

Davis, Harry Alexander, comp. *Some Huguenot Families of South Carolina and Georgia.* 2nd ed., rev. Washington DC, 1940.

Deloria, Vine, Jr., and Clifford M. Lytle. *American Indians, American Justice.* Austin: University of Texas Press, 1983.

De Vattel, Emmerich. *Law of Nations.* 1796; Philadelphia: T. & J. W. Johnson, 1863.

Dippie, Brian W. *The Vanishing American: White Attitudes and U.S. Indian Policy.* Middletown, CT: Wesleyan University Press, 1982.

Dubofsky, Melvyn. *We Shall Be All: A History of the Industrial Workers of the World.* Chicago: Quadrangle Books, 1969.

Dulles, Foster Rhea. *Labor in America.* New York: T. Y. Crowell, 1955.

Emmons, David M. *The Butte Irish: Class and Ethnicity in an American Mining Town, 1875–1925.* Urbana: University of Illinois, 1989.

Farwell, Byron. *Over There: The United States in the Great War, 1917–1918.* New York: Norton, 1999.

Fisch, Louise Ann. *All Rise: Reynaldo G. Garza, the First Mexican American Federal Judge.* College Station: Texas A&M University Press, 1996.

Foner, Philip S. *History of the Labor Movement in the United States: From the Founding of the American Federation of Labor to the Emergence of American Imperialism.* New York: International Publishers, 1955.

Foucault, Michel. *The Archaeology of Knowledge.* New York: Pantheon Books, 1972.

Freeman, Edward A. *The Growth of the English Constitution from the Earliest Times.* London: Macmillan, 1872.

Friedman, Lawrence M. *A History of American Law.* New York: Simon and Schuster, 1973.

Fritz, Christian G. *Federal Justice in California: The Court of Ogden Hoffman, 1851–1891.* Lincoln: University of Nebraska Press, 1991.

Gengarelly, Anthony W. *Distinguished Dissenters and Opposition to the 1919–1920 Red Scare.* Lewiston, NY: E. Mellen Press, 1996.

Gerhardt, Michael J. *The Federal Impeachment Process: A Constitutional and Historical Analysis.* 2nd ed. Chicago: University of Chicago Press, 2000.

Giffin, Frederick C. *Six Who Protested: Radical Opposition to the First World War.* Port Washington, NY: Kennikat Press, 1977.

Goldberg, David J. *Discontented America: The United States in the 1920s.* Baltimore: Johns Hopkins University Press, 1999.

Goldstein, Robert Justin. *Political Repression in Modern America from 1870 to 1976*. Urbana: University of Illinois Press, 2001.

Gompers, Samuel. *American Labor and the War*. New York: George H. Doran Company, 1919.

Graham, D. Kurt. *To Bring Law Home: The Federal Judiciary in Early National Rhode Island*. DeKalb: Northern Illinois University Press, 2010.

Grubbs, Frank L., Jr. *The Struggle for Labor Loyalty: Gompers, the A.F. of L., and the Pacifists, 1917–1920*. Durham, NC: Duke University Press, 1968.

Gunther, Gerald. *Learned Hand: The Man and the Judge*. 1994; New York: Oxford University Press, 2010.

Gutfeld, Arnon. *American Exceptionalism: The Effects of Plenty on the American Experience*. Brighton, UK: Sussex Academic Press, 2002.

———. *Montana's Agony: Years of War and Hysteria, 1917–1921*. Gainesville: University Presses of Florida, 1979.

Hall, Kermit, ed. *Major Problems in American Constitutional History: Documents and Essays*, vol. 1. Lexington, MA: Cengage Learning, 1992.

Harrington, Daniel. *Lessons from the Granite Mountain Shaft Fire, Butte*. Washington DC: Government Printing Office, 1922.

Hayes, Anna R. *Without Precedent: The Life of Susie Marshall Sharp*. Chapel Hill: University of North Carolina Press, 2008.

Haywood, William D. *Bill Haywood's Book: The Autobiography of William D. Haywood*. New York: International Publishers, 1929.

Hazard, Geoffrey C., Susan P. Koniak, Roger C. Cramton, George M. Cohen, and W. Bradley Wendel. *The Law and Ethics of Lawyering*. 5th ed. Foundation Press, 2010.

Heale, M. J. *American Anticommunism: Combating the Enemy Within, 1830–1970*. Baltimore: Johns Hopkins University Press, 1990.

———. *Twentieth Century America: Politics and Power in the United States, 1900–1920*. London: Hodder Arnold, 2004.

Higham, John. *Strangers in the Land: Patterns of American Nativism, 1860–1925*. New York: Atheneum, 1963.

Hofstadter, Richard. *The Paranoid Style in American Politics and Other Essays*. New York: Knopf, 1956.

Hofstadter, Richard, and Michael Wallace, eds. *American Violence: A Documentary History*. New York: Knopf, 1970.

Horwitz, Morton J. *The Transformation of American Law, 1780–1860*. Cambridge, MA: Harvard University Press, 1977.

———. *The Transformation of American Law, 1870–1960: The Crisis of Legal Orthodoxy*. New York: Oxford University Press, 1992.

Howard, Joseph K. *Montana: High, Wide and Handsome*. New Haven, CT: Yale University Press, 1943.

Hyman, Harold M. *Soldiers and Spruce: Origins of the Loyal Legion of Loggers and Lumbermen*. Los Angeles: Institute of Industrial Relations, University of California, 1963.

———. *To Try Men's Souls: Loyalty Tests in American History*. Berkeley: University of California Press, 1969.

Irons, Peter. *New Deal Lawyers*. Princeton, NJ: Princeton University Press, 1982.

Jensen, Vernon H. *Heritage of Conflict: Labor Relations in the Nonferrous Metals Industry Up to 1930*. Ithaca, NY: Cornell University Press, 1950.

Johnson, Donald. *The Challenge to American Freedoms: World War I and the Rise of the American Civil Liberties Union*. Lexington: University of Kentucky Press, 1963.

Karlin, Jules. *Joseph M. Dixon of Montana*. Part I, *Senator and Bull Moose Manager, 1867–1917*. Missoula: University of Montana Publications in History, 1974.

———. *Joseph M. Dixon of Montana*. Part II, *Governor Versus Anaconda, 1917–1934*. Missoula: University of Montana Publications in History, 1974.

Keene, Jennifer D. *The United States and the First World War*. New York: Longman, 2000.

Kennedy, David M. *Freedom from Fear: The American People in Depression and War, 1929–1945*. New York: Oxford University Press, 1999.

———. *Over Here: The First World War and American Society*. New York: Oxford University Press, 1980.

Kennedy, Kathleen. *Disloyal Mothers and Scurrilous Citizens: Women and Subversion during World War I*. Bloomington: Indiana University Press. 1999.

Kens, Paul. *Justice Stephen Field: Shaping Liberty from the Gold Rush to the Gilded Age*. Lawrence: University Press of Kansas, 1997.

Kohn, Stephen M. *American Political Prisoners: Prosecutions under the Espionage and Sedition Acts*. Westport, CT: Praeger, 1994.

Kornbluth, Joyce. *Rebel Voices: An I.W.W. Anthology*. Ann Arbor: University of Michigan Press, 1964.

Lamson, Peggy. *Roger Baldwin: Founder of the American Civil Liberties Union*. Boston: Houghton Mifflin, 1976.

Leary, William M., Jr., and Arthur S. Link. *The Progressive Era and the Great War, 1896–1920*. Arlington Heights, IL AHM, 1978.

Lee, Erica. *At America's Gates: Chinese Immigration during the Exclusion Era, 1882–1943*. Chapel Hill: University of North Carolina Press, 2003.

Lerner, Jonathan J. *The Attorney-Client Relationship after Kaye, Scholer*. New York: PLI, 1992.

Leuchtenburg, William E. *Franklin Roosevelt and the New Deal: 1932–1940*. New York: Harper and Row, 1963.

———. *The Supreme Court Reborn: The Constitutional Revolution of the Age of Roosevelt*. New York: Oxford University Press, 1995.

Levin, Louis. *The Taxation of Mines in Montana*. New York: Huebsch, 1919.

Levin, Murray. *Political Hysteria in America: The Democratic Capacity for Repression*. New York: Basic Books, 1971.

Linfield, Michael. *Freedom under Fire: U.S. Civil Liberties in Times of War*. Boston: South End Press, 1991.

Luebke, Frederick C. *Bonds of Loyalty: German-Americans and World War I.* Dekalb: Northern Illinois University Press, 1974.

MacMillan, Donald. *Smoke Wars: Anaconda Copper, Montana Air Pollution, and the Courts, 1890–1924.* Helena: Montana Historical Society, 2000.

Malone, Michael P., Richard B. Roeder, and William L. Lang. *Montana: A History of Two Centuries.* Seattle: University of Washington Press, 1991.

McDonnell, Janet A. *The Dispossession of the American Indian, 1887–1934.* Bloomington: Indiana University Press, 1991.

McKenna, Marian C. *Franklin Roosevelt and the Great Constitutional War: The Court Packing Crisis of 1937.* New York: Fordham University Press, 2002.

Merrill, Karen R. *Public Lands and Political Meaning: Ranchers, the Government, and the Property between Them.* Berkeley: University of California Press, 2002.

Mezerik, A. B. *The Revolt of the South and West.* New York, Duell, Sloan, and Pearce, 1946.

Mock, James R. *Censorship, 1917.* Princeton, NJ: Princeton University Press, 1941.

Mock, James R., and Cedric Larson. *Words That Won the War: The Story of the Committee on Public Information, 1917–1919.* Princeton, NJ: Princeton University Press, 1939.

Morlan, Robert. *Political Prairie Fire: The Nonpartisan League, 1915–1922.* Minneapolis: University of Minnesota Press, 1955.

Murphy, Mary. *Mining Cultures: Men, Women, and Leisure in Butte, 1914–1941.* Urbana: University of Illinois Press, 1997.

Murphy, Paul L. *The Constitution in Crisis Times, 1918–1969.* New York: Harper and Row, 1971.

———. *The Meaning of Freedom of Speech: First Amendment Freedoms from Wilson to FDR.* Westport, CT: Greenwood Press, 1972.

———. *World War I and the Origins of Civil Liberties in the United States.* New York: Norton, 1979.

Murray, Robert K. *Red Scare: A Study in National Hysteria, 1919–1920.* 1955. Minneapolis: University of Minnesota Press, 1964.

Novick, Sheldon N. *Honorable Justice: The Life of Oliver Wendell Holmes.* Boston: Little Brown, 1989.

O'Malley, Robert E., William Freivogel, and Brian Redding, eds. *The Kaye, Scholer Case and Other Selected Professional Liability and Ethics Issues.* Attorneys' Liability Assurance Society, 1992.

Perlman, Selig, and Philip Taft. *History of Labor in the United States, 1896–1932.* New York: Macmillan, 1935.

Peterson, Horace C., and Gilbert C. Fite. *Opponents of War, 1917–1918.* Madison: University of Wisconsin Press, 1957.

Polenberg, Richard. *Fighting Faiths: The Abrams Case, the Supreme Court, and Free Speech.* New York: Viking, 1987.

Posner, Richard A. *An Affair of State: The Investigation, Impeachment, and Trial of President Clinton.* Cambridge: Harvard University Press, 1999.

Powe, Lucas A., Jr. *The Fourth Estate and the Constitution: Freedom of the Press in America.* Berkeley: University of California Press, 1991.

Preston, William. *Aliens and Dissenters: Federal Suppression of the Radicals in the United States.* Cambridge, MA: Harvard University Press, 1941.

Price, Polly. *Judge Richard S. Arnold: A Legacy of Justice on the Federal Bench.* New York: Prometheus Books, 2009.

Prucha, Francis Paul. *American Indian Policy in Crisis: Christian Reformers and the Indians, 1865–1900.* Norman: University of Oklahoma Press, 1976.

Rabban, David M. *Free Speech in Its Forgotten Years.* New York: Cambridge University Press, 1997.

Reid, John Phillip. *Constitutional History of the American Revolution.* Madison: University of Wisconsin Press, 1995.

———. *Legitimating the Law: The Struggle for Judicial Competency in Early National New Hampshire.* DeKalb: Northern Illinois University Press, 2012.

———. *Rule of Law: The Jurisprudence of Liberty in the Seventeenth and Eighteenth Centuries.* DeKalb: Northern Illinois University Press, 2004.

Raymer, Robert G. *Montana: The Land and the People.* 3 vols. Chicago: Lewis Publishing, 1930.

Renshaw, Patrick. *America in the Era of Two World Wars, 1910–1945.* London: Longman, 1996.

Ross, Stewart Halsey. *Propaganda for War: How the United States Was Conditioned to Fight the Great War of 1914–1918.* Jefferson, NC: McFarland, 1996.

Rozell, Mark J., and Clyde Wilcox, eds. *The Clinton Scandal and the Future of American Government.* Washington DC: Georgetown University Press, 2000.

Sanders, Helen Fitzgerald. *A History of Montana.* Chicago: Lewis Publishing, 1913.

Schaffer, Ronald. *America in the Great War: The Rise of the War Welfare State.* New York: Oxford University Press, 1991.

Scheiber, Harry N. *The Wilson Administration and Civil Liberties, 1917–1921.* Ithaca, NY: Cornell University Press, 1960.

Scherer, James A. B. *The Nation at War.* Garden City, NY: Doubleday, 1918.

Schwartz, Bernard. *A History of the Supreme Court.* New York: Oxford University Press, 1993.

Semonche, John E. *Charting the Future: The Supreme Court Responds to a Changing Society, 1890–1920.* Westport, CT: Greenwood Press, 1978.

Shattuck, Petra, and Jill Norgren. *Partial Justice: Federal Indian Law in a Liberal Constitutional System.* New York: Berg, 1991.

Slotkin, Richard. *The Fatal Environment: The Myth of the Frontier in the Age of Industrialization, 1800–1890.* New York: Atheneum, 1985.

Smith, Donald L. *Zechariah Chafee, Jr.: Defender of Liberty and Law.* Cambridge, MA: Harvard University Press, 1986.

Smith, Sherry Lynn. *Reimagining Indians: Native Americans through Anglo Eyes, 1880–1940.* Oxford: Oxford University Press, 2000.

Soifer, Aviam. *Law and the Company We Keep.* Cambridge, MA: Harvard University Press, 1995.

Spence, Clark C. *Montana: A Bicentennial History*. New York: Norton, 1978.

Stein, Harry H. *Gus J. Solomon: Liberal Politics, Jews, and the Federal Courts*. Portland: Oregon Historical Society Press, 2006.

Stone, Geoffrey R. *Perilous Times: Free Speech in Wartime*. New York: Norton, 2004.

Stout, Tom Stout, ed. *Montana: Its Story and Biography: A History of Aboriginal and Territorial Montana and Three Decades of Statehood*. Chicago: American Historical Society, 1921.

Symes, Lillian, and Clement Travers. *Rebel America: The Story of Social Revolt in the United States*. New York: Harper and Brothers, 1934.

Taylor, Graham T. *The New Deal and American Tribalism: The Administration of the Indian Reorganization Act, 1934–1945*. Lincoln: University of Nebraska Press, 1980.

Thompson, Fred. *The I.W.W.: Its First Fifty Years, 1905–1955*. Chicago: Industrial Workers of the World, 1955.

Todes, Charlotte. *Labor and Lumber*. New York: International Publishers, 1931.

Toole, Kenneth Ross. *Montana: An Uncommon Land*. Norman: University of Oklahoma Press, 1959.

———. *The Rape of the Great Plains: Northwestern America and the Energy Crisis*. Boston: Little Brown, 1976.

———. *Twentieth Century Montana: A State of Extremes*. Norman: University of Oklahoma Press, 1972.

Toole, Kenneth Ross, and Merrill G. Burlingame, eds. *A History of Montana*. 3 vols. New York: Lewis Publishing, 1957.

Tuller, Roger H. *Let No Guilty Man Escape: A Judicial Biography of "Hanging Judge" Isaac C. Parker*. Norman: University of Oklahoma Press, 2001.

Tyler, Robert. *Rebels of the Woods: The I.W.W. in the Pacific Northwest*. Eugene: University of Oregon Books, 1967.

Urofsky, Melvin I. *Louis D. Brandeis: A Life*. New York: Pantheon Books, 2009.

———. *A Mind of One Piece: Brandeis and American Reform*. New York: Scribner, 1971.

Urofsky, Melvin I., and Paul Finkelman. *A March of Liberty: A Constitutional History of the United States*. Vol. 2, *From 1898 to the Present*. New York: Oxford University Press, 2002.

Waldron, Ellis. *Montana Politics since 1864: An Atlas of Elections*. Missoula: University of Montana Press, 1957.

Washburn, Wilcomb E. *The Assault on Indian Tribalism: The General Allotment Act of 1887*. Philadelphia: Lippincott, 1975.

Weaver, Jace. *Then to the Rock Let Me Fly: Luther Bohanon and Judicial Activism*. Norman: University of Oklahoma Press, 1993.

Wheeler, Burton K. *Yankee from the West: The Candid, Turbulent Life Story of the Yankee-Born U.S. Senator from Montana*. Garden City, NY: Doubleday, 1962.

White, G. Edward. *The Marshall Court and Cultural Change, 1815–1835*. New York: Oxford University Press, 1991.

Wiecek, William M. *The Lost World of Classical Legal Thought: Law and Ideology in America, 1886–1937*. New York: Oxford University Press, 1998.

Wilkinson, Charles F. *American Indians, Time, and the Law: Native Societies in a Modern Constitutional Democracy*. New Haven, CT: Yale University Press, 1987.

Williams, Lee E. *Post-War Riots in America, 1919 and 1946: How the Pressures of War Exacerbated American Urban Tensions to the Breaking Point*. Lewiston, NY: E. Mellen Press, 1991.

Williams, Robert A. *The American Indian in Western Legal Thought: The Discourse of Conquest*. New York: Oxford University Press, 1990.

Wolfskill, George. *The Revolt of the Conservatives: A History of the Liberty League, 1934–1940*. Boston: Houghton Mifflin, 1962.

Work, Clemens P. *Darkest Before Dawn: Sedition and Free Speech in the American West*. Albuquerque: University of New Mexico Press, 2005.

Zeiger, Robert H. *America's Great War: World War I and the American Experience*. Lanham, MD: Rowman and Littlefield, 2000.

Articles

Anderson, Alexis J. "New England's Experience with Punishing Political Speech during World War I: A Study in Prosecutional Discretion." *Massachusetts Legal History* 4 (1998): 83–135.

Arrington, Leonard. "The New Deal in the West: A Preliminary Statistical Inquiry." *Pacific Historical Review* 38 (1969): 311–316.

Arrington, Leonard, and Don C. Reading. "New Deal Economic Programs in the Northern Tier States, 1933–1939." In *Centennial West: Essays on the History of the Northern Tier States*, edited by William L. Lang, 227–243. Seattle: University of Washington Press, 1991.

Auerbach, Jerold. "The Patrician as Libertarian: Zechariah Chafee Jr., and Freedom of Speech." *New England Quarterly* 42 (1969): 511–531.

Baer, Judith. "Women Workers and Liberty to Contract." In *Major Problems in American Constitutional History*, vol. 1, edited by Kermit L. Hall, 118–129. Lexington, MA: Cengage Learning, 1992.

Bahmer, Robert H. "The American Society of Equity." *Agricultural History* 14 (1940): 33–63.

Ball, Milner S. "Constitution, Court, Indian Tribes." *American Bar Foundation Association Journal* 1 (1987): 1–139.

Belknap, Michal. "The Mechanics of Repression: J. Edgar Hoover, the Bureau of Investigation, and the Radicals, 1917–1925." *Crime and Social Justice* 7 (1977): 49–58.

Benedict, Michael Les. "The Libertarian Foundations of Laissez Faire Constitutionalism." In *Major Problems in American Constitutional History*, vol. 1, edited by Kermit L. Hall, 62–79. Lexington, MA: Cengage Learning, 1992.

Bevis, Harvard I. "The Deportations of Aliens." *University of Pennsylvania Law Review* 68 (January 1920): 97–119.

Brissenden, Paul F. "The Butte Miners and the Rustling Card." *American Economic Review* 10 (December 1920): 755–775.

Burke, J. C. "The Cherokee Cases: A Study in Law, Politics and Morality." *Stanford Law Journal* 21, no. 3 (1969): 500–531.

Burke, Robert E. "A Friendship in Adversity, Burton K. Wheeler and Hiram W. Johnson." *Montana: The Magazine of Western History* 36 (1986): 12–25.

Capazzola, Christopher. "The Only Badge You Need Is Your Patriotic Fervor: Vigilance, Coercion and the Law in World War I America." *Journal of American History* 84 (2002): 1354–1382.

Chafee, Zechariah, Jr. "A Contemporary State Trial: The United States v. Jacob Abrams et al." *Harvard Law Review* 33 (1920): 747–774.

———. "Freedom of Speech in Wartime." *Harvard Law Review* 32 (1919): 932–973.

Coben, Stanley. "A Study in Nativism: The American Red Scare of 1919–1920." *Political Science Quarterly* 79, no. 1 (1964): 52–75.

Colburn, David R. "Governor Alfred E. Smith and the Red Scare, 1919–1920." *Political Science Quarterly* 88 (1973): 423–444.

Gengarelly, W. Anthony. "The Abrams Case: Social Aspects of a Judicial Controversy." *Boston Bar Journal* 3 and 4 (1981).

———. "Secretary of Labor William B. Wilson and the Red Scare, 1919–1920." *Pennsylvania History* 47 (1980): 311–330.

Gross, Oren. "Chaos and Rules: Should All Responses to Violent Crises Be Constitutional?" *Yale Law Journal* 112 (2003): 1011–1134.

Groth, Clarence W. "Sowing and Reaping: Montana Banking, 1910–1925." *Montana: The Magazine of Western History* 20, no. 4 (1970): 28–35.

Gunther, Gerald. "Learned Hand and the Origins of Modern First Amendment Doctrine: Some Fragments of History." *Stanford Law Review* 27 (1975): 719–773.

Gutfeld, Arnon. "As American As Cherry Pie: Political Violence as a Persistent Theme in American History." *Israel Yearbook of Human Rights* 28 (1998): 121–170.

———. "The Deprivation of Indian Sovereignty, 1776–1871." *Israel Yearbook of Human Rights* 25 (1995): 169–192.

———. "George Bourquin: A Montana Judge's Stand against Government Despotism." *Western Legal History* 6 (1993): 51–68.

———. "History and Justice in Indian Law: An Analysis of Scheer v. Moody." *European Review of Native American Studies* 8, no. 2 (1994): 31–34.

———. "Loyalty, Treason, and Sedition in the United States during Crisis Times." In *Challenges to Democracy: Essays in Honor and in Memory of Professor Sir Isaiah Berlin*, edited by Raphael Cohen-Almagor, 55–76. London: Ashgate, 2000.

———. "Purveyors of Injustice: Bourquin on Lawyers and the Legal System." *Tel-Aviv Studies in Law* 15 (2000): 237–255.

———. "Stark Starving, Raving Mad: An Analysis of a World War I Impeachment Trial." *Yearbook of German American Studies* 30 (1995): 57–72.

———. "The Levine Affair: A Case Study in Academic Freedom." *Pacific Historical Review* 39 (1970): 19–37.

———. "The Murder of Frank Little: Radical Labor Agitation in Butte, Montana, 1917." *Labor History* 10 (Spring 1969) : 177–192.

———. "The Speculator Disaster in 1917: Labor Resurgence in Butte, Montana." *Arizona and the West* 11 (1969): 27–38.

———. "The Ves Hall Case, Judge Bourquin, and Sedition Act of 1918." *Pacific Historical Review* 38 (1968): 163–168.

———. "Western Justice and the Rule of Law: Bourquin on Loyalty, the Red Scare and Indians." *Pacific Historical Review* 64 (1996): 85–106.

Halverson, Guy, and William E. Ames. "The Butte Bulletin: Beginnings of a Labor Daily." *Montana Journalism Quarterly* 46 (1969): 260–266.

Hilton, O. A. "Public Opinion and Civil Liberties in Wartime, 1917–1919." *Southwestern Social Science Quarterly* 27 (1947): 201–224.

Himmelberg, Robert R. "The War Industries Board and the Antitrust Question in November 1918." *Journal of American History* 52 (1965): 59–74.

Irons, Peter H. "'Fighting Fair': Zechariah Chafee Jr., the Department of Justice, and the 'Trial at the Harvard Club.'" *Harvard Law Review* 94 (1981): 1218–1222.

Johnson, Donald. "The Political Career of A. Mitchell Palmer." *Pennsylvania History* 25 (1958): 345–370.

Josephson, Harold. "The Dynamics of Repression, New York During the Red Scare." *Mid-America* 59 (1977): 131–146.

Karlin, Jules A. "Progressive Politics in Montana." In *A History of Montana*, edited by Merrill G. Burlingame and K. Kenneth Ross Toole, 247–280. New York: Lewis Publishing, 1957.

Kester, Randall. B. "The War Industries Board, 1917–1918: A Study in Industrial Mobilization." *American Political Science Review* 34 (1940): 655–684.

Kettleborough, C. "War Legislation." *American Political Science Review* 12 (1918): 78–88.

Levine, Louis. "Tax Legislation in Montana." *Bulletin of the National Tax Association* 3 (1917): 191–194.

Malone, Michael. "The Montana New Dealers." In *The New Deal*, edited by John Braeman, Robert H. Brenner, and David Brody, 2:240–268. Columbus: Ohio State University Press, 1975.

———. "Montana Politics and the New Deal." *Montana: The Magazine of Western History* 21 (1971): 2–11.

———. "Montana Politics at the Crossroads, 1932–1933." *Pacific Northwest Quarterly* 69 (January 1978): 20–29.

McKenna, Marian. "Prelude to Tyranny: Wheeler, F.D.R., and the 1937 Court Fights." *Pacific Historical Review* 62 (1993): 405–431.

Murphy, Paul L. "Sources and Nature of Intolerance in the 1920's." *Journal of American History* 51 (1964): 60–76.

Murray, Robert K. "Communism and the Great Steel Strike of 1919." *Mississippi Valley Historical Review* 38 (1951): 455–468.

Noble, David W. "Herbert Croly and American Progressive Thought." *Western Political Quarterly* 7 (1954): 537–553.

———. "The New Republic and the Idea of Progress, 1914–1920." *Mississippi Valley History Review* 38 (1951): 387–402.

Novick, Sheldon M. "The Unrevised Holmes and Freedom of Expression." *Supreme Court Review* (1991): 303–390.

Ott, Franziska. "The Lynching of a German-American as Reported in the Local English Language Press." In *The Anti-German Hysteria of World War One*, vol. 1 of *German-Americans in the World Wars: A Documentary History*, edited by Don Heinrich Tolzman. Munich: K. G. Saur, 1995.

Patterson, James T. "The New Deal in the West." *Pacific Historical Review* 38 (1969): 317–327.

Paul, Arnold M. "Traditional Legal Conservatism." In *Major Problems in American Constitutional History*, vol. 1, edited by Kermit L. Hall, 54–62. Lexington, MA: Cengage Learning, 1992.

Post, Louis F. "Administrative Decisions in Connection with Immigration." *American Political Science Review* (1916): 251–261.

Prude, Jonathan. "Portrait of a Civil Libertarian: The Faith and Fear of Zechariah Chafee Jr." *Journal of American History* 60 (1973): 633–656.

Rabban, David M. "The Emergence of Modern First Amendment Doctrine." *University of Chicago Law Review* 50 (1983): 1207–1267.

Rader, Benjamin. "The Montana Lumber Strike of 1917." *Pacific Historical Review* 36 (1967): 189–207.

Ragan, Fred D. "Justice Oliver Wendell Holmes, Jr., Zechariah Chafee, Jr., and the Clear and Present Danger Test for Free Speech: The First Year, 1919." *Journal of American History* 58, no. 1 (1971): 24–45.

Reid, John Philip. "The Layers of Western Legal History." In *Law in the Western United States*, edited by Gordon Morris Bakken, 3–42. Norman: University of Oklahoma Press, 2000.

Rippley, LaVern J. "Conflict in the Classroom: Anti-Germanism in Minnesota Schools, 1917–1919." *Minnesota History* 47 (1981): 170–183.

———. "F. W. Sallet and the Dakota Freie Presse." *North Dakota History* 59 (1992): 2–20.

Roeder, Richard B. "Montana Progressivism: Sound and Fury and One Small Tax Reform." *Montana: The Magazine of Western History* 20 (1970): 18–26.

Rogers, Alan. "Judge George W. Anderson and Civil Rights in the 1920s." *The Historian* 54, no. 2 (1992): 289–304.

Ruetten, Richard T. "Anaconda Journalism: The End of an Era." *Journalism Quarterly* 37 (1960): 3–12, 104.

———. "Senator Burton K. Wheeler and Insurgency in the 1920s." In *The American West: A Reorientation*, edited by Gene M. Gressley, 111–131. Laramie: University of Wyoming Publications, 1968.

Saloutos, Theodore. "The Expansion and Decline of the Nonpartisan League in the Western Middle West, 1917–1921." *Agricultural History* 20 (1946): 235–252.

———. "The Montana Society of Equity." *Pacific Historical Review* 14 (1945): 393–408.

Saindon, Robert, and Bunky Sullivan. "Taming the Missouri and Treating the Depression: Fort Peck Dam." *Montana: The Magazine of Western History* 27 (1977): 34–57.

Schauer, Frederick. "Formalism." *Yale Law Journal* 97, no. 4 (March 1988): 509–548.

Schlitz, John M. "Montana's Captive Press." *Montana Opinion* 1 (1956): 1–11.

Simon, William H. "The Warren Court, Legalism, and Democracy: Sketch for a Critique in a Style Learned from Morton Horwitz." In *Transformations in American Legal History: Law, Ideology, and Methods*, vol. 2, edited by Daniel W. Hamilton and Alfred L. Brophy. Cambridge, MA: Harvard Law School, 2010.

Soifer, Aviam. "Objects in Mirror Are Closer Than They Appear." *Georgia Law Review* 28 (1994): 533–553.

———. "The Paradox of Paternalism and Laissez Faire Constitutionalism: The United States Supreme Court, 1888–1921." *Law and History Review* 5 (1987): 249–279.

Tyler, Robert. "The United States Government as Union Organizers: The Loyal Legion of Loggers and Lumbermen." *Mississippi Valley Historical Review* 47 (1960): 434–451.

———. "The I.W.W. and the West." *American Quarterly* 12 (1960): 175–187.

———. "The I.W.W. in the Pacific Northwest: Rebels of the Woods." *Oregon Historical Quarterly* 5 (1954): 3–44.

Urofsky, Melvin I. "The Courts and the Limits to Liberty of Contract." In *Major Problems in American Constitutional History*, vol. 1, edited by Kermit L. Hall, 129–141. Lexington, MA: Cengage Learning, 1992.

———. "Myth and Reality: The Supreme Court and Protective Legislation during the Progressive Era." *Yearbook of the Supreme Court Historical Society*, 1983: 53–72.

———. "State Courts and Protective Legislation during the Progressive Era: A Reevaluation." *Journal of American History* 72 (1985): 63–91.

Vindex, Charles. "Survival on the High Plains, 1929–1934." *Montana: The Magazine of Western History* 28 (1978): 2–11.

Walter, Dave. "Casualties of War: The Tragedy of Judge C. L. Crum." *Montana Magazine* 104 (1990): 56–63.

Williams, David. "The Bureau of Investigation and Its Critics, 1919–1921: The Origins of Federal Political Surveillance." *Journal of American History* 68 (1981): 560–579.

Wiprud, Theodore. "Butte: A Troubled Labor Paradise." *Montana: The Magazine of Western History* 21 (1971): 31–38.

Dissertations

Bates, J. Leonard. "Senator Walsh of Montana, 1918–1924: A Liberal under Pressure." PhD diss., University of North Carolina, 1952.

Deforth, Shirley J. "The Montana Press and Joseph M. Dixon, 1920–1922." MA thesis, University of Montana, 1959.

Evans, Robert E. "Montana's Role in the Enactment of Legislation Designed to Suppress the Industrial Workers of the World." MA thesis, University of Montana, 1964.

Fritz, Nancy Rice. "The Montana Council of Defense." MA thesis, University of Montana, 1966.

Garrity, Donald A. "The Frank Little Episode and the Butte Labor Troubles of 1917." Senior honors paper, Department of History, Carroll College, Helena, MT, 1957.

Gutfeld, Arnon. "The Butte Labor Strikes and Company Retaliation during World War I." MA thesis, University of Montana, 1967.

Harris, Lyle. "Dr. E. B. Craighead's *New Northwest*: 1915–1921." MA thesis, University of Montana, 1967.

Johnson, Charles S. "An Editor and a War: Will A. Campbell and the Helena Independent, 1914–1921." MA thesis, University of Montana, 1977.

McDean, Harry C. "M. L. Wilson and Agricultural Reform in Twentieth Century America." PhD diss., University of California, Los Angeles, 1969.

Ragan, Fred Donald. "The New Republic: Red Hysteria and Civil Liberties." PhD diss., University of Michigan, 1965.

Roeder, Richard B. "Montana in the Early Years of the Progressive Period." PhD diss., University of Pennsylvania, 1971.

Ruetten, Richard T. "Burton K. Wheeler, 1905–1925: An Independent Liberal under Fire." MA thesis, University of Oregon, 1957.

———. "Burton K. Wheeler of Montana: A Progressive between Wars." PhD diss., University of Oregon, 1961.

Schaffer, Ronald. "Jeannette Rankin, Progressive Isolationist." PhD diss., Princeton University, 1959.

Smith, Norma. "The Rise and Fall of the Butte Miners' Union, 1874–1914." MA thesis, Montana State College, 1961.

Toole, K. Ross. "A History of the Anaconda Copper Mining Company: A Study in the Relationship between a State, Its People, and a Corporation." PhD diss., University of California, Los Angeles, 1954.

———. "Marcus Daly: A Study of Business in Politics." MA thesis, University of Montana, 1948.

Wetzel, Kurt. "The Making of an American Radical: Bill Dunne in Butte." MA thesis, University of Montana, 1970.

INDEX

Page numbers in *italic* refer to illustrations.

favors, 94, 95
fear of Germany. *See* Germany, fear of
fear of traitors, spies, etc. (c. 1917–21).
    See Red Scare (c. 1917–21)
federal aid to Montana, 107, 109
Federal Justice in California (Fritz), xiii–
    xiv, 11
feudalism, 44, 110
Fifth Amendment, 12, 69, 70, 85, 86–87
financial reports, 100–101, 102
fines, 14, 34, 41, 43, 92, 95, 101, 128,
    129
First Amendment, xiv, 4, 6, 12, 30, 123.
    See also freedom of speech
Fisch, Louise, xiv
flag, US. *See* US flag
Flathead Indian Reservation, 24, 79–85
    passim
Flathead Indians. *See* Kootenai people;
    Pend d'Oreilles people
Flathead Valley, Montana, *89*
Flege, G., 58–59
Fong Yue Ting v. United States, 145–46n26
Ford, Sam C., 101–3
Fort Peck Dam, 109
Foucault, Michel, 48, 146n47
Founders, 6, 19, 48, 110, 113, 119,
    133. *See also* Hamilton, Alexander;
    Jefferson, Thomas; Washington,
    George
Fourteenth Amendment, 42, 62, 63, 64,
    70, 71, 74, 128
Fourth Amendment, 12, 75, 76
France, Joseph I., 37
freedom of speech, 3, 4, 6, 11, 21–51
    passim, 123–29, 145n14
Fritz, Christian G.: *Federal Justice in
    California*, xiii–xiv, 11
Fritz, Harry, 52
frontier myth, 149–50n12

Galen, A. J., 91–96 passim
Gallatin County, Montana, 65–66
Garza, Reynaldo, xiv
General Allotment Act of 1887. *See*
    Dawes Act
Genzberger, Earle N., 96–97

Georgia, 78
German Americans, 22, 23, 52–61
Germany, fear of, 23, 24, 25, 38
"goon squads," 18, 24
government aid to Montana. *See* federal
    aid to Montana
government power, 8–10 passim, 14,
    22, 46–47, 50, 62–73 passim, 112,
    115; viewed as "despotism," 4, 5, 12,
    48–49, 50, 133. *See also* checks and
    balances
government secrecy, 45
government subsidization, 76–77, 84
Graham, D. Kurt: *To Bring Law Home*, xv
grazing rights. *See* livestock grazing
    rights
Great Britain, 28, 56, 124; treaties, 74,
    75. *See also* England
Great Depression. *See* Depression
*Great Falls Gas Co. v. Public Service
    Commission of Montana*, 68, 104
Great Falls Tribune, 33, 109
greed, 76–77, 82, 97
Gregory, Thomas W., 35

habeas corpus, 41, 47, 50
Hall, Ves, 28–31, 33, 35, 36–37, 53, 54,
    57, 123–26
Halter v. Nebraska, 128
Hamilton, Alexander, 9
Hamilton, John D. M., 120
Hardwick, Thomas W., 37
Harrison, Benjamin, 16
Haymarket anarchists, 134
Haynes, Felkner (Fritz), 54, 56
Healy, Dennis, 88–89
Helena, Montana, 16, 19, 24
Helena Independent, 31, 32, 53
heresy, 54, 58
Herrig, A. L., 100–101
Higgins, Ronald, 58, 59, 60, 61
"high crimes and misdemeanors," 53,
    147n4
Hoffman, Ogden, xiv
Holmes, Oliver Wendell, Jr., 3, 9, 43, 74,
    129, 145n14
Holter Hardware Co. v. Boyle. See *A. M.
    Holter Hardware Co. v. Boyle*

New Deal, 9, 107–20 passim, 157n27
New Hampshire, xv
newspapers, 23, 31, 33, 38, 60; editorial
    cartoons, 19, 110, *121*
Nix v. Whiteside, 154n1
Nonpartisan League (NPL), 25
Norman, George, 47
Norris, George, 21–22
Northern Pacific Railway Co. et al. v.
    Board of Railroad Commissioners of
    Montana, 66–68
Norwegian immigrants, 43–44, 58–59

O'Brien, John Lord, 35, 36–37
obstruction of justice, 91–96
Oklahoma, xiv
O'Leary, John, 19, 20
One Hundred Club, 58, 60
opinion, dissenting. *See* dissent and
    dissenters; juridical dissent
Oregon, xiv
Over-Seas Club, 56
ownership, communal. *See* communal
    ownership
ownership of land. *See* landownership

Parker, Isaac Charles, xiii
paternalism, 10, 47, 88, 89–90
patriotism, 6, 10, 22–25 passim, 38, 40,
    51, 52; Bourquin on, 30, 42–43, 126;
    in Crum impeachment, 11, 52, 57,
    58; in Hall case, 123; in Jackson
    case, 49–50; press appeal to, 33; in
    Starr case, 42–43, 127–29 passim;
    Thomas Hardwick view, 37
Pend d'Oreilles people, 79, 83
peremptory challenges, 153–54n2
physicians: prescription of alcohol by,
    104–5
Pinkerton Agency, 18
Prager, Robert, 38
presidential elections, 17, 120
presidential privilege. *See* executive
    power
President's Mediation Commission
    (1917–19), 38
press. *See* newspapers

price regulation. *See* rate regulation
private enterprise. *See* business
probation denial, 98–100
Progressive movement, 8, 59–60, 120
Prohibition, 14, 33, 104–5
propaganda, 22, 26
property and property rights, 7, 8, 62,
    70–77 passim, 85, 93, 104, 105.
    See also communal ownership;
    landownership; water rights
public good, 62–73 passim, 82, 86, 120
public land use, 64–65
Public Service Commission of Montana,
    68–71
public utilities, 67–68
public works projects, 109
punishment, 33, 41, 55, 98–99, 100. *See*
    also fines

race in jury selection, 153–54n2
radicals: labeling of, 22; repression of,
    47–48, 131–35
Radivoeff, Nicholas, 44–45
railroad industry, 6, 22, 66–68, 76–77,
    107
Rankin, Wellington, 101
rate regulation, 62, 67, 69, 71
Ratigan, Mary Mitchell. *See* Bourquin,
    Mary Mitchell
Reclamation Act of 1902, 84
Red Lodge, Montana, 24
Red Scare (c. 1917–21), xvii, 6, 11, 21–
    61 passim, 117, 123–35 passim
regulatory commissions, 64–73 passim
Rehnquist, William, 78–79, 151n3
Reid, John Phillip, xv, 10
religion, 16, 21, 22, 42, 58, 128. *See also*
    Bible
repression (c. 1917–21). *See* Red Scare
    (c. 1917–21)
Republican Party, 15, 17, 101, 107–20
    passim
res judicata, 47, 146n41
restraining orders, 66–67, 68
Rhode Island, xv
rights, individual. *See* individual rights
rights, livestock grazing. *See* livestock
    grazing rights